Conservatism for the democratic age

MANCHESTER
1824

Manchester University Press

Conservatism
for the democratic age

Conservative cultures and the challenge of mass
politics in early twentieth-century England

David Thackeray

Manchester University Press

Manchester and New York

*distributed in the United States exclusively
by Palgrave Macmillan*

Published by Manchester University Press
Oxford Road, Manchester M13 9NR, UK
and Room 400, 175 Fifth Avenue, New York, NY 10010, USA
www.manchesteruniversitypress.co.uk

Distributed in the United States exclusively by
Palgrave Macmillan, 175 Fifth Avenue, New York,
NY 10010, USA

Distributed in Canada exclusively by
UBC Press, University of British Columbia, 2029 West Mall,
Vancouver, BC, Canada V6T 1Z2

British Library Cataloguing-in-Publication Data
A catalogue record for this book is available from the British Library

Library of Congress Cataloging-in-Publication Data applied for

ISBN   978 0 7190 8761 5   hardback

First published 2013

The publisher has no responsibility for the persistence or accuracy of URLs for any external or third-party internet websites referred to in this book, and does not guarantee that any content on such websites is, or will remain, accurate or appropriate.

Typeset in Aldine
by JCS Publishing Services Ltd
Printed in Great Britain by TJ International Ltd, Padstow, Cornwall

Contents

List of figures *page* vi
List of tables vii
Note on the text viii
Acknowledgements ix
Abbreviations xi

Introduction: politics in a democratic age 1

I Edwardian politics

1 Responding to the Edwardian crisis of Unionism 17
2 The working man's pint and the housewife's budget 36
3 The challenge of class politics 53
4 Cultures of Unionism 69

II The First World War

5 Rowdiness and respectability 87
6 Labour, civic associations and the new democracy 102
7 'Country before party' 117

III From the Armistice to Baldwin

8 The peaceable man and the prudent housewife 133
9 The multiple identities of anti-socialism 153
10 Baldwin's party? 171

Conclusion 190

Biographical appendix 197
Bibliography 200
Index 217

Figures

0.1 Commemorative postcard, Mid-Devon election, December 1910, Devon Record Office, Exeter, Ernest Morrison-Bell MSS, 2128   *page* xii

2.1 Commemorative postcard, Worcester by-election, February 1908, Parliamentary Archives, London, Wargrave MSS, WAR6/19   36

2.2 'The woman and the canvasser', leaflet, n.d. [1909], Bodleian Library, Oxford, Conservative Party Archive (CPA), PUB32/2   40

2.3 Henry Page Croft, election leaflet, Christchurch election, January 1910, Churchill College, Cambridge, Page Croft MSS, CRFT3/2   44

2.4 Postcard of Henry Page Croft addressing a tariff reform fete, July 1908, author's collection   46

3.1 'It's your money we want', Municipal Reform poster, 1907 London County Council elections, London Metropolitan Archives, Acc. 3606, LCC/CL/COUN/2/41-45   54

6.1 Joint advertisement by Bradford Coalition candidates, 1918 general election, *Bradford Daily Argus*, 5 December 1918, p. 6   108

8.1 Demobilised Democrat cartoon, *Popular View*, December 1921, p. 13   138

8.2 'Vote for Erskine-Bolst' handbill, Blackpool election, November 1922, LRO, Blackpool Conservative Association MSS, PLC5/14/1, Erskine-Bolst scrapbook   139

9.1 'Bonar Law and Sound Government. Vote Unionist', Conservative Party leaflet, 1922 general election, CPA, microfiche 0.396.220, pamphlet 1922/74   161

10.1 Front cover of *Popular View*, January 1924   172

10.2 'Round the fireside', Conservative Party leaflet, 1924 general election, CPA, microfiche 0.396.271, Conservative Party leaflet (1924/19)   176

Tables

0.1 Seats won by Unionist parties in general elections,
    1900–24 *page* 10

1.1 Unionists and Liberals elected unopposed at general
    elections, 1895–1906 22

4.1 Unionist auxiliary organisations, Midland Union, c. 1913 70

5.1 Radical right candidates at by-elections, January–September
    1916 90

9.1 Composition of the London County Council 157

10.1 General election results, 1918 and 1922 173

10.2 Conservative Party performance in general elections, 1918–29 174

10.3 Parliamentary seats won at Norfolk elections, 1922–24 178

Note on the text

The Liberal Unionist and Conservative parties amalgamated in 1912. These parties are referred to as the 'Unionist alliance' throughout the text when reference is being made to the pre-amalgamation period, supporters of the alliance are referred to as 'Unionists'.

Choosing a terminology to described supporters of the united party established in 1912 is more problematic. It was often referred to as the 'Unionist' party at the time of amalgamation and over subsequent years, particularly during the Irish home rule crisis of 1912–14. Here it is referred to as the Conservative Party for the post-1918 period, in line with common scholarly practice. A 'Conservative' identity became increasingly important to the party over the course of the 1920s (and remained paramount over subsequent decades), as it became the leading force for anti-socialist politics in Britain and 'Unionist' identity was reconceptualised following the creation of the Irish Free State.

Acknowledgements

When the Unionists left office in December 1905 a man decided he would not shave until they returned to power. He had a long wait. It took seventeen years before an independent Conservative administration was formed, by which time the man been rendered unrecognisable by a copious beard. At times, writing a history of early twentieth-century British Conservatism has seemed a similarly never-ending endeavour, the present work has benefited greatly from the support of friends and colleagues at my numerous institutional homes over recent years.

What follows would not be possible without the support of a Doctoral Award from the Arts and Humanities Research Council. I would like to thank Cambridge University Press for permission to reproduce material from 'Rethinking the Edwardian crisis of conservatism', *Historical Journal*, 54 (2011), 191–213 and the University of Chicago Press for permission to use material which originally appeared in 'Home and politics: women and conservatism activism in early twentieth century Britain', *Journal of British Studies*, 49 (2010), 826–48.

Chris Wrigley and David Marquand nurtured my early interest in British political history. My greatest academic debt is to Jon Lawrence, who has always provided lively intellectual debate and an exemplary eye for detail. Jon has done much to help me understand the vitality of public politics, and without his exemplary input as the supervisor of the PhD thesis on which this book is based this would be a less ambitious, and I daresay less exciting, story. My PhD examiners Paul Readman and Duncan Tanner have done much to influence this work through their helpful suggestions. Paul's constant encouragement has helped sustain this project through some difficult times. Duncan died a few months after my viva, and it is to my regret that I never had the opportunity to know him well, but his ideas did much to shape the focus of the present work.

During 2009–10 I had the good fortune to work as a college lecturer at The Queen's College, Oxford. I am grateful to my colleagues in history and politics, John Blair, John Davis, Nick Owen and Christine Peters for providing support and advice during a time in which the prospects of a job in academia sometimes looked bleak. This book has been written since I joined the University of Exeter and I am thankful to the history department for providing such a stimulating environment in which to work and for the space to write. My colleagues in modern British history have proven exemplary friends and mentors. Andrew Thorpe and Richard Toye have both been generous with their time, reading the manuscript in full, offering encouragement, and stimulating new ideas. My 'Electoral politics' special subject students at Exeter have also helped me to test out many of the concepts contained in this study and sustained my interest in the subject through their enthusiasm.

Numerous people have read parts of this work in various drafts. I am grateful for the feedback and advice provided by Laura Beers, Eugenio Biagini, Matthew Cragoe, Lucy Delap, David Monger, Robert Saunders and Frank Trentmann. The staff at Manchester University Press have overseen the development of this work with diligence and have been a pleasure to work with.

The trials of writing a PhD and converting it into a first book have also been eased by friends who have reminded me that there is a world beyond early twentieth-century Conservatism. In particular I would like to thank Gareth Atkins, Vee Barbary, Chris Cotton, Mark Crowley, Mark Freeman, Stuart Hallifax, Matt Johnson, Gary Love, Kevin Maddison, Sarah Tebbs and Geraint Thomas, as well as the Rusty Bike irregulars. Finally, my somewhat nomadic academic career to date has benefited greatly from the support of my parents, Brian and Sharon, and my brother, Owen. Without their unflagging support the writing of this book would have been a far more difficult task.

Abbreviations

AWL	Anti-Waste League
BCU	British Commonwealth Union
BCUA	Birmingham Conservative and Unionist Association
BEU	British Empire Union
BLSUU	British League for the Support of Ulster and the Union
BWL	British Workers League
CIU	Clubs and Institute Union
CPA	Conservative Party Archive
FTU	Free Trade Union
ILP	Independent Labour Party
JIL	Junior Imperial League
LCC	London County Council
LNU	League of Nations Union
LRO	Lancashire Record Office
MCU	Middle Classes Union
NFDSS	National Federation of Discharged Sailors and Soldiers
NFWI	National Federation of Women's Institutes
NPH	New Political History
NSL	National Service League
NUCA	National Union of Conservative Associations
NWAC	National War Aims Committee
PHA	Petworth House Archive
PLG	*Primrose League Gazette*
SCUA	Scottish Conservative and Unionist Association
TRL	Tariff Reform League
TUTRA	Trade Union and Tariff Reform Association
USRC	Unionist Social Reform Committee
WI	Women's Institute
WUA	Women's Unionist Association
WUO	Women's Unionist Organisation
WUTRA	Women's Unionist and Tariff Reform Association

Figure 0.1: Commemorative postcard, Mid-Devon election, December 1910

Introduction: politics in a democratic age

Today it is hard to imagine mid-Devon as a hotbed of political ferment. The Conservative Party has tended to dominate politics here since 1918 and it made a clean sweep of the region's seats at the 2010 elections. Things were quite different a century ago. Towns like Newton Abbot and Bovey Tracey were centres of Radical politics where a Conservative politician risked physical assault if he chose to hold a public meeting. One man who dared to do so was Captain Ernest Morrison-Bell, a distinguished soldier who, at six foot two, towered over most of his constituents. During the 1908 by-election a Newton Abbott mob rewarded Morrison-Bell for his impudence by attempting to sweep him off a platform with a giant pole, and the irate Liberals pursued the Conservative candidate to his hotel, where he had to eject an intruder. Such details were apparently not enough for the *Daily Mail*, which fabricated a story claiming that the captain had picked the Liberal up and thrown him over his shoulders through a glass door! Others fared worse. Emmeline Pankhurst, drumming up publicity for the suffragette cause at the by-election, attracted the attention of a gang who pelted her with rotten eggs and rolled her in the winter mud.[1]

Yet within a few years mid-Devon had a thriving Conservative organisation and was celebrated for its peaceable politics. The successor constituency, Totnes, elected an almost unbroken line of Conservative MPs after 1918. When Morrison-Bell and his supporters sought to explain the transformation of mid-Devon, they offered a story rooted in local endeavour. Morrison-Bell's apparent efforts to tone down the fractious politics of the area were celebrated, as were the achievements that the Women's Unionist and Tariff Reform Association (WUTRA) had made in widening the appeal of Conservative politics.[2] This is an organisation which is almost forgotten today, even though it formed the backbone of the Conservative women's organisation after 1918. On the eve of the First World War there were 4,800 members of the mid-Devon women's tariff association, at least on paper, in a constituency with only 12,000 voters.[3]

Given that the Conservative Party held power either alone or in coalitions for all but twenty years between 1915 and 1997, the question of how it was able to adapt to democratic politics is one of the most significant in modern British political history.

This later electoral hegemony appeared unlikely during the early years of the twentieth century as the Unionist alliance fell to three successive election defeats during the Edwardian period. Yet by 1924 the Conservative Party had established itself as the dominant force in British politics, a position which was rarely challenged until the outbreak of the Second World War. This reversal was all the more remarkable, given that Britain became a significantly more democratic polity following the 1918 Representation of the People Act. The ranks of the parliamentary electorate, which had stood at around seven million before the First World War, were now swelled to over twenty million, and included all men aged over twenty-one. Female candidates could stand for parliament for the first time in 1918, and most women aged over thirty gained the vote.

Where historians have offered explanations for the Conservatives' revival during the early twentieth century their attention has focused on narratives of national politics; local perspectives such as those provided by Morrison-Bell have received little attention in the existing literature. John Ramsden's *The Age of Balfour and Baldwin, 1902–1940* (1978) highlighted the importance of organisational modernisation in reviving the Conservative Party's fortunes. The 1911 Unionist Reorganisation Committee is presented as an important step towards making Conservative Central Office into an effective unit which could orchestrate party campaigns.[4] In Ramsden's reading, the Conservatives' electoral revival was also aided by changes within the electoral system which occurred during the First World War and its aftermath. After the 1918 general election the Conservatives no longer had to face a block of seventy to eighty anti-Unionist Irish MPs on the benches at Westminster. They were also the main beneficiaries of an expansion of plural voting and a redistribution of seats which favoured suburbs in the Home Counties.[5]

Other scholars have highlighted the importance of the First World War in reshaping the Conservative Party's identity in ways which widened the appeal of its politics. John Stubbs claims that the party had been gripped by a 'reactionary and totally negative mood' in the years immediately before the war. Whereas Joseph Chamberlain's tariff reform campaign divided Unionist activists after 1903, the renewed primacy of the defence of the union had created a more cohesive party by 1914. This issue ultimately proved unproductive because a home rule settlement for Ireland, in some form, became a fait accompli during the war.[6] By contrast, the patriotic imperatives of the war united Conservatives and set the stall for the development of the party's anti-socialist strategy during the 1920s.[7]

Nonetheless, each of these historians has also demonstrated that the First World War had ambivalent effects on the Conservative Party's identity, removing old problems, but also creating new challenges – most notably a significant expansion in the influence of organised labour, and an electorate in which the working classes were now overwhelmingly in the majority. After 1918 the influence of issues which had previously galvanised and united Conservatives was gradually weakened, as was the case with defence of the union and the established church, or issues were redefined and no longer proved able to generate support in the ways they had done formerly, as was the case with tariff reform.[8] For Ramsden 'only after 1922, with the war at last receding from memory and coalition over, did the party take the decisions that led to its successes of the next twenty years'.[9]

A number of historians have pointed to changes in the Conservative Party's strategy after 1918 as laying the foundations for its inter-war electoral ascendancy. Charting both high political party diplomacy and the grassroots struggles of the anti-waste movement, Maurice Cowling's *The Impact of Labour* characterised the 1920–24 period as the time in which the Conservatives established themselves as the key anti-socialist force in British politics.[10] Building on this theme, Ross McKibbin claimed that the Conservative Party's post-war electoral success was rooted in portraying itself as the defender of 'the public' against the sectional interests of organised labour. As part of this strategy, Conservative propaganda nurtured 'conventional wisdoms' critical of unionised working-class culture.[11] The success of the anti-waste agitation between 1919 and 1921 played an important part in rallying support for the deflationary policies followed by Conservative administrations.[12] As well as gaining the support of most of the middle class, this anti-socialist discourse had a strong resonance for many working-class women who struggled to identify their own interests with organised labour.[13]

Philip Williamson has presented the 'ideological stereotypes' which underlined the Conservatives' success in somewhat different terms. In his reading, Baldwin's leadership of the Conservatives was key to their success. Baldwin was able to reform the party, promoting constructive policies and a consensual language, presenting the Conservatives as a moderating force in British politics, standing in the national interest.[14] Nonetheless, Williamson claims that it was not until after Baldwin became leader in 1923 that the party was able to shed the reactionary image associated with the politics of anti-waste.[15] By mastering the newsreel and radio, Baldwin played an increasingly central role in shaping the Conservatives' public image over the course of his premiership.[16] The moderate and cross-denominational aspects of Baldwin's identity did much to attract former Liberals and many of those without traditional party ties into voting Conservative.[17]

David Jarvis builds on McKibbin and Williamson's work, demonstrating that the Conservatives were able to widen the appeal of their politics during the 1920s and 1930s by targeting multiple interest groups and focusing in particular on attracting the new female electorate. Anti-socialist messages were spread in party literature after 1918, such as the 'Mrs Maggs and Betty' stories, which celebrated commonsensical working women distrustful of socialist schemes.[18] As Neal McCrillis's detailed study of Conservative organisation demonstrates, the party developed a variety of means to reach out to the new electorate, including the development of Unionist Labour Committees and the Women's Unionist Organisation.[19]

Although a great deal has been written about the changing identity of early twentieth-century Unionism, major studies have tended to focus chiefly on party organisation or individual facets of ideology. Much of this literature downplays long-term developments in Unionist culture. Studies tend to end sharply in 1914, or begin in 1918, with few major works transcending the First World War, and even fewer actually engaging directly with wartime developments in the country, rather than just at Westminster.[20] Whilst the existing literature has provided us with a sure understanding of the currents of ideas running through British Unionism it also raises several questions: How was the Unionist message spread in the localities? How did local activists respond to central office appeals from London? How did the Unionists respond to their opponents' rhetoric? It has recently been demonstrated that Labour combated Conservative anti-socialism assiduously during the inter-war period. In particular, the party sought to dispel claims that a Labour government would engage in wild socialist schemes. Labour activists argued that they would govern in the interests of the vast majority of working people, whereas the Conservatives shored up the authority of elites.[21] To date, we know little of how the Conservatives responded to these evolving Labour strategies after 1918.[22]

This study seeks to provide a new understanding of the foundations of the Conservatives' unique success in twentieth-century British politics by exploring the dramatic cultural transformation which occurred within the party between 1900 and 1924. At the beginning of this period the Conservative Party as we know it today did not exist. Following the split of the Liberal Party over Irish home rule in 1886, Lord Salisbury led a Unionist alliance in parliament, which consisted of two parties: the Liberal Unionists and the Conservatives. Tensions existed between the two wings of the Unionist alliance throughout the 1890s and 1900s. Opposition to Irish home rule was integral to the continuation of the alliance into the Edwardian period, and a formal merger between the parties was not completed until 1912.[23] This newly formed party was commonly referred to as the 'Unionist Party', such was the importance of opposition to Irish home rule to its supporters. It was only after 1918 that the alternative term 'Conservative' came to be widely used in England and Wales, as anti-socialism became integral to the party's identity. Even then, supporters of the party in Scotland continued to be chiefly known as 'Unionists', at least up until the 1960s, when a formal merger with the English Conservative Party occurred.

Aside from this transition in identity, several other key features of the modern Conservative Party emerged during the early decades of the twentieth century: a party organisation for women, a focus on addressing the voter as a consumer, targeted electioneering strategies and the use of modern media to speak to a mass audience. This was an era when British politics was in upheaval. The rise of new forms of mass media and commercial entertainment both challenged the centrality of party politics to civic life and provided new opportunities for politicians to connect with the public. Furthermore, the boundaries of what politics meant were contested from various directions: the emergence of consumer movements, the rise of non-party organisations, the growing visibility of the female political activist and challenges to traditional forms of demonstrative public politics. This study provides the first substantial attempt to assess the Unionists' adaptation to democracy across the early twentieth century from a cultural perspective. Rather than offering a conventional party political history, it locates the growth in appeal of Unionist politics within the context of the party's interactions with emerging forms of civic life. Attention will also be paid to the competitive dialogue which existed between Unionists and their Liberal and Labour rivals in developing new means to appeal to the electorate, and responding to innovations made by their opponents.

The Unionists' successful transition to politics in a democratic age was rooted in their ability to gradually develop a variety of popular appeals after 1900, rooted in class, gender and regional identities. Unionist leaders and grassroots activists worked in symbiosis to develop a party culture with a wider appeal, effectively using new forms of media, and shaping, as well as adapting to, new ideas about public politics and responsible citizenship. In studying this transition we need recognise the importance of backbenchers like Morrison-Bell and the new female politicians who came through the women's tariff association, as well as more familiar figures like Stanley Baldwin and Neville Chamberlain, whose own political outlooks were shaped by their political apprenticeships served in the backwaters of local Unionist activism.

Our understanding of late Victorian politics has been transformed by a variety of studies of local politics, many of them influenced by the 'New Political History' (NPH). Scholars have analysed how individual politicians developed support bases through appeals founded on gender, class and imperial patriotism.[24] In much of this literature the support base of the Conservative Party in the localities appears to have owed little to the rhetoric and policies of the national party leadership. During the 1870s and 1880s populist Tory politicians created a social culture which united working- and middle-class supporters. Conservative parliamentary candidates took care to associate themselves with masculine civic cultures by championing local sports teams and the drink trade.[25] At the same time, women's integration into the party was facilitated by the respectable, cross-community social culture of the Primrose League.[26] However, there has been a reluctance to follow up these studies and analyse how late Victorian traditions of popular politics influenced Unionists during the 1900s. It has been claimed that earlier cultures of popular Tory politics lost their authority, given the divisions caused by Joseph Chamberlain's tariff reform crusade, the populist appeal of Edwardian Liberalism, and the emergence of Labour.[27]

This study of early twentieth-century England builds on the approaches developed by advocates of the NPH. An understanding that politics is a fundamentally cultural practice is inherent to this work. Building on the approaches developed by scholars of 'high politics' such as Maurice Cowling, the NPH has sought to understand how politicians actively construct constituencies of support by articulating plausible representations of 'interest' and 'identity' through language.[28] Although the NPH has its roots in earlier forms of political history writing, its advocates have tended to employ a wider source base than traditional political historians, using visual means of communication such as posters and paying particular attention to how politics is played out in public spaces through forms of activism such as election rituals, which are crucial to constructing relations between leaders and the led.[29]

Aside from a few studies of the tariff reform movement, analyses of local Unionism during the early twentieth century have largely been confined to studies of the Conservative Party organisation and the Primrose League, which was beginning its decline at this time.[30] But constituency organisation records offer only a glimpse of how Unionism operated in the localities. Often they are largely concerned with routine administrative procedures linked to the running of party organisation.[31] As Stuart Ball has observed, constituency organisations tended to debate a narrow range of topics; it is 'surprisingly rare [to find] discussion of such burning issues as tariff reform' in Edwardian minutes.[32] Yet the most vibrant and dynamic Unionist-affiliated organisations of the early twentieth century operated outside the official Conservative Party apparatus. The Tariff Reform League (TRL) and WUTRA played a vital role in widening the appeal of Unionist politics in the localities during the Edwardian period. They were only part of a wide culture of popular conservative leagues which emerged between the 1890s and 1914, including the Navy League, National Service League (NSL) and League of British Covenanters.

The relative neglect of the culture of these auxiliary conservative leagues largely stems from the assumption that they lacked a genuine popular appeal and relied on an aristocratic male leadership for their sustenance. Some historians have portrayed these leagues as a haven for the 'radical right', a hardcore of disaffected Tory zealots.[33] Frans Coetzee, who has provided the most detailed study of the Edwardian conservative leagues to date, claims that their rank-and-file membership participated in political activism in a way which 'was superficial and largely passive'.[34] This study influenced Ewen Green in turn, who argued that such organisations played a marginal role in the Unionist alliance's attempts to adapt to the challenge of mass politics.[35] The leagues' emergence has been seen as a result of the Edwardian 'crisis of conservatism'. Activists created and supported such movements due to their frustrations with the Conservative hierarchy.[36] With a revival in the party organisation after 1911, following major structural reforms, the independent leagues withered.[37]

Yet during the Edwardian period auxiliary organisations grew rapidly in number, not merely within the Unionist ranks, but across the political spectrum. This had much to do with the issue of finance: organisations such as the TRL and Free Trade Union (FTU), nominally independent of party, could spend vast sums during election campaigns without affecting the expenditure of candidates by claiming that they were promoting their policy rather than any specific party nominee. The competing organisations in the tariff reform debate appear to have been well financed; indeed, their resources arguably rivalled those of the official party organisations at the height of their campaigning. The profusion of extra-parliamentary movements enabled the de facto spending of the competing party forces to exceed by far the limits set out by the Corrupt Practices Act.[38] It has been estimated that the monthly spending of the FTU in its early months of activity was similar to the annual budget of the National Liberal Federation, and in 1907 the secretary of former Prime Minister Arthur Balfour claimed that the TRL had better finances and organisational resources than local Conservative associations.[39] The development of the popular conservative leagues was therefore not necessarily an indication of Unionist fractiousness, for it made sound financial sense.

While organisations like the Navy League and NSL were hierarchical and authoritarian, the same cannot be said of the tariff reform movement launched by Joseph Chamberlain in 1903. Chamberlain's supporters were at the heart of attempts to revitalise Unionist politics in the Edwardian period, and to widen its appeal to both sexes. Tariff reform organisations promoted an inclusive form of activism, delegating power to local activists through their decentralised structures. They did not simply wish to promote heterodox economic policies; they attempted to transform the culture of Unionism in Edwardian Britain. These popular conservative leagues often offered a much richer programme of regular events outside the heat of election campaigns than local Unionist associations could provide.

This study seeks to revise our understanding of the development of British Conservatism. But its story is also framed within wider debates about how conceptions of British political culture and citizenship were reformulated during the early decades of the twentieth century. A great deal of work has focused on the 'marketisation' of British politics, exploring how new forms of advertising and media reshaped political culture during the early decades of the twentieth century.[40] By the 1920s party leaders could reach an audience of millions through radio broadcasting and cinema newsreel. But we should not assume that there was a direct shift in focus from localised to national campaigning. Traditional and 'modern' forms of campaign meshed together throughout the early twentieth century. This was an era when a local party activist could write a play in response to a free trade film, publish it as a cheap pamphlet, and eventually see it performed nationally at tariff reform demonstrations, with characters added to suit local tastes.

Recent work has demonstrated that unruly traditions of public politics came under challenge and were replaced by a new concern with promoting 'peaceableness', especially after 1918.[41] It has also been suggested that the rise of non-party organisations after the First World War contributed to shifts in conceptions about responsible citizenship and challenged the former centrality of political parties to civic life.[42] This study provides the first substantial attempt to map out how these transformations in the culture of political life affected the fortunes of the leading parties in Britain. Conservative activists responded effectively to these shifts in public politics, thereby widening the appeal of their politics. After 1917 the Conservative Party was at the forefront of attempts to challenge traditions of unruly public politics. Moreover, rather than responding passively to the growth of non-party activism during and after the First World War, Conservative activists often participated in non-party organisations and sought to imitate their democratic culture in an attempt to expand the popular appeal of Unionist politics.

We will explore the Unionists' attempts to widen the purchase of their politics in England from three chief perspectives: gender, class and appeals to nation and locality, with individual chapters addressing each of these themes for the Edwardian, First World War, and post-war periods. It could be argued that the discussion of religious issues in politics merits study in separate chapters, rather than being discussed more generally under other headings. After all, as Ross McKibbin has recently noted, denominational identification was one of the most important elements in party affiliation before 1914, and it remained important throughout the 1920s.[43] Nonetheless, whilst religious issues were a bedrock of Unionist identity, they were not a factor which significantly expanded the Conservative Party's appeal to new groups of voters in England, and this was especially the case after 1914. During the First World War and its aftermath, traditional bonds between Nonconformist identity and the Liberal Party were ruptured. The free churches split over the running of the war and were divided over whether to support Lloyd George or Asquith's leadership when the Liberal Party split after 1916.[44] With English political Nonconformity in decline, the influence of religious issues in politics in the 1920s, whilst still noticeable, particularly during the Prayer Book controversy, was by no means as consistently apparent as it had been before the war. Moreover, the rise of a vibrant culture of non-party activism challenged the traditional hold that church and chapel had held over associational life in many regions. While Baldwin's Christian identity may have appealed to many erstwhile Liberals, the Conservatives' success after 1918 was rooted in a largely secular programme of anti-socialism and social reform.

All the same, whilst the influence of religious issues may have waned in much of England, they continued to play a vital role in shaping party identification in many parts of the 'Celtic fringe' of Scotland, Wales and Northern Ireland (as well as Cornwall) after the First World War. The continued strength of the Liberal Party in parts of rural Wales and Scotland during the 1920s and 1930s owed much to the survival of political Nonconformity in these regions.[45] A wider study of the United Kingdom would need to take into account the continued centrality of denominational identification in shaping party politics in the Celtic fringe. It would also require a detailed exploration of the emergence of a distinctive Welsh and Scottish politics during this period, which developed around issues of language and culture, as well as the politics of the specific industrial bases of these nations.[46]

Given this, attention will focus on England, which provided the core of Unionist MPs at Westminster throughout the early twentieth century (see table 0.1).

The following analysis draws heavily on Unionist printed and pictorial ephemera, as well as the surviving records of organisers and activists. However, the regional dimension of Unionist politics is also explored through a series of local case studies, using constituency records and local newspapers. This study focuses chiefly on seven areas which broadly reflect the experiences of Unionism across England: Birmingham, central Lancashire, Norfolk, Sussex, west London, west Yorkshire and Worcestershire. The choice of these particular case studies is dictated by concerns to cover a wide geographical range, urban and rural areas, regions of Unionist dynamism and weakness, and by the (rare) survival of substantial party records for these localities covering the whole of the 1900–24 period. Studies of the Conservative Party's revival during the early twentieth century have largely provided national perspectives. Yet

Table 0.1 *Seats won by Unionist parties in general elections, 1900–24*

Election	Lib. Unst England	Conservative England	Combined England	Lib. Unst Other	Conservative Other	Combined Other
1900	45	287	332	23	47	70
1906	16	106	122	8	27	35
1910 (J)	24	210	234	8	31	39
1910 (D)	27	208	235	9	29	38
1918	–	–	312	–	–	71
1922	–	–	308	–	–	37
1923	–	–	220	–	–	37
1924	–	–	354	–	–	65

1900–10 figures based on F.W.S. Craig (ed.), *British Parliamentary Election Results 1885–1918* (Chichester, 1974); 1918–24 figures based on David Butler and Gareth Butler, *British Political Facts 1900–1994* (London, 1994), pp. 214–15, 222. 'Other' seats are classified as Scotland, Wales, Ireland/ Northern Ireland and university seats.

in several respects the mass activism of post-1903 grassroots Unionism laid the foundations for the Conservative Party's successful negotiation of democracy and paved the way for Baldwinite Conservatism to flourish as the dominant force in inter-war politics.

Notes

1 Devon Record Office, Exeter, Ernest Morrison-Bell MSS, 2128, Ernest Morrison-Bell speech, n.d. [mid-1950s].
2 *Totnes Unionist*, February 1926, p. 1, cutting in Ernest Morrison-Bell MSS, 2128.
3 *Outlook*, 8 November 1913, p. 633.
4 John Ramsden, *The Age of Balfour and Baldwin, 1902–1940* (London, 1978), pp. 56–62.
5 Ramsden, *Age of Balfour and Baldwin*, pp. 121–3.
6 John Stubbs, 'The impact of the Great War on the Conservative Party', in Gillian Peele and Chris Cook (eds), *The Politics of Reappraisal, 1918–39* (London, 1975), pp. 14–38 at p. 14.
7 Stubbs, 'Impact of the Great War'; Nigel Keohane, *The Party of Patriotism: The Conservative Party and the First World War* (Farnham, 2010), pp. 128, 212; John Turner, *British Politics and the Great War: Coalition and Conflict, 1915–1918* (New Haven, CT, 1992), p. 391.
8 Stubbs, 'Impact of the Great War', pp. 31–5; Ramsden, *Age of Balfour and Baldwin*, pp. 116, 126; Keohane, *Party of Patriotism*, pp. 213–14; Turner, *British Politics and the Great War*, pp. 51, 318.
9 Ramsden, *Age of Balfour and Baldwin*, p. 110: Ewen Green has developed the idea that the end of the Lloyd George coalition in October 1922 played an important part in the development of Conservative anti-socialist politics, see E.H.H. Green, 'Conservatism, anti-socialism, and the end of the Lloyd George Coalition', in his *Ideologies of Conservatism* (Oxford, 2002), pp. 114–34 at p. 134.

10 Maurice Cowling, *The Impact of Labour, 1920–1924: The Beginning of Modern British Politics* (Cambridge, 1971).

11 Ross McKibbin, 'Class and conventional wisdom: the Conservative Party and the 'public' in inter-war Britain', in his *The Ideologies of Class: Social Relations in Britain, 1880–1950* (Oxford, 1990), pp. 259–93 at pp. 267, 273, 292–3.

12 Ibid., pp. 268–9.

13 Ibid., p. 285.

14 Philip Williamson, 'The doctrinal politics of Stanley Baldwin', in Michael Bentley (ed.), *Public and Private Doctrine: Essays in British History Presented to Maurice Cowling* (Cambridge, 1993), pp. 181–208 at p. 195; see also Williamson's *Stanley Baldwin: Conservative Leadership and National Values* (Cambridge, 1999), pp. 32–3; There has been a rapprochement between these perspectives in recent surveys by McKibbin and Williamson, with both acknowledging that the Conservatives' appeal was widened by their ability to use multiple anti-socialist languages during the 1920s. See Philip Williamson, 'The Conservative Party, 1900–1939: from crisis to ascendancy', in Chris Wrigley (ed.), *A Companion to Early Twentieth-Century Britain* (Oxford, 2003), pp. 3–22 at p. 16; Ross McKibbin, *Parties and People: England, 1914–1951* (Oxford, 2010), pp. 62–3.

15 Williamson, *Stanley Baldwin*, p. 206.

16 Ibid., pp. 83–7.

17 Williamson, *Stanley Baldwin*, p. 33; Ramsden also stresses the centrality of Baldwin to the Conservative Party's identity after 1924, see his *Age of Balfour and Baldwin*, pp. 203, 206–11.

18 David Jarvis, 'Mrs. Maggs and Betty: the Conservative appeal to women voters in the 1920s', *Twentieth Century British History*, 5:2 (1994), 129–52; David Jarvis, 'British Conservatism and class politics in the 1920s', *English Historical Review*, 111 (1996), 59–84 at 73–5, 80.

19 Neal McCrillis, *The British Conservative Party in the Age of Universal Suffrage: Popular Conservatism, 1918–1929* (Columbus, OH, 1998).

20 Ramsden's *Age of Balfour and Baldwin* provides an important exception to this trend.

21 Laura Beers, 'Counter-Toryism: Labour's response to anti-socialist propaganda, 1918–1939', in Matthew Worley (ed.), *The Foundations of the Labour Party: Identities, Cultures and Perspectives, 1900–39* (Aldershot, 2009), pp. 231–54; Jon Lawrence, 'Labour and the politics of class, 1900–1940', in David Feldman and Jon Lawrence (eds), *Structures and Transformations in Modern British History: Papers for Gareth Stedman Jones* (Cambridge, 2011), pp. 237–60.

22 An important exception here is Richard Toye's ongoing work on the culture of the House of Commons after 1918: Richard Toye, '"Perfectly parliamentary"? The Labour Party and the House of Commons after 1918' (unpublished MS).

23 Ian Cawood, 'Joseph Chamberlain, the Conservative Party and the Leamington Spa candidature dispute of 1895', *Historical Research*, 79 (2006), 554–77; Victoria Barbary, '"From Platform to the Polling Booth"': Political Leadership and Popular Politics in Bolton and Bury, 1868–1906' (PhD dissertation, University of Cambridge, 2007), chs 5–6.

24 Much of this literature has focused on popular Conservatism, but see also James Moore, *The Transformation of Urban Liberalism: Party Politics and Urban Governance in Late-Nineteenth Century England* (Aldershot, 2006); Paul Readman, 'The 1895 election and political change in late Victorian Britain', *Historical Journal*, 42:2 (1999), 467–93; see also his 'The Conservative Party, patriotism, and British

politics: the case of the General Election of 1900', *Journal of British Studies*, 40:1 (2001), 107–45.

25   Jon Lawrence, 'Class and gender in the making of urban Toryism, 1880–1914', *English Historical Review*, 108 (1993), 629–52; Alex Windscheffel, *Popular Conservatism in Imperial London, 1868–1906* (Woodbridge, 2007); Matthew Roberts, '"Villa Toryism" and popular Conservatism in Leeds, 1885–1902', *Historical Journal*, 94:1 (2006), 217–46; see also his 'Constructing a Tory world-view: popular politics and the Conservative press in late-Victorian Leeds', *Historical Research*, 79 (2006), 115–43.

26   Frans Coetzee, 'Villa Toryism reconsidered: Conservatism and suburban sensibilities in late-Victorian Croydon', in E.H.H. Green (ed.), *An Age of Transition: British Politics, 1880–1914* (Edinburgh, 1997), pp. 29–47 at pp. 44–5; Roberts, '"Villa Toryism" and Popular Conservatism in Leeds', p. 235.

27   Windscheffel, *Imperial London*, ch. 8; Coetzee, 'Villa Toryism reconsidered', pp. 40–1; Lawrence, 'Class and gender', pp. 645, 648–51; Frank Trentmann, *Free Trade Nation: Commerce, Consumption, and Civil Society in Modern Britain* (Oxford, 2008), p. 76.

28   For a perceptive discussion of the similarities between the 'New Political History' and earlier histories of 'high politics' see David M. Craig, '"High politics" and the "New Political History"', *Historical Journal*, 53 (2010), 453–75.

29   See, for example, James Thompson, '"Pictorial lies"? Posters and politics in Britain, c. 1880–1914', *Past and Present*, 197 (2007), 177–210; James Vernon, *Politics and the People: A Study in English Political Culture, c. 1815–1867* (Cambridge, 1993).

30   The local culture of tariff reform is explored in Alan Sykes, 'The Confederacy and the purge of the Unionist free traders, 1906–1910', *Historical Journal*, 18:1 (1975), 349–66; Larry L. Witherell, 'Political cannibalism among Edwardian Conservatives: Henry Page Croft, the confederacy and the campaign for East Hertfordshire, 1906–10', *Twentieth Century British History*, 8:2 (1997), 1–26; for the Conservative Party organisation see Ramsden, *Age of Balfour and Baldwin*; McCrillis, *Age of Universal Suffrage*; Stuart Ball, *Baldwin and the Conservative Party: The Crisis of 1929–1931* (New Haven, CT, 1988); see also his 'Local Conservatism and the evolution of the party organization', in Stuart Ball and Anthony Seldon (eds), *Conservative Century: The Conservative Party since 1900* (Oxford, 1994), pp. 261–314; for the Primrose League see Martin Pugh, *The Tories and the People* (Oxford, 1985); Philippe Vervaecke, 'Dieu, la couronne et l'Empire la Primrose League, 1883–2000: culture et pratiques politiques d'un movement Conservateur' (PhD dissertation, University of Lille, 2003).

31   Ball, 'Local Conservatism', p. 264.

32   Stuart Ball, 'National politics and local history: the regional and local archives of the Conservative Party, 1867–1945', *Archives*, 22 (1996), 27–59 at 56–7.

33   G.R. Searle, 'Critics of Edwardian society: the case of the Radical Right', in Alan O' Day (ed.), *The Edwardian Age: Conflict and Stability* (London, 1979), pp. 79–96 at p. 85; Anne Summers, 'The character of Edwardian nationalism: three popular leagues', in Paul Kennedy and Anthony Nicholls (eds), *Nationalist and Racialist Movements in Britain and Germany before 1914* (London, 1981), pp. 68–87; Ewen Green has pointed out that several of these groups had a moderate ideology and can be better described as 'Radical Conservative', see E.H.H. Green, *The Crisis of Conservatism: The Politics, Economics and Ideology of the British Conservative Party, 1880–1914* (London, 1995), pp. 23, 318–22, 329–32.

34   Frans Coetzee and Marilyn Shevin Coetzee, 'Rethinking the Radical Right in Germany and Britain before 1914', *Journal of Contemporary History*, 21:4 (1986), 515–37 at 518, 524–6.

35   E.H.H. Green, 'The strange death of Tory England', *Twentieth Century British History*, 2:1 (1991), 67–88 at 82.

36   Alan Sykes, 'The radical right and the crisis of conservatism before the First World War', *Historical Journal*, 26:3 (1983), 661–76; Green, 'Strange death of Tory England', 80–2; Searle, 'Critics of Edwardian society', pp. 79–96.

37   Ramsden, *Age of Balfour and Baldwin*, pp. 62, 72; Frans Coetzee, *For Party or Country: Nationalism and the Dilemmas of Popular Conservatism in Edwardian England* (Oxford, 1990), pp. 7–8.

38   P.G. Cambray, *The Game of Politics: A Study of the Principles of British Political Strategy* (London, 1932), p. 155.

39   John W. Hancock, 'The anatomy of the British Liberal Party, 1908–1918: a study of its character and disintergration' (PhD dissertation, University of Cambridge, 1992), p. 29; Robert Sandars to Arthur Balfour, 22 January 1907, British Library, London, Balfour MSS, Add. MSS 49765, fols 10–16.

40   Sian Nicholas, 'The construction of a national identity: Stanley Baldwin, "Englishness" and the mass media in inter-war Britain', in Martin Francis and Ina Zweiniger-Bargielowska (eds), *The Conservatives and British Society, 1880–1990* (Cardiff, 1996), pp. 127–46; Trentmann, *Free Trade Nation*; Thompson, 'Pictorial lies'; Jon Lawrence, *Electing Our Masters: The Hustings in British Politics from Hogarth to Blair* (Oxford, 2009), chs 3–4; Laura Beers, *Your Britain: Media and the Making of the Labour Party* (Cambridge, MA, 2010).

41   Jon Lawrence, 'The transformation of British public politics after the First World War', *Past and Present*, 190 (2006), 185–216.

42   Helen McCarthy, 'Parties, voluntary associations and democratic politics in interwar Britain', *Historical Journal*, 50:4 (2007), 891–912.

43   McKibbin, *Parties and People*, pp. 5, 13–14.

44   Trevor Wilson, *The Downfall of the Liberal Party, 1914–1935* (London, 1966), pp. 24–8; Stephen Koss, *Nonconformity in Modern British Politics* (London, 1975), ch. 6.

45   Felix Aubel, 'The Conservatives in Wales, 1880–1935', in Martin Francis and Ina Zweiniger-Bargielowska (eds), *The Conservatives and British Society, 1880–1990* (Cardiff, 1996), pp. 96–110; Koss, *Nonconformity in Politics*, p. 175.

46   For the importance of these issues see Andrew Edwards and Wil Griffith, 'Welsh national identity and governance, 1918–1945', in Duncan Tanner, Chris Williams, W.P. Griffiths and Andrew Edwards (eds), *Debating Nationhood and Governance in Britain, 1885–1939: Perspectives from the Four Nations* (Manchester, 2006), pp. 118–45; Kenneth Morgan, *Rebirth of a Nation: Wales 1880–1980* (Oxford, 1980), chs 7–9; Richard Finlay, 'Scottish Conservatism and Unionism since 1918', in Martin Francis and Ina Zweiniger-Bargielowska (eds), *The Conservatives and British Society, 1880–1990* (Cardiff, 1996), pp. 111–26 at pp. 114–19.

PART I

Edwardian politics

1

Responding to the Edwardian crisis of Unionism

One dreary day, whilst eating dinner, the Perring family had an unexpected guest. Ignoring the unfinished meal, wailing babies and the piles of washing around the room, Mrs Balkwill swept into the Perrings' humble home, dressed in silk petticoats and trailed by her maid. Exchanging the briefest of pleasantries, the well-to-do lady canvasser showed undue haste in wishing to put Mr Perring down as a vote for her side, evidently keen to quit the house for more salubrious surroundings. When questioned, Balkwill seemed unsure of her candidate's programme, but assured the family, 'he's such a nice man; a thorough gentleman' who went by the motto 'trust the people'. Seemingly unaware of the family's meal gone cold, the lady canvasser made her exit, anxious to get home to her warm lunch.[1]

This skit appeared in *Seems So!*, an extraordinary book published in 1911 by Stephen Reynolds in collaboration with two Devon fishermen, Tom and Bob Woolley. Their Mrs Balkwill was a variation on a familiar stereotype: the well-to-do 'Lady Bountiful' who would only enter the slums at election time to preach at the working classes on how her party of choice cared for their welfare. Mercifully freed from the attention of Mrs Balkwill, Dave Perring damns the 'parcel o' women' who canvass during elections to get their men in, but made little attempt to educate either themselves or the public on politics in the meantime.[2]

The year after *Seems So!* appeared, the Conservative Party merged with the Liberal Unionist Party which had been created in 1886 by Liberals such as Joseph Chamberlain who opposed Gladstone's plans to introduce home rule for Ireland. Although the Unionist alliance had been the dominant force in British politics for much of the late Victorian period under Lord Salisbury's leadership, it had slumped to three consecutive election defeats between 1906 and 1910. Unsurprisingly then, scholars have often referred to the Edwardian years as witnessing a 'crisis of conservatism', a subject explored most authoritatively by Ewen Green.[3]

During the late nineteenth century the Unionists had developed a broad coalition of support, transcending class and gender boundaries. Populist politicians celebrated Britain's imperial might and championed the respectable working man who could be trusted to enjoy a drink and a flutter in moderation. At the core of Conservative attempts to develop a mass support base in late Victorian Britain was the Primrose League, an organisation which sought to bridge the traditionally class-bound cultures of Conservative life. Founded in 1883, the Primrose League promoted values of domesticity and family life, and afforded women the opportunity to participate in Conservative activism.[4]

Given that the late Victorian Conservatives' social culture appeared to have a wide appeal, the enthusiasm with which many Unionists greeted Joseph Chamberlain's decision to take up the cause of tariff reform in 1903 may seem puzzling. Chamberlain's campaign, which attracted the support of thousands of activists, has been blamed for causing chronic divisions within party constituency associations during the 1900s, and is also viewed as a precipitating factor in triggering the Primrose League's gradual decline in influence.[5] In trying to make sense of the decision to adopt tariff reform, Ewen Green argued that many Unionists felt they needed to adopt a 'positive' electoral policy which could secure their long-term future by stopping the country from dividing along class lines. Chamberlain's supporters fervently promoted tariff reform, even though it divided the Unionist ranks, as they believed that it was the only major policy that could surmount the party's apparent crisis and enable it to consolidate its appeal amongst the working classes.[6]

Whereas Green focused chiefly on policy-making, this chapter explores the cultural reasons behind the rapid development of the grassroots tariff reform movement during the early years of the twentieth century. In focusing on the harmful effects that the tariff reform campaign had on the cohesion of Unionist constituency associations, historians have largely overlooked the fact that many activists were frustrated by the limited opportunities that existing conservative organisations provided for political education in the early 1900s. These resentments were expressed most keenly by the Liberal Unionists. It is clear that Green's thesis underestimates the extent to which the two partners within the Unionist alliance retained distinct identities which fuelled enthusiasm for an overhaul of party organisation.[7] Chamberlain's supporters thought that there were too many people like Mrs Balkwill in the Conservative rank-and-file who showed more concern with parading their social respectability than engaging meaningfully in the political battles of the day.

The development of tariff reform as a popular movement was not only based on Unionists' desire to find a policy which could secure their electoral future. In fact, tariff reform was not promoted as a panacea to fend off the Unionists' ills. In 1907, Violet Brooke-Hunt, secretary of the Women's Unionist and Tariff Reform Association, stated that her organisation had four objects: promoting political education, supporting tariff reform, supporting social reforms and opposing Irish home rule.[8] The development of the tariff reform campaign reflected a widespread desire amongst Unionists to shape a new ethos of activism better suited to dealing with the challenges of democratic politics. Chamberlain's supporters sought to forge a genuinely Unionist identity combining the Liberal Unionists' concern to promote political education with the Conservatives' focus on developing a popular social culture.

In 1902, the year before the tariff reform controversy flared up, *Lady's Realm* published an eleven-page article on the progress of the Primrose League, the majority of which was given over to opulent portraits of titled women connected with that organisation's work. The Primrose League, it claimed, was faring more successfully than the Women's Liberal Federation because the latter body had 'minor masculine' characteristics and used 'caucusing' tactics to win over the voter. By contrast, the 'eternally feminine' Primrose Dame used her 'social charms' and understood the importance of entertainments to the successful political organisation.[9] Nonetheless, many other commentators did not share this optimism about the Primrose League's position. Indeed, the characteristics that the *Lady's Realm* lauded were often seen as hampering Unionist prospects.

By the early 1900s there were indications that the Primrose League was struggling to function effectively as a political auxiliary of the Conservative Party in several regions. True, it continued to attract large numbers of members and played a key role in Conservative life, particularly in rural constituencies where its branch network of 'habitations' acted as a social centre for scattered villages, albeit one which was increasingly reliant on an ageing membership in some cases.[10] Nevertheless, by the turn of the century concerns were growing that the Primrose League was placing too much focus on social events, at the expense of educational activities.[11]

Primrose League reports from these years suggest that many habitations were struggling to attract new members who could take a lead in providing political education. An investigation in Lancashire during 1901, the findings of which were circulated privately, confirmed that only just over half of the county's habitations were active.[12] The following year head office staff recorded that around a third of habitations in Sussex were 'inert or practically dead'. Little enthusiasm was shown for reviving these branches: 'There is not one that could not be reorganised if those in the district who have some leisure would come forward and give the necessary lead.'[13] The Liberals' landslide election victory in 1906 led to further soul-searching about the state of the Primrose League.[14] A central office report commissioned in the wake of the Unionists' defeat concluded: 'It frequently happens that the political character of the League is not mentioned at Primrose League gatherings…The efforts of Habitation officials are directed more towards the provision of amusement than of political instruction.'[15]

There were three key reasons why the Primrose League's focus on social activities was coming under criticism: a narrowing gap between Liberal and Conservative social cultures, the hostility of Liberal Unionists, and evidence of an incipient Liberal revival after 1902. These factors, combined with the electoral disaster of 1906, led the leaders of the tariff reform campaign to attempt to overhaul the culture of popular Unionism. Whereas the Primrose League's social activities had been important to the Conservatives' appeal, particularly in county constituencies, Patricia Lynch's study of rural England suggests that the Liberal Party developed an increasingly effective organisation in agricultural communities during the late 1890s and early 1900s, imitating the Primrose League's culture of teas, soirees and garden parties.[16] More generally, the social bases of populist male Conservatism, with its links to sport and the drink trade, were coming under challenge at this time. The rise of the Clubs and Institute Union meant that working men's clubs, which had formed a bulwark of urban Conservatism, were increasingly presenting themselves as non-political.[17] Growing numbers of Liberal clubs chose to sell alcohol in the 1890s, further undermining the Conservatives' position as the champion of the working man's pint.[18] Liberal papers also began to reflect the tastes of the populist Tory press in paying attention to sports and betting.[19] By the turn of the century it was becoming increasingly obvious that the Conservatives could not rely solely on their social culture to maintain an electoral appeal, given that they were losing a distinct cultural identity.

Whilst the social culture of late Victorian Conservatism has received a great deal of attention, we know much less of the experiences of activists who supported the junior partner within Lord Salisbury's alliance, the Liberal Unionists. Yet recent valuable work has demonstrated that significant tensions existed between the two wings of the Unionist alliance at the local level into the 1890s and beyond.[20] Writing in 1906, the former chairman of the East Worcestershire Conservative Association, John Bridges, provided a vivid recollection of the differences between the Unionist parties' social cultures in his constituency. Recounting the Conservative smoking concerts he had organised in King's Norton from the 1880s onwards, Bridges noted that they had to make sure the political speech was not too long 'or the room would speedily have emptied'.[21] The smoking concerts were: 'An abomination to the Liberal Unionists. I have seen a few of them there, but if not always like skeletons at a feast, they never seemed comfortable. They gave the idea of condescending to what they considered a regrettable waste of their valuable time.'[22]

Bridges' vituperative attack on the Liberal Unionists was no doubt coloured by his hostility to Joseph Chamberlain following the alliance's disastrous showing at the 1906 election. All the same, Bridges had a point. The Liberal Unionists' character reflected the more earnest traditions of Gladstonian Liberalism, and the party's leaders were at the forefront of calls for a more progressive and ideologically focused Unionist programme.[23] The Women's Liberal Unionist Association, in particular, devoted great attention to educational work, encouraging discussion meetings, with the assistance of guest speakers, to train efficient political workers.[24] Unsurprisingly then, the ethos of Chamberlain's party sat uneasily with the decorous social culture of the Primrose League. Bridges believed that Liberal Unionist women in his division 'would have laughed to scorn the idea of developing into political personages like our Primrose Dames'.[25] As leader of the Birmingham Liberal Unionists, Chamberlain did little to ease such tensions, not appearing on a platform in connection with the Primrose League until 1899.[26]

Liberal Unionist hostility to the Primrose League was not merely a West Midlands phenomenon. Habitations in Scotland appear to have experienced similarly frosty relations in their dealings with Liberal Unionists. In Lancashire too, the strength of the Primrose League appears to have been largely confined to pockets of Conservative support. Bolton had a series of flourishing habitations with close connections to the local Conservative leadership; the Primrose League claimed that it had over seven thousand members in the town in 1902. Despite this, in nearby Bury, where the Liberal Unionists dominated the alliance, the Primrose League struggled to gain a foothold in the town's life.[27]

When a Liberal revival began after 1902, existing conservative organisations appeared unable to take effective steps to rejuvenate Unionism. The Education Act introduced that year frustrated Liberal Unionists, who feared that it would alienate their substantial Nonconformist support. At the heart of the controversy was the government's decision to abolish the school boards which had been set up by the 1870 Education Act, enabling Nonconformists to gain influence in the running of schools. Furthermore, it was decided that denominational schools would henceforth be funded by local taxation. Given that the majority of such schools were Anglican, many Nonconformists resented having to fund a form of religious education which they disagreed with.[28] Joseph Chamberlain articulated his party's frustrations with the Education Bill in an August 1902 letter to Arthur Balfour:

To my view it is clear that the Bill has brought all the fighting Nonconformists out into the field and made of them active instead of merely passive opponents. Their representation and appeals to the old war cries have influenced large numbers of the lower middle and upper working classes who have hitherto supported the Unionist Party without joining the Conservative organization. The transfer of their votes will undoubtedly have immense importance at a general election…I do not think that any seat where there is a strong Nonconformist electorate can be considered absolutely safe.[29]

In Devon and Cornwall, the main stronghold of English Liberal Unionism outside the West Midlands, the party had a particularly close association with the free churches, and it appears to have lost several seats at the 1906 election as a result of Nonconformist defections to the Liberal Party.[30]

Aside from the Education Act, the Liberals' claim that Chinese labourers had been kept in dire conditions on the Rand also proved problematic for the Unionist alliance. The 'Chinese slavery' cry undermined an argument which Unionists had regularly employed at the 1900 election, namely that the Boer War had been fought for democratic reasons. Appeals to protect British subjects in South Africa had played an important part in the alliance's success in winning the 'Khaki election'.[31]

Finally, and most importantly, a remarkable campaign was staged in defence of free trade following Chamberlain's proclamation of support for tariff reform in May 1903. Propagandists spread their message through films, plays, speaking campaigns, shop exhibitions and study circles, amongst other means.[32] Faced with this onslaught, existing conservative organisations were ill-prepared to wage a fight against the resurgent Liberal forces. Through adopting a policy of neutrality on the fiscal question, the Primrose League Grand Council hampered the ability of local habitations to participate in tariff reform activism.

The Conservative organisation more generally appears to have stagnated in the early 1900s. During the 1895 and 1900 elections Unionist candidates had been able to stand unopposed in much larger numbers than their rivals, breeding a mood of complacency which left them poorly prepared when faced by a Liberal or Labour candidate in nearly every seat they contested in 1906.[33] A memorandum on Conservative organisation in London noted that the party lacked a 'practical working organisation' in twenty-five seats; several constituencies in the capital had no Conservative agent at the time of the election.[34] Furthermore, the Conservative Club movement did not provide an adequate basis for a fight back, being almost solely social in focus.[35]

Table 1.1 *Unionists and Liberals elected unopposed at general elections, 1895–1906*

Year	Unionist	Liberal
1895	123	12
1900	153	23
1906	5	32

Figures based on A.K. Russell, *Liberal Landslide: The General Election of 1906* (Newton Abbot, 1973), p. 44.

Conservative Central Office struggled to modernise in response to the Liberal resurgence. If anything, this body became less effectively managed under the direction of Lionel Wells, the Conservative Party's principal agent between 1903 and 1905. Wells was seen as heavy-handed in his leadership, neglecting to consult the National Union of Conservative Associations (NUCA), and losing touch with local constituency branches. Wells' leadership came under attack at the NUCA conference in November 1905, where a resolution was adopted which complained that the management of the central office in London was defective and needed revising.[36] Wells subsequently quit his post, but the party reorganisation that followed in 1906 was far from satisfactory. Provincial divisions were abolished, which meant that each county had to appoint its own secretary and agent rather than using the central office district agents as previously, stymying professionalism.[37] During the 1910 elections the Liberal Party Central Office enjoyed close relations with the press, with Sir Henry Norman, the secretary of the Budget League and a former journalist, providing material to news agencies. By contrast, Conservative Central Office had a much more haphazard relationship with the press and had no form of press bureau, with the result that campaign speeches by leading Unionist speakers appear to have received less coverage that the meetings of prominent Liberals like Winston Churchill in papers such as *The Times*.[38]

Following a third successive election defeat, a Unionist Reorganisation Committee was appointed in 1911, interviewing 103 witnesses and receiving written testimony from 289 others. In the months before the committee sat, leading tariff reformers had been vocal in their criticisms of the Conservative hierarchy. Leo Amery wrote to Bonar Law, stating they 'must at all costs…reconstruct the whole party organisation'. He claimed that local associations 'pay no attention whatever to the central office, and the central office has no control over them'.[39] Mary Maxse, chairman of the WUTRA, expressed herself in a similar vein. She claimed that amongst her supporters 'there is a universal feeling, which I share, that changes are necessary in the Central Organisation of the Conservative party'; they wanted 'newer, brisker, more democratic methods'.[40]

The Unionist Reorganisation Committee presented forms of propaganda which were centrally organised by the Conservative Party in London as inefficient. Testimonials were highly critical of Conservative touring vans, which did 'not justify the expense of their maintenance' and were 'absolutely useless in a manufacturing centre'.[41] Constituency association records reveal that local party leaders shared these frustrations. The North Norfolk Conservative Association reported that the vans 'had no good results' and that the money would be better spent on recruiting touring working men speakers employed by the TRL.[42] Likewise, in contrast to its hostility to the propaganda efforts of Conservative Central Office, the reorganisation committee praised the work that tariff reform organisations were playing in enhancing Unionism's electoral prospects.[43]

Joseph Chamberlain's supporters responded to the emerging crisis of Unionism by creating a range of new organisations that encouraged a more ideologically committed, activist mentality. Chamberlain had a reputation as an organisational moderniser through pressure group activities, having established the National Liberal Federation in 1877. This organisation sought to widen the influence and representation of local Liberal associations. At its outset the National Liberal Federation proclaimed its mission to 'take the people at large into the counsels of the party, to share its control and management'.[44] Chamberlain's tariff organisations similarly aimed to widen popular participation in organised politics. A Tariff Reform League appeared in 1903, which created a nationwide network of branches for male supporters of Chamberlain's campaign. The TRL's functions in the West Midlands were performed by the Imperial Tariff Committee, which had close links to the region's Liberal Unionist leadership. A Women's Tariff Reform League was formed in 1904. By 1906 the Women's Liberal Unionist Association had been shorn of its free trade membership; it subsequently amalgamated with this body to create the WUTRA.[45] Many of the figures who emerged as the tariff leagues' grassroots leaders during the 1900s were aged under thirty-five when they began to campaign actively in support of Chamberlain's fiscal programme. Henry Page Croft started his involvement in the tariff reform campaign at twenty-two, Leo Amery aged twenty-nine. Mary Maxse and Violet Brooke-Hunt were both thirty-four when they took their respective positions as chairman and secretary of the women's tariff association. Caroline Bridgeman began work for this organisation at the age of thirty-one. These figures represented a new generation who were frustrated by the Conservative status quo.[46]

To understand truly the nature of Chamberlain's supporters' response to the Unionist alliance's malaise, we need to explore how activists used a variety of forms of media to promote political causes on the ground. Recent years have seen a flourishing of interest in the culture of popular politics in Edwardian Britain; the often-sensational politics of the period are brought to life in studies of the public meeting, political posters and explorations of the novel campaign methods of the time, such as seaside meetings and shopping exhibitions.[47] Nonetheless, the existing literature has tended to neglect the activities of Unionist activists in the localities.

Frank Trentmann has explored the culture of the free trade campaign at length, convincingly presenting it as, at heart, a popular movement which mobilised thousands of Britons in its defence.[48] Chamberlain's supporters sought to develop a comparable democratic culture to free trade, offering new opportunities for men and women to participate in Unionist activism in the process. The way in which tariff reformers deployed media was crucial to their strategy of developing a more demotic form of Unionism, which could appeal beyond the traditional activist minority. Chamberlain's supporters took pains to encourage forms of activism which the public could participate in en masse.

Jan Rüger's recent study of the popular cult of the navy provides one of the most detailed analyses of popular political ritual in Edwardian Britain. Rüger stresses the role that new forms of mass media played in shaping the political culture of the time, concluding that the burgeoning film industry and popular press, rather than organised pressure groups, played the chief role in shaping mass enthusiasm for naval culture.[49] Yet the same conclusions cannot be drawn in regard to the tariff reform campaign. Whilst commercial actors helped to shape the fiscal debate, their message could at times be outflanked by cruder forms of campaign developed autonomously by local activists. The culture of the tariff reform movement demonstrates that the most prominent debate in Edwardian politics revolved around a rich interaction between national and local, and modern and traditional forms of campaign.

One of the most effective ways to explore how various actors shaped the public identity of tariff reform is to analyse the use they made of Joseph Chamberlain, a figure highly recognisable in popular culture. As colonial secretary, Chamberlain had been one of the chief architects behind the Boer War. Celebrating his martial qualities, a 1900 election poster depicted him as a wrestling champion, and he was lauded as 'fightin' Joe' in the music hall.[50] Cinema was quick to utilise the image of Chamberlain when addressing the tariff reform controversy. In *John Bull's Hearth* (1903), the first tariff reform film, a Briton is ejected from his fireside by foreign traders. In the pivotal scene a colonial enters, bearing a portrait of Chamberlain, to whom John Bull, the archetypal patriot, doffs his hat. They proceed to banish the foreigners and replace free trade with fair trade.[51]

Cinema increasingly came to be seen as a useful political tool in early twentieth-century Britain. Mr F. Payne, Unionist agent for Barnstaple, wrote to the *Conservative Agents' Journal* noting the value of films for political lectures. He singled out *John Bull's Hearth* as a useful production.[52] Nonetheless, cinema played a limited role in furthering the tariff cause. It was common for film-makers such as Gaumont to produce movies for both sides of the fiscal debate. The cinema journal *Bioscope* encouraged proprietors to buy Gaumont's opposing films during the January 1910 election campaign: 'We think it would be a good "draw" for any showman to show both of these. It would create further interest in the show without hurting the feelings of any of the patrons.'[53] Cinema acted as a new forum for political theatre in which audiences could boo and cheer the opposing sides of the political debate, much as they did in the music hall. Election results shown at the end of presentations were cheered loudly by audiences.[54]

The cinema of 'naval theatre' which Rüger explores utilised iconic images of huge warships being launched in front of large crowds. It was a theme well suited to the age of silent film. Cinema audiences could feel that they were taking part in an event based around patriotically celebrating the majesty of the imperial fleet and the achievements of British industry.[55] By contrast, silent movies could present little of the complex nature of the fiscal debate or of the specific industrial concerns of local communities. Gaumont's tariff reform film for the 1910 elections, a thinly disguised remake of *John Bull's Hearth* from 1903, appears clichéd and simplistic next to the company's free trade production.[56]

Amy Moreton, a tariff reform activist from Nuneaton, wrote a play entitled *Freedom in Happy England* (1911) as a more potent riposte to Gaumont's free trade film. The Gaumont film depicts the home of an English workman made affluent by free trade, 'he has a poster on the wall, depicting old age pensions, and crowns Mr Lloyd George, [the Liberal chancellor of the Exchequer], with a halo of flowers'.[57] Moreton's play mocks this scenario. We are introduced to the scantily furnished home of Tom Smith, a workman. On the wall is the ironic motto 'God bless Lloyd George, the people's friend'. Tom is eventually convinced of the errors of free trade by his friend, Bill. He proceeds to tear down the motto, and the play ends with Bill's appeal to the audience: 'you'll curse the day Lloyd George was born and bless kind Providence for giving to England the Statesman who sacrificed 'ealth and strength for Tariff Reform to benefit not one particular class, but all classes and the Empire at large – Joseph Chamberlain'.[58] Unlike cinema, fiscal plays were well attuned to the changing politics of Edwardian Britain. They enabled local activists to mould and shape the presentation of their cause. Successful productions were published in pamphlet form and came to be widely imitated, topical allusions could be thrown in and songs and characters added to suit the concerns of local audiences.[59]

Rank-and-file activists played a vital role in shaping the public identity of tariff reform, especially through the TRL's celebration of Chamberlain Day. Every year tens of thousands of supporters participated in celebrations on Chamberlain's birthday, 8 July, or attended fetes later in the month. We can view it as an 'invented tradition' which enabled tariff reformers to renew their faith in the cause through a communal celebration of their chief's work.[60] There was often a rousing speech in which Chamberlain was portrayed as a great champion of empire, and a call was made for activists to follow his patriotic example. This might be followed by a rendition of the 'Chamberlain Celebration Song', in which the audience pledged to 'follow Joe through weal and woe'.[61]

Amateur companies of women performing educational tariff reform plays became a familiar sight at Unionist social events such as Chamberlain

Day.[62] Such performances often deployed slapstick humour. Audiences of the play *That Foreigner* were requested not to throw vegetables at the repulsive German trader, Herr Smit von Squeeze, who 'will be deported under the Undesirable Aliens Acts subsequent to the performance'. Chamberlain's opponents likewise had a taste for pantomime. The *Free Trader* reported on one performance of *Tried and True*: 'The peals of laughter at the discomfiture of the tariff reform characters and the cheers as the sturdy workman "Jim Burton" and his wife put them to rout lengthened the play by a full ten minutes.'[63] Dramatic entertainments had been a common feature of Victorian Primrose League meetings, but they rarely had a specific political focus. By contrast, Edwardian fiscal plays aimed at spreading a serious message, albeit by light-hearted means. The *Free Trader* argued that 'people can be induced to go to a play when they cannot be tempted into a meeting. Ideas and principles seen, as it were, in the concrete appeal more powerfully and directly to many minds.'[64] In effect, by promoting such entertainments, tariff reformers were able to retain the social appeal which had been intrinsic to the culture of existing Unionist auxiliary organisations, but align it effectively with a more serious political ethos.

In July 1904 William Bridgeman, a convinced supporter of Chamberlain's tariff reform campaign, stood as Conservative candidate for Oswestry, Shropshire, a seat which had been held by the party since its creation in 1885. Bridgeman had played a prominent role in a local Primrose League habitation and could expect success given his party's pedigree in the constituency.[65] Yet the Shropshire Primrose Leaguers on whom Bridgeman relied to promote his cause appear to have offered only feeble efforts to combat a Free Trade Union (FTU) campaign which targeted housewives and sought to present Bridgeman as a squire out of touch with the mood of local people. The FTU speaker, Francis Soutter, delighted in speaking in clothes dirtied by fly-posting so that he could address Bridgeman's tenants 'in their own garb', in sharp contrast to the Conservative candidate, who arrived at his meetings in a starched suit and panama hat.[66] Free traders like Soutter sought to present themselves as the champions of rural interests, claiming that tariff reform would sacrifice British agriculture in the interests of Tory plutocrats determined to find new markets for their manufactures.[67] Unable to mount an effective counter-attack, the Conservatives lost the seat by 385 votes.

Stung by this defeat, William Bridgeman moved quickly to modernise the Oswestry association with the aid of Joseph Chamberlain and Liberal Unionist organisers, laying the basis for a Conservative victory in the constituency at the 1906 election. Their innovations provide an indication of how tariff reformers sought to distance themselves from earlier cultures of Unionist activism. Within days of the defeat Chamberlain provided Bridgeman with the assistance of William Jenkins of the Imperial Tariff Committee to reorganise the constituency party's structure.[68] Over the next year working men's associations were formed in several polling districts.[69]

At the forefront of the revitalised Oswestry Conservative organisation was the new women's association chaired by Caroline Bridgeman, the candidate's wife. Jenkins had identified the lack of 'lady helpers' as one of the key defects in the recent election campaign.[70] Whereas the Primrose League had paid little attention to politics in the intervals between elections, Caroline Bridgeman's Women's Unionist Association sought to run a continuous campaign. Informal 'cottage meetings' were arranged on a regular basis in the villages, and a Conservative magazine was distributed once a month.[71] Caroline Bridgeman believed that such efforts were necessary as existing conservative organisations had failed to educate housewives effectively, and consequently, they were attracted by Liberal 'bogies' about tariff reform such as 'your bread will cost you more' and 'the big and little loaf'.[72] Having established a dynamic movement in Oswestry, Caroline Bridgeman became the vice-chairman of the WUTRA, arguably the most innovative and successful of the auxiliary organisations formed by supporters of Joseph Chamberlain.

The impetus to develop WUTRA grew from women's frustrations with the undemocratic culture of the Primrose League. The Duchess of Atholl, who became the first Conservative female Cabinet minister, later recounted that the Primrose League 'had not found favourable soil' in Scotland, with people 'not altogether understanding the League's hierarchy of Knights and Dames'.[73] Of particular concern for tariff reformers were the limited opportunities which the Primrose League provided for female leadership, which had become vital given that free traders placed the female consumer at the heart of their campaigning.[74] The Liberals could draw on substantial support from the Women's Liberal Federation, whose leaders had become used to addressing predominantly male meetings from the 1880s onwards.[75] Liberal women also participated in local government in much greater numbers than their Primrose League counterparts in the 1890s.[76] The Primrose League Ladies Grand Council had no formal powers and was purely an advisory body dominated by aristocrats. True, at local level, some habitations were solely confined to women, but they do not generally seem to have provided the necessary impetus to challenge free traders' claims to represent the housewives' interest. The Brighton Dames habitation, which was one of the most high-profile female-only branches in southern England, had to wait until 1896 for its first meeting addressed solely by women speakers. Even then, the Dames insisted that they would 'always avail themselves of those male Leaguers whose experience in organisation, demonstration, and agitation is necessarily far more varied and far more extensive' than their own.[77]

By contrast, the women's tariff association aimed to promote a vibrant local culture of activism so that Unionist workers would be well informed on the political issues of the day. Speaking at a meeting of the WUTRA-led Women's League for Municipal Reform, Mrs E.P. Nicholson noted that 'the day had gone by when it was only necessary that a canvasser for votes should be able to pat children upon the head and talk prettily. Canvassers must now be people of information.'[78] Study circles became central to WUTRA's new brand of politically aware female activist. In spring 1910 *Monthly Notes on Tariff Reform* publicised a newspaper interview with Mrs Fletcher, wife of the MP for Hampstead. She believed that Conservatives 'suffer from a want of organisation in many constituencies' and that the work of female tariff activists could make up for this deficiency. Fletcher ran a debating class, where she encouraged women to bring along political literature to discuss and 'contribute to our store of knowledge'. She attributed high Unionist majorities in the counties surrounding London at the January 1910 election to 'the education of the village people by women workers...having debates, delivering speeches and giving Tariff Reform plays'. According to Fletcher, the advent of the tariff leagues created a sea change in these constituencies. Previously they had often become used to holding a handful of Conservative meetings between elections.[79] Following the creation of WUTRA, a woman could commonly attend over twenty meetings in her constituency annually.[80]

Key to the tariff leagues' attempts to revitalise the Unionist cause was their promotion of a decentralised power structure, empowering local activists. Mary Maxse was a keen believer in letting branches act as the female voice of tariff reform in their localities. She limited the role of salaried organisers to 'inspection, advice and guidance divested of direct executive control'.[81] Maxse saw continuous political education by local bodies as key to Unionist fortunes; merely canvassing during election campaigns could have little effect on political opinions.[82] In 1912 she noted: 'it is now generally recognised that the real burden of political work, during the quiet time between elections...rests upon the sub-committees in the towns and villages, the men and women who go from house to house arousing and keeping alive the interest of the voter'.[83]

At their most dynamic, the tariff leagues' campaigning in the localities proved a match for the ingenuity of their free trade rivals. In Sussex, for instance, the Tariff Reform League organised village campaigns, weekly lectures in Brighton and beach-front meetings. Audiences of up to three thousand were attracted to the seaside demonstrations, which often featured rival free trade and tariff reform platforms positioned within shouting distance of each other.[84] The Brighton and Sussex branches were essentially self-contained units. They held instruction classes to train local orators, who spoke at the bulk of TRL meetings in the county.[85] Promoting Sussex speakers meant that the league was better able to claim that it represented local opinion. It was felt that farm labourers 'would pay much more attention to the local man than they would to a paid speaker' touring the country.[86]

John Ramsden saw the TRL and WUTRA as part of a 'legion of [extra-parliamentary] leagues' which grew to prominence in Edwardian Britain as a result of Unionist activists' frustrations with the Conservative hierarchy.[87] In this reading, there was an inverse relationship between the fortunes of the tariff leagues and the party organisation.[88] Following the report of the Unionist Reorganisation Committee and the appointment of Andrew Bonar Law as party leader in 1911, the efficiency of the Conservative Party organisation increased dramatically, diminishing the need for the leagues' continued existence.[89] Ramsden produces an essentially top-down view of the Unionist revival, portraying the party leaderships' reorganisation efforts as marking 'the beginning of the climb back to power'.[90]

Yet, as we have seen, the tariff leagues were at the forefront of attempts to revive Unionist politics in Edwardian Britain. They sought to widen the opportunities for previously marginalised groups, such as women, to participate in political activism. By the early 1900s it was commonly felt that existing conservative organisations could not compete effectively in modern politics due to their lack of a democratic structure and neglect of political education. At the heart of the tariff leagues' development as a mass movement was a widespread desire amongst rank-and-file activists to modernise and revive Unionist politics. The tariff reform campaign, and the defection of leading Liberal Unionist free traders such as the Duke of Devonshire and Sir Henry James, effectively ended the traditional division between Conservatives and Liberal Unionists, paving the way for the merger of these parties in 1912.[91] Whereas the Unionist Reorganisation Committee was highly critical of the Conservative Central Office's propaganda efforts, it praised the work of the tariff leagues for 'performing most valuable work both during and between elections'.[92] Moreover, high office was given to the Liberal Unionist organisers William Jenkins and John Boraston, who became joint principal agents to the Conservative Party. Both had been heavily involved in the operations of the Imperial Tariff Committee. We can see the 1911 reorganisation as an attempt on the part of the Conservative Party leadership to harness the dynamism which the tariff leagues had sought to inject into Unionist activism since 1903.

Notes

1   Stephen Reynolds, Bob Woolley and Tom Woolley, *Seems So! A Working Class View of Politics* (London, 1911), pp. 3–12.
2   Ibid., pp. 9–10.
3   Green, *Crisis of Conservatism*.
4   Lawrence, 'Class and gender'; Roberts, '"Villa Toryism" and Popular Conservatism in Leeds'; Windscheffel, *Popular Conservatism in Imperial London*.
5   Roberts, '"Villa Toryism" and Popular Conservatism in Leeds', 244; Pugh, *Tories and the People*, p. 160.
6   E.H.H. Green, 'Radical Conservatism: the electoral genesis of tariff reform', *Historical Journal*, 28:3 (1985), 667–92 at 672, 686–92.
7   Green, *Crisis of Conservatism*, pp. 6–8.
8   Tariff Reform League (hereafter TRL), *Monthly Notes*, 6:4 (1907), p. 353.
9   *Lady's Realm*, Spring 1902, pp. 3, 8.
10 Patricia Lynch, *The Liberal Party in Rural England, 1885–1910: Radicalism and Community* (Oxford, 2003), pp. 51, 85; Janet Howarth, 'The Liberal revival in Northamptonshire, 1880–1895: a case study in late nineteenth century elections', *Historical Journal*, 12:1 (1969), 78–118 at 96–7. The minutes of the Garstang habitation in rural Lancashire reveal that when it disbanded in 1911 only half the members had joined since 1900. Virtually all paid only the nominal associate fee, Lancashire Record Office (hereafter LRO), Preston, Garstang Primrose League Habitation minutes and register, DDFz.
11 This has been a perennial dilemma for the Conservative Party; for example, Young Conservatives keenly debated the proper balance between political and social activities during the 1950s and 1960s. Lawrence Black, 'The lost world of Young Conservatism', *Historical Journal*, 51 (2008), 991–1024.
12 Forty-nine habitations were recorded as being active, thirteen 'absolutely dead', thirty habitations provided no information or were in a dormant and unsatisfactory state. Bodleian Library, Oxford, Primrose League MSS, MS3, Grand Council minutes, Agency Committee report, 19 December 1901.
13 *Primrose League Gazette* (hereafter *PLG*), 1 May 1902, p. 6.
14 *PLG*, March 1906, p. 19; for Conservative frustrations with the culture of the Primrose League see also January 1904, p. 10; H.C. Richards, *The Candidates' and Agents' Guide in Contested Elections* (London, 4th edition, 1904), p. 67.
15 Primrose League MSS, MS4, General Purposes Committee Special Report, 2 February 1906.
16 Lynch, *Liberal Party in Rural England*, pp. 86–7; at this time the *Liberal Agent* regularly instructed its readers to pay attention to social activities, claiming they had played an important role in the Conservatives' success, *Liberal Agent*, January 1900, 27; October 1900–January 1901, pp. 68–9; April 1902, p. 25.
17 Jon Lawrence, *Speaking for the People: Party, Language and Popular Politics in England, 1867–1914* (Cambridge, 1998), pp. 140–1.
18 Kathryn Rix, 'The party agent and English electoral culture, 1880–1906' (PhD dissertation, University of Cambridge, 2001), pp. 186, 236–7; for the Unionists' defence of the working man's pint during the late Victorian period see Lawrence, 'Class and gender', 639–40, 644.
19 Roberts, 'Constructing a Tory world-view', 140.
20 Cawood, 'Leamington Spa candidature dispute'.

21 John A. Bridges, *Reminiscences of a Country Politician* (London, 1906), p. 53.

22 Ibid., pp. 169–70.

23 For a brief account of the Liberal Unionists' culture see Eugenio F. Biagini, *British Democracy and Irish Nationalism 1876–1906* (Cambridge, 2007), ch. 5; At the 1895 election Liberal Unionists had focused on the need to enact social reforms such as old age pensions and workers' compensation. Readman, '1895 Election and political change', 477–8, 493.

24 Helen Blackburn (ed.), *A Handbook for Women Engaged in Social and Political Work* (London, 2nd edition, 1895), p. 85.

25 Bridges, *Reminiscences of a Country Politician*, p. 170.

26 It should be emphasised that this meeting was convened by the Primrose League in cooperation with Leicester's Liberal Unionist and Conservative organisations. Chamberlain's speech focused on foreign policy and at no point did he mention the Primrose League. Janet Henderson Robb, *The Primrose League, 1883–1906* (New York, 1942), p. 80.

27 Barbary, 'From platform to the polling booth', pp. 100, 189; Bolton's membership figures come from *PLG*, 1 May 1902, p. 6; the Scottish Primrose League Grand Council claimed that Liberal Unionists had been hostile to its operations, National Library of Scotland, Edinburgh, Scottish Conservative and Unionist Association (SCUA) MSS, Acc.10424/1, Grand Council (Scotland) minutes, report of Joint Committee [with English Council], 10 May 1900.

28 G.I.T. Machin, *Politics and the Churches in Great Britain, 1869 to 1921* (Oxford, 1987), pp. 262–72.

29 Balfour MSS, Add. MSS 49774, fols 7–12, Joseph Chamberlain to Arthur Balfour, 4 August 1902.

30 At the 1906 election the Liberal Unionists were nearly wiped out in the region, losing seats in Bodmin; St Ives; Truro (all Cornwall); Tavistock (Devon); only one seat was retained – Totnes (Devon); A.M. Dawson, 'Politics in Devon and Cornwall, 1900–1931' (PhD dissertation, University of London, 1991), pp. 135–7; Ian Cawood, 'The lost party: Liberal Unionism, 1886–1895' (PhD dissertation, University of Leicester, 2009), p. 216.

31 Biagini, *British Democracy and Irish Nationalism*, pp. 343–4. The share of British subjects within the 'Uitlander' community in the Transvaal and Orange Free State was often exaggerated in Unionist election addresses. Readman, 'Conservative Party, patriotism and British politics', 120–1.

32 Trentmann, *Free Trade Nation*, chs 1–2.

33 Coetzee, 'Villa Toryism reconsidered', 40.

34 Bodleian Library, Oxford, Sandars MSS, c.753, fol. 189, Memorandum on London parliamentary representation, n.d. [1906].

35 In 1908 one London organiser claimed that of the 1,400 clubs in existence across the country only thirty had a political sub-committee and most were 'practically useless as political fighting machines', *Walsall Observer*, 5 December 1908, cited in Kenneth J. Dean, *Town and Westminster: A Political History of Walsall from 1906–1945* (Walsall, 1972), p. 11.

36 A. Lawrence Lowell, *The Government of England* (New York, 2 vols, 2nd edition, 1912), vol. 1, pp. 578–9.

37 Ramsden, *Age of Balfour and Baldwin*, p. 26.

38 Neal Blewett, *The Peers, the Parties and the People: The General Elections of 1910* (London, 1972), pp. 303–4.

39 For Amery see biographical appendix; Churchill College, Cambridge, Amery MSS, AMEL2/3/1, Leo Amery to Andrew Bonar Law, 16 December 1910.

40 For Maxse see biographical appendix; Parliamentary Archives, London, Bonar Law MSS, BL18/6/148, Mary Maxse to Andrew Bonar Law, 19 December 1910.

41 For the touring vans see Kathryn Rix, '"Go out into the highways and hedges": The diary of Michael Sykes, Conservative political lecturer, 1895 and 1907–8', *Parliamentary History*, 20:2 (2001), 209–31; National Archives of Scotland, Edinburgh, Steel-Maitland MSS, GD193/80/4, Unionist Organisation Committee report, June 1911, pp. 35, 46; Bodleian Library, Oxford, Conservative Party Archive (hereafter CPA), Microfilm 2923, Unionist Organisation Committee Index of Proceedings to 31 March 1911, pp. 24, 53.

42 Norfolk Record Office, Norwich, Upcher of Sheringham MSS, North Norfolk Conservative Association Executive Committee Minutes, 7 November 1910; for hostility to Conservative touring vans in rural areas see also Oxfordshire Record Office, Oxford, South Oxfordshire Conservative Association MSS, S. Oxon. Con. 3/1, NUCA Oxfordshire Provincial Division minutes, 21 March 1908.

43 Steel-Maitland MSS, GD193/80/4, Unionist Organisation Committee Report, June 1911, pp. 35, 46; CPA, Microfilm 2923, Unionist Organisation Committee Index of Proceedings to 31 March 1911, pp. 24, 53.

44 National Liberal Federation, *Proceedings Attending the Formation of the National Liberal Federation of Local Associations* (Birmingham, 1877), p. 14 cited in Patricia Auspos, 'Radicalism, pressure groups, and party politics: From the National Education League to the National Liberal Federation', *Journal of British Studies*, 20:1 (1980), 184–204 at 200.

45 Liberal Unionist divisions over the tariff issue at local level are explored in Barbary, 'Platform to polling booth', ch. 5.

46 For Page Croft and Bridgeman – see biographical appendix.

47 Lawrence, *Electing our Masters*, ch. 3; Thompson, 'Pictorial lies'; Trentmann, *Free Trade Nation*.

48 Trentmann, *Free Trade Nation*, chs 1–2.

49 Jan Rüger, *The Great Naval Game: Britain and Germany in the Age of Empire* (Cambridge, 2007) , pp. 9, 52–4, 96–8.

50 Readman, 'Conservative Party, patriotism and British politics', 124.

51 *John Bull's Hearth* (1903), www.screenonline.org.uk/film/id/1186859/index.html, accessed on 8 October 2012.

52 *Conservative Agent's Journal*, January 1904, p. 3.

53 *Bioscope*, 13 January 1910, p. 11.

54 Ibid., 27 January 1910, pp. 34–5; on the animated nature of Edwardian cinema audiences see 11 November 1909, pp. 25, 31.

55 Jan Rüger, 'Nation, empire and navy: identity politics in the United Kingdom, 1887–1914', *Past and Present*, 185 (2004), 159–88 and Rüger, *Great Naval Game*, pp. 99–139.

56 *Bioscope*, 13 January 1910, p. 61.

57 Ibid.

58 Amy H. Moreton, *Freedom in Happy England: A Tariff Reform Play* (Nuneaton, 1911).

59 *PLG*, October 1911, p. 16; *Free Trader*, new series, 1 (1908), p. 23.

60 For the concept of 'invented tradition' see David Cannadine, 'The context, performance and meaning of ritual: the British monarchy and the "invention

of tradition", c. 1820–1977', in Eric Hobsbawm and Terence Ranger (eds), *The Invention of Tradition* (Cambridge, 1983), pp. 263–307; on attempts to develop Chamberlain Day into a permanent annual event see TRL, *Notes for Speakers*, 6 July 1912, pp. 1–2.

61 TRL, *Monthly Notes*, 5:2 (1906), pp. 118, 121, 125, 132, 135.

62 Several WUTRA branches formed their own companies to perform educational plays. *Our Flag*, January 1913, 15; for discussions of tariff plays see, for example *PLG*, December 1911, p. 14; *Wellington Journal*, 27 June 1914, cutting in Churchill College, Cambridge, Lloyd MSS, GLLD16/64.

63 *Free Trader*, new series, 3, February 1909, p. 72; *PLG*, March 1908, p. 6.

64 *Free Trader*, new series, 1, December 1908, p. 23.

65 *PLG*, January 1904, p. 10.

66 Francis William Soutter, *Fights for Freedom: The Story of My Life* (London, 1925), pp. 48–51.

67 Lynch, *Liberal Party in Rural England*, p. 179.

68 Shropshire Archives, Shrewsbury, William Bridgeman MSS, 4629/1/1904/14, Joseph Chamberlain to William Bridgeman, 2 August 1904.

69 William Bridgeman MSS, 4629/1/1905/21, Oswestry and West Shropshire Conservative circular, n.d. [1905].

70 William Bridgeman MSS, 4629/1/1904/17, William Jenkins to William Bridgeman, 3 August 1904.

71 William Bridgeman MSS, 4629/1/1904/1, 'Hints to Workers' for members of the West Salop Women's Unionist Association, n.d. [1904].

72 John Gore (ed.), *Mary Maxse, 1870–1944: A Record Compiled by her Family and Friends* (London, 1946), p. 100.

73 For Atholl – see biographical appendix; ibid., p. 98.

74 Trentmann, *Free Trade Nation*, pp. 69–75.

75 Biagini, *British Democracy and Irish Nationalism*, pp. 89–93.

76 Christine Jesman, 'Conservative Women, the Primrose League and public activity in Surrey and Sussex, c. 1880–1902' (DPhil dissertation, University of Sussex, 2008), pp. 78, 138 180; Patricia Hollis, *Ladies Elect: Women in English Local Government, 1865–1914* (Oxford, 1987), p. 58.

77 *Brighton Gazette*, 23 April 1896, cited in Jesman, 'Conservative women and public activity', p. 63.

78 *The Times*, 15 February 1910, p. 10.

79 TRL, *Monthly Notes*, 12:4 (1910), pp. 351–52.

80 Ibid., 19:1 (1913), p. 68.

81 Leo Amery, 'Women and the National Service League', *Morning Post*, 15 July 1910, cutting in Amery MSS, AMEL5/10.

82 West Sussex Record Office, Chichester, Maxse family MSS, C. Uncatalogued 225, Mary Maxse to Ivor Maxse, 25 January 1906.

83 Mary Maxse, foreword to Lillian Mary Bagge (ed.), *The Unionist Workers Handbook* (London, 1912), p. xxii.

84 Petworth House Archive (hereafter PHA), West Sussex Record Office, Chichester, Brighton and Hove TRL minutes, PA9582, March 1908 report; for the seaside campaigns see TRL, *Monthly Notes*, 9:4 (1908), pp. 315–16; 11:1 (1909), p. 58; 12:5 (1910), p. 426.

85 PHA, PA9582, Brighton and Hove TRL minutes, 19 March 1907, 1 April 1908, 14 April 1909.

86 PHA, PA11807, Sussex County TRL minutes, 11 May 1904,

87 Ramsden, *Balfour and Baldwin*, p. 41.

88 Ibid., pp. 48, 51.

89 Ibid., pp. 72, 115; this conclusion is supported by Coetzee, *Party or Country*, ch. 5.

90 Ramsden, *Balfour and Baldwin*, p. 62.

91 These defections also appear to have occurred amongst local activists. The Liberal Unionist organisation in Bury, Lancashire, was badly hit by free traders defecting to the Liberal Party, see Barbary, 'Platform to polling booth', ch. 6.

92 Steel-Maitland MSS, GD193/80/4, Unionist Organisation Committee Report, June 1911, pp. 35, 46; CPA, Microfilm 2923, Unionist Organisation Committee Index of Proceedings to 31 March 1911, pp. 24, 53.

2

The working man's pint and the housewife's budget

On polling day at the Worcester by-election of 1908 a group of men processed through the city's streets, banging a drum and chanting slogans in support of the Unionist candidate, Edward Goulding, a leading figure within the Tariff Reform League. The parade was vividly described in the local press: 'on a large dray, drawn by a horse…a jovial party dressed in red suits and hats [the local Unionist colour], were around a table spread with prodigious loaves, British beef and bottles of stout. Red poles in four corners supported the inscriptions "Made in Worcester, England. Vote for Goulding and have more work and food"'.[1] Goulding was presented as a champion of the local working man. In the commemorative photograph staged outside the candidate's election headquarters a serviceman takes pride of place at the front of the dray, and the slogan 'Goulding's your man' is visible on placards. Another sign asked voters to remember the successful Liberal petition against the constituency's 1906 general election result. The

Figure 2.1: Commemorative postcard, Worcester by-election, February 1908

petition proved unpopular as the expenses led to a rise in the local rates and was seen as a slur against Worcester's civic pride.[2]

Historians have paid little attention to how Unionists sought to develop appeals to gendered identities on the ground in Edwardian Britain. In a 1993 article Jon Lawrence argued that the Conservative Party encouraged a more domesticated social culture in response to the rising influence of women in political activism, shedding its earlier association with beer-barrel politics.[3] Nonetheless, the article paid little attention to the culture of the tariff reform campaign, concluding that it 'helped to undermine popular Toryism's greatest strength, its local, community based character'.[4] Yet the demonstration by Goulding's supporters, with its focus on restoring a sense of masculine civic pride in response to alleged Liberal slights, suggests otherwise.

Building on Lawrence's conclusions, Frank Trentmann has recently argued that the failure of Joseph Chamberlain's tariff reform campaign was based substantially on shortcomings in his supporters' use of political communication. Whereas populist Conservatives had sought to defend the rights of working men to enjoy an occasional pint without undue interference from the state during the 1870s and 1880s, in Edwardian Britain free traders alone were able to develop a popular language of the consumer which could appeal to a wide public of both sexes. According to Trentmann, tariff reformers set themselves up in opposition as defenders of producers' interests.[5] Despite the merits of this work, it appears to see tariff reform through its opponents' eyes.

In 1905 a Liberal agent and Free Trade Union speaker told a Walsall audience that Chamberlain's Birmingham organisation 'was exclusively a manufacturers' movement, made up largely of employers who were behind the times'.[6] And yet the Goulding demonstration indicates that earlier Tory appeals to the manly ale-drinking consumer were integrated into the wider discourse of tariff reform. The procession was designed to provide a 'moving object lesson on a elaborate scale' as a witty riposte to Liberal skulduggery. A Free Trade Union pamphlet circulating the constituency at the time proclaimed: 'Do you want to live on rye bread instead of white bread and horseflesh instead of beef? If not you must vote for Free Trade'.[7] Black bread and horseflesh were supposedly staple foods for impoverished working families in tariff-protected Germany.[8] Whilst the Liberals claimed that Chamberlain's fiscal policy would force Britons to subsist on a foreign diet, Goulding's supporters portrayed themselves as the true patriots. The 'made in Worcester' sign and the display of hearty English food and drink underscored how tariff reform would rejuvenate British agriculture and industry.

If the culture of the Unionist working man in Edwardian Britain has received little historical attention we know even less of the world of the female activists who joined the Women's Unionist and Tariff Reform Association. Julia Bush's study of anti-suffragism dismisses the organisation as 'merely an auxiliary of the male Tariff Reform League'.[9] Such conclusions are unwarranted. As we saw in the previous chapter, WUTRA encouraged women to engage more seriously in day-to-day Unionist activism than they had done in the Primrose League. Edwardian Unionists were not merely concerned with appealing to the male voter. The tariff reform movement sought to develop a new culture of Unionist public politics, more amenable to women than the rowdy traditions of the Victorian hustings. All the same, these efforts met with ambiguous results. Whilst female Unionist activism flourished in Edwardian Britain, there are signs that some male Conservative leaders grew uneasy with the increasing encroachment by women into their activities.

Following their by-election stunt in 1908, Goulding's Worcester supporters staged another parade on polling day during the January 1910 general election. A local paper noted: 'Quite the feature of the street scenes during the morning was the procession of poor children bearing aloft a banner on which were the words: "Our parents want work and we want food, Vote for Goulding and happy homes"'.[10] Goulding's supporters were challenging Liberal claims that maintaining free trade was the only way to promote social justice.[11] 'An Englishman's home', a Unionist poster produced for the election campaign, sought to convey a similar message. It depicted a shabby and anaemic-looking family walking past the dilapidated gates of their cottage, which is to be sold. In the distance is a palatial mansion, which appears to be the venue for celebratory 'Budget Fete Dancing'. The message was clear: Lloyd George's 'People's Budget' was no cure for Britain's economic woes, which could only be solved by tariff reform. Liberals did not represent the working family and were celebrating free trade whilst it was ruining the country.[12]

Tariff reformers used the imagery of the family to demonstrate that they were not upholding the sectional interests of wealthy businessmen who sought to gain from the defeat of free trade. For example, Leo Amery's 1908 by-election campaign in East Wolverhampton focused heavily on addressing the plight of Willenhall lock-makers, who were suffering from cheap German and American imports.[13] A series of cartoons published in the *Midland Evening News* during the campaign depicted Amery as the guardian of working families. In one he tells the voter to listen to an unemployed colleague who implores him to 'employ your fellow workman' and gain 'better wages and happier homes!' A vote for the Liberal was presented as one in the interests of foreign industry.[14] Echoing the earlier election culture of 'chairing', Amery was carried aloft to the poll by men from the Axle-Box works. Their children followed, cheering the candidate in Unionist supporters' cars, presenting the Wolverhampton public with a display of the deprived working families that Amery claimed to represent.[15]

In the tariff reform play, *Freedom in Happy England*, which was performed across the country, the idea of masculine protection of the home is linked with guarding the nation. The action takes place in the home of Tom Jones, an unemployed motor mechanic. Tom and his friend Bill Smith are confronted by a canvasser, working on behalf of a Liberal candidate, Karl Schutzman. Bill, whose firm has been struggling to compete with a tariff-protected German rival, becomes irate with the Radical sent to canvass 'for a carpet-bagger with a foreign name'. He persuades Tom to kick out the German, showing him that 'there's still one right left to us, and that's the right o' the Englishman to be master in 'is own 'ome'.[16]

In part, this strategy of presenting a more domesticated image of masculinity resulted from the increasing problems that Unionists faced in presenting themselves as the defenders of working men's clubs against interference from Liberal teetotallers. The 1908 Licensing Bill appeared to offer a fruitful opportunity for Tories to revitalise their links with beer-barrel politics. Contemporary Unionist posters and literature implied that the Liberals did not understand working men's lifestyles. One poster focused on the injustices of the existing fiscal system, alleging that it heavily taxed the British beer and whisky enjoyed by working men, whilst levying little or no duties on foreign luxuries commonly consumed by the rich.[17]

Yet, the fight against the Liberal Licensing Bill demonstrated that non-party groups could make just as much of a claim to represent the working men's club movement as the Conservatives did. Opposition was chiefly orchestrated by the non-party Clubs and Institute Union (CIU), which spent £10,000 campaigning against licensing reform. The CIU was particularly concerned by the ambiguously phrased threat in the bill that clubs could be struck off the register if they were used 'mainly as a drinking club'.[18] In introducing a special issue on the bill the CIU journal was keen to emphasise that it drew support from across the political spectrum. In fact, it claimed that roughly 75 per cent of Union clubmen had voted for the incumbent government.[19]

Unionists were concerned with developing a wider appeal to working men in response to their weakening hold on the politics of drink. Nonetheless, their increasing focus on home and family life can also be explained by the need to counter free traders' claims to represent the female consumers' interest. It appears that the beer-barrel politics, with their associations with the 'old corruption' of unreformed politics could act as an incubus towards gaining women's support.[20] At the January 1910 election mid-Devon Liberals produced a leaflet in which their candidate's wife, Dorothy Buxton, addressed her 'women friends'. Buxton claimed that the Unionist victory at the mid-Devon by-election in 1908 had been won by corrupt means. She presented her opponents as working hand in hand with the liquor interest, doing 'evil work' using 'beer and gifts' to win votes. It was implied that Unionists employed these tactics to blind people to the deleterious effects that tariff reform would have on the household budget: 'a farthing more on every loaf would soon more than cover the value of these Xmas charities'.[21]

The opinions of the housewife became a highly contested battleground in the fiscal debate. During the 1906 election, free trade literature portrayed tariff reform as a policy which would effectively rob from the home cupboard, increasing food prices.[22] At the next election, in January 1910, Liberals claimed that Lloyd George's ambitious economic reforms were effectively a 'Women's Budget', which aided the housewife.[23] The Unionists retaliated during that campaign, producing images of assertive housewives who were tired of false claims that free trade was the only way to a cheap diet.[24] In fact, as the women's tariff association repeatedly argued, the price of living had risen substantially since the Liberals came to power.[25]

Through championing the educated female consumer who was wise to Liberal tricks, WUTRA distanced itself from the largely peripheral role that women had performed in the Primrose League during the Victorian era.

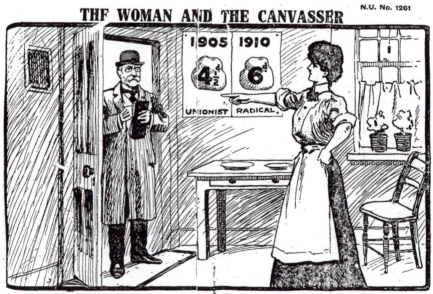

CANVASSER : I say, missis, don't you let your man vote for the Tory : he will tax your bread.

WOMAN : Get out---you've told me that for the last five years and look at the price of bread now under your folk.

Published by The National Union of Conservative & Constitutional Associations, St. Stephen's Chambers, Westminster, S.W. ; & Printed by DAVID ALLEN & SONS, Ltd., 180, Fleet Street, E.C.

Figure 2.2: 'The woman and the canvasser' leaflet, n.d. [1909]

The domestic sphere and the concerns of the housewife were now seen as a key combat zone in political debate.

Throughout the Edwardian era WUTRA's speakers were intent on spreading one message above all others: tariff reform was a housewife's question and, as the family's chief consumer, she needed to educate herself about it. A speaker told the Lincoln women's tariff association that it 'was their bounden duty as housekeepers' to take an interest in fiscal debates: 'she thought as it so especially referred to their homes they might in a great measure be able to influence men to think seriously about it'.[26] Despite the focus here on encouraging women to influence male voters on the fiscal question, female tariff activists were also concerned with offering women a greater prominence in Unionist politics.

WUTRA argued that, by taking an intelligent interest in the fiscal question, women could play a permanent and substantial role in political activism. In a talk on 'the influence of women in politics', St Clair Townsend stated that they could no longer decorously 'draw aside their skirts, lest they become soiled, and focus all their powers and energies on their own domestic circles'. Townsend argued that political activism could enhance the capabilities of housewives in their domestic tasks: 'The home need not suffer; rather should it gain in dignity and completeness by the broader outlook its women gain…In her relations to her home and family, her powers for good must be increased.' Engagement with tariff activism was equated with respectability by Townsend. She argued that it would enhance women's 'mental horizon', noting that 'it is the capable, well-equipped, wholesome twentieth century woman whose help is evoked by all [politicians]'.[27] By highlighting the value of the female consumer within the fiscal debate, Chamberlain's supporters encouraged women to take a keener and more assertive role in Unionist activism. Before 1903 the Primrose League's respectability had an essentially social meaning; its claims to gentility rested on distancing itself from the public house-centred culture of earlier forms of popular Conservatism.[28] Conversely, WUTRA activists such as St Clair Townsend argued that the modern woman needed to involve herself in serious politics if she were to maintain her claims to respectability.

WUTRA gained support from both sides of the women's suffrage debate. Divisions were avoided over the issue as leading Conservative 'Antis' within WUTRA, such as Katherine Tullibardine, later Duchess of Atholl, supported a progressive 'forward policy' focused on advancing women's position in municipal politics and social work. Municipal politics played a vital role in the activities of Edwardian Conservatives and its importance has been unfairly overlooked. Alfred Bird, a supporter of Joseph Chamberlain, introduced the practice of systematically fighting municipal elections in Wolverhampton. For Bird these were: 'the equivalent of autumn manoeuvres in military affairs; they are the best means we possess of keeping our fighting forces in the highest efficiency'. When ward committees had a good prospect of success Bird felt that 'to deprive them of a chance of a fight must have a disastrous influence upon our forces and bring about certain discouragement and slackness when a Parliamentary election comes along'.[29]

In his recent studies of London Conservatism, Alex Windscheffel claimed that there was a 'Tory backlash' against women's involvement in municipal elections during the 1900s.[30] If so, it was not particularly effective. Female activists found a new voice in local politics during the Edwardian era, especially after the formation of the Women's League for Municipal Reform in 1909. This body was linked to the London Municipal Society, which sponsored 'Municipal Reform' candidates and acted as the voice of Unionism in London borough elections. A WUTRA organiser assisted the Women's League in the capital, contacting female Unionists in each constituency and calling personally on all agents.[31] Local elections were a crucial arena for female activism as over one million women exercised the municipal franchise. WUTRA's leaders, such as Lady Ilchester, president of the association, spoke on behalf of Municipal Reform candidates and gave vigorous support to their two female nominees at the 1910 London borough elections.[32] They presented municipal politics as a housewife's question, much like tariff reform, arguing that an increase in the rates made it more difficult for them to maintain the household.[33]

All the same, WUTRA was not merely concerned with fiscal policy. Indeed, it caught the imagination of Unionists when it stood in defence of Ulster following the introduction of the Third Irish Home Rule Bill in 1912. Female canvassers became a familiar sight in streets across the country during spring 1914, promoting WUTRA's 'Help the Ulster Women' campaign. In a leaflet distributed house-to-house, readers were asked to visualise the grim spectacle of Ulster families turned out of their homes and left to starve in the event of an Irish civil war, with 'no resting place for those who love the Union Jack' in the rest of the country.[34] British women were encouraged to offer promises of shelter to potential Ulster refugees. A key part of the campaign's massive popular appeal was that it emphasised the importance of traditional female roles of philanthropy and care for the family. If Conservatives were to introduce tariff reform they would have to convert an exclusively male electorate. By contrast, the Ulster campaign's leaders presented it as being dependent on the goodwill of English women and relied on female activists to promote the cause.[35] The response was impressive: by April 1914 the campaign had already received promises of over £12,000 in cash and hospitality for over five thousand refugees in the event of the government using force to coerce Ulster into accepting the authority of a Dublin parliament.[36] A member of the organising committee later claimed that pledges were eventually received to host the 'whole female and infant population of Ulster'.[37]

The Ulster Women campaign was also significant because it had the full cooperation of the Primrose League, which commanded a substantial membership. Lord Desborough, the league's chancellor, claimed that two hundred thousand members of his organisation acted as canvassers at the January 1910 election, and it was claimed in 1912 that the league had nearly five hundred thousand supporters. Both figures are no doubt exaggerations, but they testify to the continued importance of this auxiliary organisation.[38] The Primrose League had not always supported WUTRA's assertive style of female activism. George Lane-Fox, the league's vice-chancellor until 1912, was keen to portray the Women's Tariff Reform League (the forerunner of WUTRA) as an unnecessary association that was undermining the work of his organisation. In 1906 he wrote to Balfour's secretary, claiming that in several areas branches were being formed 'to work against the Primrose League'.[39] Such allegations had a kernel of truth. There are certainly examples of rival Primrose League and WUTRA branches operating in the same constituency, divided over the question of tariff reform.[40] Yet claims that the Primrose League and the women's tariff association 'fought a kind of civil war' across the nation are wide of the mark.[41]

There is plenty of evidence to suggest that the relationship between the Primrose League and the tariff organisations became increasingly amicable as the Edwardian period progressed. Even though the Primrose League Grand Council adopted a policy of neutrality on the fiscal question, in practice many habitations eventually came to support tariff reform enthusiastically and sometimes shared administrators with WUTRA branches.[42] Local Primrose League leaders could see statements by Arthur Balfour, the Conservative Party leader, as overriding the Grand Council's calls for neutrality on fiscal matters. For example, Lady Hardman spoke at the opening meeting of the Paddington WUTRA in 1907:

> She came to the meeting with great pleasure as a member of the Primrose League, for those that belonged to that body were now able to take part in the Tariff Reform movement...Mr. Balfour has declared that fiscal reform would and must remain the first constructive work of the Unionist Party. It therefore behoved all Unionist women to work for Tariff Reform.[43]

In areas of Scotland where both organisations operated, they gave each other notice of meetings or agreed on areas where each body could work to avoid clashes of interest.[44]

In England WUTRA held discussions with the Primrose League on cooperation from 1908 onwards. A Joint Consultative Committee was formed in 1912, to coordinate campaigning efforts.[45] These long-standing attempts at cooperation culminated in the two organisations working together to promote the Help the Ulster Women campaign.[46]

Supporters of Chamberlain's tariff campaign sought to create a new culture of Unionist activism that would widen the bounds of the politically active nation. In some respects tariff reformers' attitudes towards public politics reflected existing conventions. Leaders supported open-air meetings as they were seen as an opportunity for the local public to engage vigorously with politics, with interruptions forming part of a legitimate sporting

Figure 2.3: Henry Page Croft, election leaflet, Christchurch election, January 1910

combat between speaker and audience.[47] In another continuation of earlier cultures, tariff reformers presented their command of the platform as a sign of manly vigour.[48] For example, Henry Page Croft, the Conservative MP for Christchurch, developed a reputation for his verbal sparring with hecklers.[49] This was exploited by a 1910 Conservative election poster that presented cameo portraits of Page Croft and his opponent inside boxing gloves, with the caption: 'Who will be counted out on January 14th? What are the odds and on whom?' Page Croft was presented as a man who could fight energetically for Christchurch's interests, employing the same robustness in parliament that he displayed on the platform.

The depiction of leading tariff reformers as boxers offered Conservatives a way to present their leaders as upholders of both populist and genteel forms of public politics.[50] As well as uniting the classes, the rules of boxing were presented by their advocates as instilling martial qualities of self-control under the most trying of circumstances – ideal qualities for the platform speaker.[51]

Rather than glorying in the rowdy traditions of the Victorian hustings, the tariff leagues' leaders portrayed themselves as respectable politicians who were nonetheless willing to engage with mass politics. The Tariff Reform League regularly criticised Liberal 'rowdyism' by claiming that it was being organised by outside auxiliary organisations rather than reflecting local opinion. Following a disrupted meeting, Exeter tariff reformers claimed that if such scenes were repeated they would 'procure the arrest and prosecution of the ringleaders of the "Free Trade" rowdies'.[52] Similar threats were made against alleged organised interruptions from Socialists in Battersea.[53]

There are some instances of disruption at TRL and FTU meetings. The *Free Trader* accused the Brighton branch of the TRL of organising interruptions at free trade demonstrations on the city's beachfront. Likewise, tariff reformers claimed that opponents engaged in systematic heckling at their meetings.[54] All the same, very few of these incidents led to major breaches of the peace. In contrast to the sometimes turbulent atmosphere of elections, ordinary TRL gatherings were characterised by their orderliness. *Monthly Notes on Tariff Reform* provided regular detailed coverage of meetings across the country, recording several attempts by Liberals and Socialists to start rival meetings at TRL gatherings.[55] However, on only one occasion did the police feel the need to intervene to keep order.[56]

Edwardian tariff reformers' concern with taming the rougher elements of public politics resulted partly from the need to integrate women more thoroughly into day-to-day Conservative activism in response to the advance of the Women's Free Trade Union.[57] Speaking and debating classes aimed at women became a common feature of constituency activities in Edwardian Britain.[58] The educated female tariff reform speaker challenged

Figure 2.4: Postcard of Henry Page Croft addressing a tariff reform fete, July 1908

traditional ideas that command of the platform was an indication of manly character. By 1911 the Mid-Devon women's tariff association was organising over a dozen meetings a month. As a local newspaper noted: 'in most cases these are addressed by ladies, who are well able to hold their own in the heckling encounters' which were a common feature of meetings in this marginal seat.[59] There was no simple process of feminisation of public politics in early twentieth-century Britain. Rather, early women MPs such as Margaret Bondfield and Katherine Tullibardine were praised for conforming to traditional expectations of the male orator and displaying self-restraint and good humour when faced with a baying crowd when they stood for parliament in the 1920s.[60]

Whilst tariff reformers like Page Croft used vigorously masculine imagery in their electioneering material, they came to rely heavily on female activists to support their constituency activities, and subsequently presented a more genteel image when addressing women supporters. Tariff reform meetings with mixed audiences and platforms were common, and the men's and women's tariff reform associations often jointly organised summer fetes.[61] Page Croft's keenness to attend such events should come as no surprise. His election campaigns in Christchurch were heavily reliant on the support of women from the local branch of the Primrose League. They distributed literature extensively and enabled Page Croft to canvass over 95 per cent of voters during the January 1910 election campaign.[62]

★

By 1914 women had become indispensable to Unionist activities at the local level. The most detailed information we have on constituency-level organisation in Edwardian Britain survives in a notebook in the Bodleian Library which provides details of which Unionist auxiliary organisations were operating in thirty-three constituencies covering Herefordshire, Staffordshire, Shropshire and Worcestershire, shortly before the First World War.[63] Twenty-four of the constituencies contained branches of the women's tariff association, most of which were praised effusively for their services to the party. Stanley Baldwin, MP for West Worcestershire from 1908, was one of those who saw the women's tariff association as a great boon.[64] By 1914 there were over two thousand members of this organisation in his constituency. The women were active in nearly every polling district, held extensive campaigns in outlying villages, participated in registration work and organised fundraising social events.[65]

Edwardian tariff reformers clearly made significant advances in developing a new culture of Unionist activism where supporters of both sexes could play a substantial role in campaigning. Nonetheless, it is far from clear that male politicians were fully reconciled to women's growing influence within Unionist activism. Yes, it was fine for women to engage in political discussions about the household budget, but what if they sought to meddle in military affairs? Buoyed by the increasing threat posed by Germany to Europe, militarist organisations such as the Navy League and National Service League ballooned in support during the late Edwardian period. The former's membership grew from 20,000 in 1908 to 125,000 in 1913.[66] On the eve of the First World War the NSL claimed 100,000 members and 270,000 adherents, although it would be dubious to claim that the latter group played a significant role in its activism.[67] These were organisations where women were expected to fall in line with the decisions of male leaders.

In 1910 the *Morning Post* censured two female Unionist leaders, Mary Maxse and Violet Cecil, for critical comments they made at a NSL meeting regarding local organisation. Leo Amery wrote to the paper, criticising suggestions it had raised in an editorial that the women's conduct was inspired by 'disruptionist tendencies' and 'an objection to authority itself'.[68] As chairman of the women's tariff association, Maxse was arguably the country's most influential female Unionist. However, she was treated by the *Morning Post* as a shrew. The paper compared the women's actions at the meeting with recent suffragette outrages, claiming that 'the terror of the one is hardly less than that of the other for men who are stirring to the best of their ability to bring about reforms which are urgently needed in the interests of national safety'. Given that Maxse and Cecil had 'had a run for their money', it hoped that they would now rally behind the executive.[69] By linking their actions to suffragette militancy, which it deplored, the *Morning*

Post was claiming that the women were producing an unwarranted and unfeminine intrusion into military affairs.

Jan Rüger's study of naval launches demonstrates that women also had a circumscribed role in the public politics of the Navy League. Ships were often named after cities during the Edwardian period. The local women's branch of the Navy League would usually raise a subscription for a gift to the crew of the ship bearing their city's name, to be presented at the launch. Rüger argues that the female role at these public spectacles was one of 'complaisance and admiration' rather than a more assertive form of participation.[70] Furthermore, Julia Bush's work on Conservative anti-suffragism indicates that there were wider cultural tensions amongst Conservative leaders regarding women's sphere in politics during the late Edwardian period. A section of aristocratic male leaders, led by Viscount Curzon, a member of the NSL, proved reluctant to provide women with leadership opportunities within the anti-suffrage movement. They were also grudging in their support for the 'forward policy' promoted by female anti-suffragists, which called for a more constructive role for women in public politics through local government work and social service.[71] By 1914 strains were developing between the tariff leagues' desire to create a more populist appeal, empowering women and local activists, and the military leagues' defence of traditional male elites' role as exclusive policymakers.

The free trade/tariff reform controversy refashioned political debate in Edwardian Britain; each side focused attention on the effects of fiscal policy on domestic life and claimed to represent the housewife. This meant that they had to encourage women to play a prominent role in their campaigns as activists. Subsequently, although they continued to champion the ale-drinking male consumer, Unionist appeals needed to be more varied, coded and subtle than the Tories' traditional associations with beer-barrel politics, which were already becoming of increasingly doubtful value before 1900. In their efforts to develop a social culture which could appeal to women, organisations such as the TRL and WUTRA sought to distance themselves from unruly traditions of masculine politics and developed a consumerist politics.

This was clearly a strategy which met with success in Unionist heartlands, where the women's tariff association flourished and a revitalised Primrose League came to play an important role in political education. Despite this, it should emphasised that two cultures of public politics sat together uneasily in Edwardian Britain. The tariff leagues' efforts to develop a peaceable culture, which integrated male and female activists, laid the basis for the Conservatives' post-war efforts to present themselves as the party which represented an orderly politics, as opposed to the rowdyism of Labour militants. All the same, the tariff leagues' efforts appear to have had little immediate effect on the culture of electoral meetings, which, if anything, became more violent in Edwardian Britain than they had been in the 1880s and 1890s. Lawrence estimates that at least one-third of election meetings involved opposition from the floor in January 1910.[72] The campaigns of the militant suffragettes demonstrated that full participation in public politics remained a male privilege in Edwardian Britain and served to narrow female involvement further as some leading Liberals banned women from their meetings to avoid disruption.[73] Conservative leaders' unease at the growing influence of women within 'manly' spheres of politics, such as military affairs, manifested itself in the politics of organisations such as the NSL and in male anti-suffragists' attempts to limit the role of female leadership within their cause. These two cultures of public politics would clash during the First World War, with the Conservative Party ultimately distancing itself from exclusionary forms of masculine politics.

Notes

1 For Goulding see biographical appendix; *Berrow's Worcester Journal*, 8 February 1908, p. 5.
2 For the unpopularity of the Liberal petition see Denise Mylechreest, 'A singular Liberal: Richard Robert Fairbairn and Worcester politics, 1899–1941' (MPhil dissertation, University of Coventry, 2007), pp. 23–4, 30.
3 Lawrence, 'Class and gender', 634, 645–7, 652.
4 Ibid., 650.
5 Trentmann, *Free Trade Nation*, pp. 16–17, 69–71, 76.
6 Dean, *Town and Westminster*, p. 24.
7 *Berrow's Worcester Journal*, 8 February 1908, p. 4.
8 Dean, *Town and Westminster*, p. 24.
9 Julia Bush, *Women Against the Vote: Female Anti-suffragism in Britain* (Oxford, 2008), p. 133.
10 *Berrow's Worcester Journal*, 22 January 1910, p. 3.
11 Trentmann, *Free Trade Nation*, pp. 16, 71.
12 Budget Protest League poster (1909), CPA, 1909/10-21.
13 For Amery's lunchtime meetings at factory works see *Midland Evening News (Wolverhampton)*, 22 April 1908, p. 2; 25 April 1908, p. 4; 28 April 1908, p. 4; 30 April 1908, p. 4.
14 *Midland Evening News (Wolverhampton)*, 4 May 1908, p. 4; see also 24 April 1908, p. 2; Amery presented a similar discourse to that employed in the paper's campaign. *Conservative and Unionist*, September 1911, p. 136.
15 On the traditional importance of chairings in electoral culture see Frank O' Gorman, 'Campaign rituals and ceremonies: the social meaning of elections in England, 1780–1860', *Past and Present*, 135 (1992), 79–115 at 89–91, 114; The Wolverhampton polling day is covered in Leo Amery, *My Political Life, Vol. 1: England before the Storm, 1896–1914* (London, 1953), p. 332; *Midland Evening News (Wolverhampton)*, 5 May 1908, p. 4.
16 Moreton, *Freedom in Happy England*.
17 'Unfair preference', January 1910 election poster, CPA 1909/10-09; for the

Unionists' defence of the beer and tobacco enjoyed by working men see also Imperial Tariff Committee, *General Election 1910: A Handbook for Unionist Canvassers* (Birmingham, 1909), p. 11; Amery MSS, AMEL4/5, Leo Amery election leaflet, 22 April 1908.

18 B.T. Hall, *Our Fifty Years: The Story of the Working Men's Club and Institute Union* (London, 1912), pp. 218–20.

19 Ibid., pp. 217–20.

20 For the role of beer in corrupt electioneering during the Victorian period, and the isolated survival of electoral bribery into the Edwardian period, see Kathryn Rix, '"The elimination of corrupt practices in British elections"? Reassessing the impact of the 1883 Corrupt Practices Act', *English Historical Review*, 123 (2008), 65–97 at 67–8, 88–9.

21 Ernest Morrison-Bell MSS, 2128, leaflet letter from Dorothy Buxton, 22 December 1909.

22 Free Trade Union, *Photographic Reproductions of our Brilliantly Coloured Picture and Word Posters* (London, n.d., c. 1905), p. 11.

23 'Vote for Dunne! and the women's budget', Walsall Local History Centre Special Collections, election material, January 1910/42.

24 CPA, Microfiche 0.396, card 148, National Union of Conservative Associations, *The Woman and the Canvasser*, leaflet no.1261, n.d. [1909].

25 Mary Maxse, *Tariff Reform and Cheap Living* (London, 1910), pp. 8, 11.

26 Churchill College, Cambridge, Page Croft MSS, *Nottingham Daily Guardian*, 28 June 1905, cutting in CRFT3/1; *Bournemouth Echo*, 9 November 1909, cutting in CRFT3/2.

27 Women's Library, London, St Clair Townsend MSS, 7SCT/05, box FL679, Mrs Walter [St Clair] Townsend, *The Influence of Women in Politics: An Address Read at the Annual General Meeting of the Barnard Castle Women's Unionist Association branch, 5th May 1909* (1909); Elizabeth Collum of the WUTRA likewise argued that the domestic nature of contemporary politics made it imperative for women to participate in political activism, regardless of whether they sought the vote or not. *North Wales Guardian*, 14 June 1907, p. 6.

28 Coetzee, 'Villa Toryism reconsidered', p. 44; Matthew Roberts, 'W.L. Jackson, Leeds Conservatism and the world of Villa Toryism, c.1867–1900' (PhD dissertation, University of York, 2003), p. 223.

29 Bird to Marston, 12 October 1912, West Wolverhampton Conservative Association Management Committee minutes, cited in G.W. Jones, *Borough Politics: A Study of the Wolverhampton Town Council, 1888–1964* (London, 1969), p. 47.

30 Alex Windscheffel, 'Villa Toryism? The making of London Conservatism, 1868–1906' (PhD dissertation, University of London, 2000), p. 275 and *Popular Conservatism in Imperial London*, pp. 156–7.

31 Guildhall Library, London, London Municipal Society MSS, Women's League for Municipal Reform, Executive Committee report, 8 June 1909.

32 *The Times*, 11 February 1907, p. 12; 15 February 1910, p. 10.

33 Ibid., 15 February 1910, p. 10.

34 Amery MSS, AMEL6/3/29, file 2, WUTRA, *Help the Women and Children*, n.d. [1914].

35 *Berrow's Worcester Journal*, 24 January 1914, p. 4.

36 Primrose League MSS, MS5/1, Grand Council minutes, 3 April 1914.

37 Imperial War Museum, London, Women at Work Collection (microfilm),

BEL2/2/14, reel 4, Edith Lyttelton, 'Some Personal Experiences and Accounts of Individual Belgian Refugees', p. 5.

38 *The Times*, 31 January 1910, p. 7; the membership figure of 495,463 was based on communications between Grand Council and provincial secretaries. Yet it should be emphasised that habitations were reluctant to strike off their lists members who no longer contributed subscriptions. It is also questionable how committed many associates, who paid nominal subscription fees, were to the league's political activities. Primrose League MSS, MS5/1, Grand Council minutes, 21 November 1912.

39 Sandars MSS, c.751, fols 73–4, George Lane-Fox to Jack Sandars, 4 January 1906.

40 See Vervaecke, 'Dieu, la couronne et l'Empire la Primrose League', pp. 93–188; Pugh, *Tories and the People*, pp. 160, 170.

41 G.E. Maguire, *Conservative Women: A History of Women and the Conservative Party, 1884–1997* (Basingstoke, 2000), p. 61.

42 The two organisations shared staff in Henley-on-Thames, Oxfordshire, *Henley and South Oxfordshire Standard*, 1 May 1908, p. 2; in Blackburn, Lancashire, TRL speakers were invited to address Primrose League meetings, Lancashire Record Office, Preston, PLC2/2/1, Darwen Conservative Association MSS, memorandum of Cranborne (Blackburn) Primrose League meetings addressed by TRL speakers, enclosed in Thomas Robinson to Arthur Longworth, 11 August 1910 (loose).

43 Women's Library, London, Women's Suffrage Autograph Collection (microfilm), AL/289, *Morning Post*, 27 June 1907, cutting.

44 SCUA MSS, Acc. 10424/1, Primrose League Grand Council (Scotland) minutes, 19 April 1910, 19 July 1910, 30 May 1911; Acc. 10424/39, Eastern Organisation Committee of NUCA for Scotland minutes, 7 March 1906.

45 Primrose League MSS, MS4, Grand Council minutes, 4 June 1908, 31 October 1912, 6 November 1913.

46 For cooperation between the two organisations at a local level during the campaign see, for example, *Berrow's Worcester Journal*, 24 January 1914, p. 4; *West London Observer*, 3 July 1914, p. 11.

47 For contemporary appraisals of the value of open-air meetings see J. Seymour Lloyd, *Elections and How to Fight Them* (London, revised edition, 1909), pp. 20, 32–3; TRL, *Notes for Speakers*, September 1911, p. 381.

48 *Conservative and Unionist*, February 1908, p. 31; Lawrence, *Electing our Masters*, p. 61.

49 Page Croft MSS, CRFT3/2, *Bournemouth Echo*, 31 December 1909, cutting.

50 TRL, *Notes for Speakers*, 6 July 1912, pp. 1–2; in the cartoon 'A strong lead', Bonar Law is portrayed as a lean tariff reform boxer who has floored the flabby free trader, Asquith, TRL, *Monthly Notes*, 13:2 (1910), p. ii.

51 J.G. Bohun Lynch, *The Complete Amateur Boxer* (London, 1913), pp. 15, 194.

52 TRL, *Monthly Notes*, 15:1 (1907), p. 71.

53 *The Times*, 24 September 1909, p. 8.

54 *Free Trader*, new series, 11, 15 October 1909, p. 292; *Conservative Agent's Journal*, January 1904, p. 2.

55 See, for example, TRL, *Monthly Notes*, 6:1 (1907), pp. 75–6; 15:1 (1911), p. 71; 15:3 (1911), p. 381.

56 TRL, *Monthly Notes*, 6:2 (1907), p. 151.

57 Trentmann, *Free Trade Nation*, pp. 69–75.

58   TRL, *Monthly Notes*, 12:4 (1910), pp. 351–2.

59   Parliamentary Archives, London, Arthur Morrison-Bell MSS, *Western Morning News*, n.d. [1911], cutting.

60   *The Conservative Woman (Leeds)*, April 1924, p. 1; M.A. Hamilton (Iconoclast), *Margaret Bondfield* (London, 1924), pp. 9–15.

61   TRL, *Monthly Notes*, 6:3 (1907), p. 241; 6:4 (1907), pp. 352–3.

62   G.A. Arbuthnot (ed.), *The Primrose League Election Guide* (London, 1914), p. 23; *Primrose League Gazette*, January 1912, p. 5.

63   Midland Union notebook, 1907–17, CPA, ARE MU 29/3 (hereafter Midland Union notebook, CPA). Cross referencing of membership figures suggests that they were compiled around 1913.

64   *Berrow's Worcester Journal*, 3 May 1913, p. 3.

65   Ibid., 3 May 1913, p. 3; 23 May 1914, p. 6.

66   Coetzee, *Party or Country*, p. 138; for the growing culture of militarism in Edwardian Britain see Anne Summers, 'Militarism in Britain before the Great War', *History Workshop Journal*, 2 (1976), 104–23.

67   Matthew Hendley, '"Help us to secure a strong, healthy, prosperous and peaceful Britain": the social arguments of the campaign for compulsory military service in Britain, 1899–1914', *Canadian Journal of History*, 30 (1995), 262–88 at 262; it has been show that in Birmingham factories there was an element of employer coercion in getting workers to sign adherent forms. These were passed round for signature at the end of works meetings. M.D. Blanch, 'Nation, Empire and the Birmingham working-class, 1899–1914' (PhD dissertation, University of Birmingham, 1975), p. 272.

68   *Morning Post*, 15 July 1910, p. 6.

69   Ibid., 14 July 1910, p. 6.

70   Jan Rüger, 'The celebration of the fleet in Britain and Germany, 1897–1914' (PhD dissertation, University of Cambridge, 2003), p. 222.

71   Bush, *Women against the Vote*, pp. 23, 199, 208–9.

72   Lawrence, 'Transformation of public politics', pp. 202–3.

73   Lawrence, *Electing our Masters*, pp. 84–5.

3

The challenge of class politics

A week before polling at the 1907 London County Council (LCC) election, the London Municipal Society held a rally in Trafalgar Square. Municipal Reform supporters processed past Nelson's Column carrying banners bearing messages attacking the record of the incumbent Liberal-linked Progressive administration. Amongst the slogans were: 'Every vote given for the Progressives is a vote for Socialism' and 'Wastrels pay their men three and a half pence an hour but throw away £100,000 on steamboats', a reference to the council's bungled attempts to maintain a municipal boat service on the Thames.[1] Political tensions were running high in the capital, not least as a result of the London Municipal Society's propaganda campaign. One notorious poster depicted the Progressive threat as an ugly Semitic-featured man with hand outstretched, the caption stated: 'It's your money we want'.[2]

Progressives made their opinion about these tactics clear at the Trafalgar Square rally. Fighting broke out and banners were torn to shreds. *The Times* referred to the gathering as 'the largest and most uproarious meeting held in Trafalgar Square since the pro-Boer demonstration at the time of the South African war'.[3] But if the Progressives had won this fight, they did not win the battle at the polling booth. In 1907 the Unionist-linked Municipal Reform Party took control of local government in the metropolis for the first time. Charles Masterman, a Liberal politician, claimed that the Municipal Reformers' breakthrough had resulted from their ability to harness class interests. According to Masterman, the suburban middle classes swarmed to the polls 'in feverish hordes...to vote against a truculent proletariat'. The Conservative cause apparently appealed in the villas of suburbia because it was 'supposed to be the party favoured by Court, society, and the wealthy and fashionable classes'.[4]

In spite of Masterman's observations, recent research has challenged previous assumptions that middle-class 'Villa Toryism' was a key contributor to the electoral success of the Unionist alliance.[5] Work on late Victorian Conservatism stresses that Salisbury's party developed a wide support base by promoting a heterogeneous programme, appealing to both working- and middle-class social cultures.[6] Furthermore, Ross McKibbin suggests that the anti-expropriation discourse which Municipal Reformers utilised in London was likely to have had a unique appeal in the capital, given its large financial and commercial sector, and should

Figure 3.1: 'It's your money we want', Municipal Reform poster, 1907 London County Council elections

not be seen as necessarily representative of anti-socialist politics across Edwardian Britain.[7]

While anti-socialist appeals to suburbia may have had a limited purchase, Edwardian Unionists also appear to have struggled to develop effective links to working-class interests. David Jarvis claims that whilst Unionists achieved significant success in municipal elections as a result of their ability to mobilise ratepayers, they struggled to repeat such success in parliamentary contests, in part as a result of their deterministic reading of class.[8] According to Jarvis, the politics of tariff reform was 'couched in an intellectual framework that posited the existence of a homogenous industrial proletariat'.[9]

There is certainly some truth in this. Tariff reformers often sought to present themselves as the defenders of depressed local industries, but they did not develop the targeted appeals to varied interest groups which were a hallmark of Conservative Party campaigning in the 1920s.[10] In 1911 a correspondent in *The Times* bemoaned the deficiencies in the Conservative organisation and complained that 'at present in many cases little or no discrimination is shown as to the kind of literature distributed, and appeals which might influence artisans are made to agricultural labourers and vice-versa'.[11] Free traders ultimately developed a more democratic appeal than their opponents, championing working-class families who needed to buy their necessities at the cheapest possible price.[12] And yet, despite its central importance to its advocates' political creed, tariff reform was only one of several campaigns that Chamberlain's supporters waged as they sought to create a Unionist politics with a wider cultural purchase. After 1912 Unionists took substantial steps to reduce their dependence on tariff reform, promoting populist campaigns in support of rural smallholdings, an overhaul of National Insurance and opposition to Irish home rule.

McKibbin has claimed that the Unionists' residual strength in late Edwardian Britain owed much to the Conservatives' 'status as the party of the dominant social order of England', an assessment which has echoes of Masterman.[13] Certainly, there was a strong correlation between Anglican voting and support for the Conservative Party, and this helps explain why the Unionist alliance still retained over 43 per cent of the popular vote during the nadir of the 1906 election. The Unionists may also have benefited from the prominence of the church schools question at the 1910 elections, which helped rally Anglican support.[14] But it should be remembered that Unionism remained an alliance of two parties with distinct identities throughout most of the Edwardian period; The Liberal Unionists drew heavily on the support of Nonconformists, many of whom saw their interests as being antithetical to members of the established church on the education question. More generally, as we have seen, many Edwardian Unionists felt that they could not rely on traditional cries, which had served them well in the Victorian era but had been undermined by Liberal counter-appeals. Unionist attempts to engage with class identities in Edwardian Britain were far from one dimensional and grew in sophistication after 1912 as the Conservative Party developed a targeted, pluralistic campaign strategy across the nation.

In the run-up to the 1907 LCC elections the London Municipal Society distributed sixteen million leaflets and 369,000 copies of posters.[15] Both the scale of the campaign and the Municipal Reform victory at this contest were exceptional. Economic conditions in the capital made an anti-expropriation campaign peculiarly effective during that year as voters were confronted with rising interest rates and a sharp decline in the London property market. At this time the rent of an average working-class dwelling in the capital was 70 per cent higher than in Birmingham and twice that of Wigan.[16]

Despite Masterman's assessment of the 1907 LCC contest, it was far from clear that Unionists could rely on suburban wards to achieve success in local and parliamentary politics consistently. For one thing, London's suburbs lacked a homogenous class identity. Frans Coetzee's study of Croydon highlights how the town's politics in the late Victorian period was divided between commuters' interests, largely represented by Conservatives, and existing residents, who formed the bedrock of local Liberalism.[17] Qualification for the franchise was haphazard, with several working-class tenants who lived in subdivided houses holding the vote, even in 'slum quarters'.[18] In 1892 the Liberal candidate for the supposedly 'villa' constituency of Dulwich estimated that the working classes made up around 4,000 of the 10,500 voters.[19] Furthermore, recent research on the London region and Lancashire has demonstrated that the Liberal Party was able to develop strong roots in some suburban constituencies in the late Victorian and Edwardian periods by promoting social reforms, free trade and Nonconformist politics.[20] Given the lack of an assured and homogenous support base, it should come as no surprise that the Municipal Reform Party struggled to hold onto the gains it had made in the 1907 LCC elections. Whereas the Municipal Reform Party won seventy-nine seats compared to the Progressive Party's thirty-five in 1907, the respective figures for 1910 were sixty and fifty-five.

The strategies pursued by the London Municipal Society do not appear to have had a substantial influence on the direction of local politics in other regions, despite the creation of the Anti-Socialist Union in 1908. This body's initial activities appear to have been largely confined to London and it did not establish an extensive branch network.[21] In any case, developing a nationwide anti-socialist organisation at this time would have been difficult, given the significant variations in the conduct of municipal politics that existed across Edwardian Britain. In some English towns like

Brighton and Newcastle, and in several Scottish cities, candidates were not formally affiliated to party labels. Elsewhere, independent candidates remained common and pacts were sometimes made to share seats between Liberals and Unionists. Official Labour nominees who intervened against sitting councillors were sometimes criticised for supposedly introducing divisive party politics into municipal contests.[22] In a general survey of British government first published in 1908, A. Lawrence Lowell observed that 'clearly marked differences between the parties on municipal policy are not common in English boroughs'.[23] Whilst the Liberals tended to be the keenest supporters of expanding the functions of municipal government this was not always the case: 'in some places the Conservatives are the more progressive body in local matters, and in many more it is impossible to draw any distinction between the parties on that basis'.[24]

It should be emphasised that few Edwardian Unionists voiced wholesale opposition to municipalism. Despite its sensationalist attacks on London's 'Progressive-Socialist' administration, the Municipal Reform Party was chiefly concerned with restricting the expansion of municipal responsibilities to areas where private enterprise could not perform such activities efficiently. The party's programme came to be strongly influenced by the tariff reform campaign. Several Chamberlainites were active in the London Municipal Society and Anti-Socialist Union, and made efforts made to develop an appeal to working-class voters through municipal policy. Speaking at a rally during the 1907 LCC campaign, William Hayes Fisher claimed that it was in the working classes' interest to maintain low municipal expenditure, 'for it was the ever-increasing rates which depressed the industries by which working men lived, which industries were being driven out of London'.[25] On taking power the Municipal Reform administration sought to protect local jobs by giving a preference to British contractors over cheaper foreign rivals.[26]

The Unionist need to craft a viable appeal to the working classes became all the more pressing after Lloyd George introduced his 'People's Budget' in 1909. This acted as a direct challenge to claims by Chamberlain's supporters that social reforms and rising government expenditure could only be paid for by imposing tariffs on imports. Lloyd George's budget proposals included an increase in death duties on estates valued above £5,000, a 20 per cent tax on the increment value of land whenever it changed hands and a tax on the site value of undeveloped land. Approximately 75 per cent of the tax increase would be paid by the wealthiest 10 per cent of the population.[27] Leading Liberals such as Winston Churchill claimed that these measures targeted unproductive and inherited wealth and were ultimately more democratic than Unionist plans to introduce tariffs on imports, which would act as a 'food tax', hitting the poorest families most severely.[28]

During the 1910 elections Liberal election literature presented the Unionist-dominated House of Lords, which had thrown out the budget, as a body hostile to working-class interests. Mid-Devon Liberals produced a leaflet in the form of a letter from the candidate's wife, Dorothy Buxton, which claimed that the voters' choice was between: 'whether we are to be really free to govern ourselves and improve the conditions of the working classes by legislation, or whether we are to kept in leading strings by the House of Lords'. According to Buxton, the Lords held no regard 'for the interests of the poor. They have bitterly opposed, and in most cases defeated, every attempt of our Liberal Government to help the working men and the working women.'[29] Liberal posters presented the Lords' opposition to the budget as resulting solely from concerns to protect their own wealth.[30]

The Unionist counter-attack implied that Liberal claims to represent the people's interests were disingenuous. Rises in drink and tobacco duties were used to suggest that the budget would harm the working man's interests.[31] A series of Unionist posters produced for the 1910 elections presented the budget as 'the poor man's burden'. Not only would he have less money to spend on his pleasures, but lower consumption of tobacco and beer would also lead to an increase in unemployment.[32] In one poster an exasperated working man stands with hand outstretched. The caption states: 'Less beer, less baccy, less employment – and they call this the people's budget'.[33] Chamberlain's followers argued that tariffs would provide revenue for social reforms such as old age pensions, without having to place further burdens on British taxpayers, as the Liberals' proposals would entail. They played a vital role in forming the Unionist Social Reform Committee in 1911.[34]

It is difficult to judge how effective the Liberals' and Unionists' respective appeals were. The immediate effect of the tariff reform campaign had been to create division and confusion amongst Unionists. Whilst the Conservative Party leader Arthur Balfour was willing to support a retaliatory tariff to defend British industry, he steered clear of a commitment to the central plank of Chamberlain's scheme: imperial preference. Russell estimates that 55 per cent of Unionist candidates at the 1906 election took a Balfourite line in their election addresses, 40 per cent stood in support of Chamberlain's plans for a general tariff and preference on corn to aid producers in the empire, and 3 per cent advocated free trade.[35] Such divisions meant that the Unionists stood in stark contrast to a Liberal Party united around free trade. Nonetheless, the Unionists made an impressive electoral recovery following the Liberal landslide victory of 1906, with the effective collapse of the Unionist free trade faction in parliament.[36] At the December 1910 election Unionists returned 271 MPs, as opposed to the Liberals' 272. Nonetheless, Labour's 42 MPs meant that there was still a comfortable free trade majority in parliament.

Whilst Britain may have remained a free trade nation, the 1910 elections suggested that its faith in the doctrine had grown uncertain. The failure of tariff reform probably owed more to economic self-interest than to any inadequacies in the campaigning strategies of Chamberlain's supporters. Tariff reform was always at a disadvantage in that it was a visionary programme: electors had the choice of keeping the free trade status quo or risking an uncertain economic future under tariff reform. Unionists did well in by-elections during the economic downturn of 1908, which gave resonance to their appeals to overhaul the fiscal system. However, for much of the Edwardian period their prognosis of systemic economic crisis appeared to belie reality.[37]

As has been well established, Chamberlain's movement struggled in northern industrial districts, where leaders in key industries such as cotton, steel, shipbuilding and wool argued that the introduction of tariffs would hamper their trade, and repudiated Unionist claims that they were being ruined by the existing fiscal system.[38] The Tariff Reform League and Women's Unionist and Tariff Reform Association found it particularly difficult to develop a vigorous culture of local activism in Lancashire and Yorkshire. A north-west counties division of the TRL was formed in 1910, and organised the majority of public meetings and exhibitions in Lancashire.[39] Little spontaneous effort had previously been directed to organising tariff associations in the north-west. In 1906 there had only been six TRL branches covering Lancashire, Cheshire, and Cumberland, before a concerted push was made to employ external organisers.[40] WUTRA did not make a parallel effort to introduce leaders from outside the region. Tellingly, Leigh was the only Lancashire spinning town where a new Women's Unionist Association was formed after 1906, and even here mining was the chief industry.[41] Similar problems were experienced in West Yorkshire. F.C. Thomas, secretary of the West Riding Tariff Reform Federation, wrote to the *Yorkshire Post* in September 1912, claiming that a recent meeting in Leeds had been a fraud. It 'consisted of a mere handful of people, a number of loafers having been given 6d. each to stand around and form a crowd'. He noted that 'as to the League's numerous branches…no-one in the West Riding can discover them as they exist only on paper'.[42] Following this debacle, Viscount Ridley, the TRL chairman, privately admitted that the West Yorkshire organisation had been 'a complete failure'.[43]

Tariff reformers were ultimately inhibited by existing regional cultures of political identity, which their rhetorical appeals failed to break down. Peter Clarke notes that the cotton industry played a major role in the politics of Edwardian Lancashire, even in towns such as Blackburn and Burnley, where it employed less than a third of the adult male population.[44] In addition, Savage and Miles point to the development of a highly cohesive neighbourhood identity in working-class districts during this era.[45] Given the neighbourhood structure of working-class districts, key industries' influence expanded well beyond their own workforce. This meant that tariff reformers struggled in several constituencies in the north where industrial structures and conditions were similar to Unionist heartlands in the West Midlands and southern England.[46]

By dropping imperial preference from its immediate programme in 1913, the Unionist Party angered many of Chamberlain's supporters, who believed that this policy was integral to tariff reform. Contrary to Ewen Green's argument, however, this does not mean that Unionists were left without an effective populist programme from 1913.[47] Given that the issue of introducing tariffs on imported food had proved so divisive, dropping imperial preference substantially enhanced the Conservative Party's prospects. After 1913 the party was able to utilise the dynamic culture of grassroots activism created by the tariff leagues, but harnessed it to promote a broader Unionist programme, with a wider appeal.

During the late Edwardian period the Conservative Party made systematic efforts to target by-election issues to suit the differing characteristics of constituencies. Whilst David Jarvis claimed that the party's attempts at targeted electioneering began in the 1920s, Alex Windscheffel has demonstrated that the Conservatives were already making strides to promote targeted campaigning in the 1890s. In particular, populist Tories in London made great efforts to appeal to East End working men by attacking the local rise of alien immigration.[48]

The Conservative Party's experiments with targeted electioneering grew more sophisticated in the immediate pre-war years. By-election candidates focused on criticising Lloyd George's land policies in rural areas, whilst the Liberal National Insurance Act bore the brunt of attacks in the cities. The Conservatives also experimented with specialised pamphlets appealing to different interest groups. A 1913 leaflet on land taxes, for example, was published in seven editions, targeting agricultural workers, transport workers, building workers, engineers, miners, printers and textile workers.[49]

The land issue has been seen as an indicator that the Unionists' malaise showed few signs of easing in the years before the First World War. Ian Packer has argued that Lloyd George's land campaign, launched in October 1913, developed significant rural support. Given the apparent popularity of the Liberals' plans for agricultural wage boards and state encouragement of cottage building, Packer suggested that the Liberals could expect to gain at least twenty seats in rural England at the next general election.[50] Green concurred with this pessimistic view of Unionist prospects in the countryside, claiming that aside from supporting Jesse Collings's plans for smallholdings, Unionists lacked consensus on how to provide a competing strategy to Liberal proposals.[51] However, Readman's recent research has offered a valuable corrective in demonstrating that there was more enthusiasm for Collings's land reform programme within the Conservative Party than Green and Packer allow, and that such ideas provided a basis for an alternative programme.[52] Notwithstanding, Readman pays little attention to the important issue of how Conservatives presented their land policies in election campaigns.

Far from seeing the issue of land reform as a handicap to be played down, rural Unionists often placed Collings's programme at the centre of their by-election campaigning. In May 1913 John Dennison-Pender, Conservative candidate for East Cambridgeshire, highlighted his support for the Rural Housing Bill, recently proposed by his party and rejected by the Liberals. Dennison-Pender contended that Collings's plans to encourage smallholdings would be far more beneficial for the working classes than Liberal proposals for the taxation of land values: 'if the Radicals taxed land up to the hilt the people could not have cheap cottages'.[53] In the event, Bonar Law's party won the seat, benefiting from a 6.6 per cent swing against the Liberals. Conservatives also criticised Lloyd George's land valuation at the Reading by-election in November, where it was claimed that the Liberal plan to introduce land courts would lead to rent rises, thereby harming tenant farmers. By contrast, Collings's alternative of encouraging English tenants to buy land through low-interest state loans was presented as a more effective means to promote the development of smallholdings.[54] Collings's programme was also portrayed as a policy that would enhance the nation's 'efficiency'. By promoting rural regeneration, Unionists sought to check the high level of migration to the cities, which was supposedly contributing to the development of slum populations.[55]

Whilst rural Conservatives fought on the land issue, urban Tories focused their attacks on the workings of the National Insurance Act. This was especially the case in February 1914, when by-elections occurred at Poplar and South-West Bethnal Green in London's East End, where Charles Masterman, one of the act's main architects, stood for the Liberals in the latter constituency. Much as Unionists claimed to represent the interests of lowly tenant farmers in the countryside, urban Tories championed casual workers, whose interests were allegedly harmed by National Insurance. Masterman's Conservative opponent Mathew Wilson argued at an election meeting: 'The really poor people who should be assisted were badly treated under the act, and some who paid their contributions got no benefit.' Instead of the current compulsory system, Wilson supported Bonar Law's proposal to appoint a select committee to investigate the feasibility of converting National Insurance into a voluntary scheme. The Conservative candidate felt that the act infringed the liberty of the individual, effectively acting as an 'identification card' for workers.[56] Wilson's criticisms were echoed by supporters of the independent Labour candidate, who claimed that National Insurance, as it stood, made workers little more than 'poll tax serfs'.[57]

The campaign against National Insurance demonstrates that Unionists could construct new campaigns rooted in the material concerns of urban working-class communities. Given the nature of local employment patterns, opposition to National Insurance was a particularly emotive cry in Poplar and Bethnal Green. Poplar had a large casual workforce, many of whom were dockworkers who were disadvantaged when seeking work if their insurance cards were not fully stamped.[58] Bethnal Green likewise had many casual workers, and the Conservatives drew support from several small employers in the constituency who were struggling to make the contributory payments required by the National Insurance Act.[59] The Conservatives took Bethnal Green from the Liberals, who suffered a 2.8 per cent decline from their poll at the constituency's previous contest in July 1911. Although the Liberals managed to retain radical Poplar, their majority was reduced by 18.9 per cent.

In short, the claim that Unionists failed to develop an electorally appealing cause to replace tariff reform is unconvincing. In the immediate pre-war years, Unionist politicians developed a broad appeal to working-class men. They claimed that an overhaul of National Insurance legislation would aid the casual worker, and stated that tenant farmers would benefit from their plans for smallholdings.

Yet how far had Unionist social cultures been reconciled to democratic politics by 1914? Certainly there was a disparity between the party's rhetoric, which was often focused on appealing to working-class audiences, and the actual composition of constituency associations, which remained dominated by elites. Following his election defeat at Bow and Bromley in December 1910, Leo Amery wrote to Bonar Law, voicing his frustration with the way in which the Conservative Party functioned at the local level: 'each constituency is a little autonomous oligarchy of half a dozen men, very often of only two men, the chairman and the agent...the one thing they bother about is a candidate who will pay for the whole organisation, and if they can get that they have no use for the central office or anything else'.[60]

The demands of 'nursing' a constituency increased the appeal of a wealthy candidate. When George Lloyd, Conservative MP for West Staffordshire, became prospective candidate for Shrewsbury, he cut his ties with forty-six local clubs and societies. Aside from acting as a patron for several Staffordshire voluntary associations, Lloyd estimated that he had contributed at least a third of the constituency association's expenses.[61] The advent of a new MP who was able to pay a full-time agent could lead to a surge in the activities of the constituency association. This happened in

West Wolverhampton, under the stewardship of Alfred Bird, the custard manufacturer, after 1908. Under Bird's influence, there was a significant expansion of propaganda work: a branch of the Trade Union Tariff Reform Association, aimed at working men, was founded, and a constituency women's organisation was set up.[62]

At a regional level the Conservative Party also appears to have relied heavily on the largesse of wealthy subscribers. Almeric Paget, Conservative MP for Cambridge, heavily subsidised the educational work of the Eastern area of the NUCA (Cambridgeshire, Norfolk and Huntingdonshire), which included van tours of villages and speaking campaigns.[63] Nor was the influence of local grandees confined to the formal Conservative Party organisation. It was quite common for regional or county tariff associations to rely chiefly on the patronage of a handful of donors.[64] In 1912 TRL organisers considered disbanding the Sussex division because of the strong support for tariff reform across Unionist organisations in the county, and because that Lord Leconfield had become virtually the sole contributor towards expenses.[65]

John Ramsden has suggested that 'the gradual consolidation of wealth in the [Conservative] party was making it more difficult to preserve the classless, "one-nation" appeal to working-class voters' at this time.[66] However, the Liberal Party also seems to have relied heavily on wealthy benefactors during the Edwardian period. Central party funds accounted for around only one-quarter of reported Liberal candidates' election expenses in 1906 and January 1910.[67] Furthermore, regional studies of Edwardian politics indicate that minor forms of 'treating' by both Liberal and Conservative candidates remained prevalent. In Devon and Cornwall it appears to have been common practice for Liberal candidates in the region to subscribe between £300 and £400 a year to constituency associations.[68] The growth of extra-parliamentary leagues – which could spend unlimited sums at elections without counting as part of the candidate's expenses – provided new opportunities for the wealthy to influence politics. The Free Trade Union's nationwide lecture campaign during 1909–10, notable for its series of seaside meetings which harassed holidaymakers, was funded by a £10,000 donation from James Caird, the Dundee jute baron.[69]

Ultimately the development of extra-parliamentary leagues like the TRL and WUTRA had ambiguous effects on the culture of Unionist activism. As we have seen, the tariff leagues provided new opportunities for previously marginalised groups, especially women, to participate in Unionist politics. Nonetheless, by relying largely on local initiative, the tariff leagues came to reflect the class-bound social cultures of their heartlands in southern England and the West Midlands, taking on some hierarchical and inegalitarian characteristics in the process. WUTRA drew much of its leadership from traditional elites. The chairman of the women's tariff association, Mary Maxse, was the daughter of the Sussex grandee and acolyte of Joseph Chamberlain, Lord Leconfield. At a local level WUTRA was often led by the wives or daughters of Unionist MPs such as Caroline Bridgeman, Beatrice Chamberlain and Edith Lyttleton.

The influence of class divisions also trickled down into activist cultures. Although WUTRA created a more progressive ethos than the previous generation of female Unionists, it still distinguished the roles that it expected activists of different classes to undertake. When WUTRA made a request for Ulster women to cross the Irish Sea and speak against home rule in 1911 it asked for: 'Ladies capable of speaking at small cottage meetings, in village schools, or in ladies' drawing rooms…second, women of any class who will be content to go from house to house talking to each individual occupier.'[70] The position of woman agent was largely the preserve of 'ladies' at this time, as WUTRA's regional organisers could only claim limited expenses from a fund set up by Lord Ebury to cover travel and accommodation expenses.[71]

While WUTRA focused on the plight of working families, it made few substantial efforts to accommodate itself to the social culture of industrial areas. The 'Help the Ulster Women' campaign, for example, was predicated on the idea that families would have spare accommodation to house Irish refugees. This meant that it received an enthusiastic response from the affluent in rural areas of counties such as Sussex.[72] Conversely, such pledges of housing were unrealistic in the terraced districts of a northern town like Darwen in Lancashire.[73] WUTRA's strategy tended to revitalise and consolidate female Unionist activism in existing heartlands, rather than advancing the party's appeal in marginal urban seats. This put it at a disadvantage in appealing to the hearts and minds of working women.

By comparison with the women's tariff association, the TRL made substantial attempts to broaden its support beyond its middle-class strongholds. Even so, the league found it hard to develop an activist base amongst the unionised working class. Formed in 1909 by TRL supporters, the Workers' Defence Union explicitly focused on attracting working men to Chamberlain's cause. It collapsed in 1912, having formed a handful of branches, several of which struggled to gain a significant popular following.[74] Similar problems were experienced by the Trade Union Tariff Reform Association (TUTRA), a related organisation. Leo Amery, one of this body's architects, hoped that it 'might at the end of a few years stand entirely on its own feet and compete effectively with the existing Labour party'.[75] And yet, the TUTRA only had ten thousand supporters at its peak in 1909.[76]

After 1912 Unionist politicians took significant strides to widen their appeal, adopting a broad populist programme. Rather than being merely passive beneficiaries of existing hostility to Liberal policies, Unionists crafted campaigns to reflect the characteristics of different constituencies, thereby constructing, rather than simply reflecting, popular antipathy towards Liberal reforms. The targeted electioneering developed during these years laid the basis for the successful campaign strategies nurtured by the Conservative Party in the 1920s.

Nonetheless, Unionists still had much to do to reconcile themselves truly to democratic politics in the years before the First World War. Constituency associations continued to be dominated by narrow elites. In turn, the tariff leagues' activism was shaped by class-bound social cultures which limited working-class participation. Despite the failure of attempts to develop a strong tariff reform organisation for trade unionists, Unionists still held on to the hope that a 'patriotic labour' movement could be formed to counteract the growing influence of the Labour Party. These concerns were to play an important factor in explaining why the 'radical right' British Workers League gained widespread sympathy amongst Unionists during the First World War.

Notes

1   *The Times*, 25 February 1907, p. 4.
2   'Ratepayers. It's your money we want' (1907), London Metropolitan Archives, Acc. 3606, LCC/CL/COUN/2/41-45.
3   *The Times*, 25 February 1907, p. 4.
4   C.F.G. Masterman, *The Condition of England* (London, 1909), pp. 71, 80.
5   For the traditional view see James Cornford, 'The transformation of Conservatism in the late nineteenth century', *Victorian Studies*, 7:1 (1963), 35–66.
6   For the debate see Roberts, 'Villa Toryism', 217–18; amongst the key revisionist works are Lawrence, 'Class and gender'; Windscheffel, *Popular Conservatism in Imperial London*; Coetzee, 'Villa Toryism reconsidered'.
7   McKibbin, *Parties and People*, p. 10.
8   Jarvis, 'British Conservatism and class politics', 66–7, 79.
9   Ibid., 79.
10 For examples of Unionist claims to represent local industrial workers see, for example, Imperial Tariff Committee, *Monthly Notes*, 8:3 (1908), p. 92; Mid-Worcestershire Tariff Reform Association, *The Carpet Trade and the Fiscal Question* (Kidderminster, 1904); *Bioscope*, 25 November 1909, p. 11; 13 January 1910, p. 11.
11 *The Times*, 30 January 1911, p. 9.
12 Trentmann, *Free Trade Nation*, p. 55.
13 McKibbin, *Parties and People*, p. 13.
14 Blewett, *Peers, Parties and People*, p. 343.
15 London Municipal Society MSS, Publication Department report, 6 March 1907.
16 Susan D. Pennybacker, *A Vision for London, 1889–1914: Labour, Everyday Life and the LCC Experiment* (London, 1995), p. 15; Avner Offer, *Property and Politics, 1870–1914: Landownership, Law, Ideology and Urban Development in England* (Cambridge, 1981), p. 255.

17 Duncan Tanner, *Political Change and the Labour Party, 1900–1918* (Cambridge, 1990), p. 166; Coetzee, 'Villa Toryism reconsidered', p. 36.

18 John Davis, 'The enfranchisement of the urban poor in late-Victorian Britain', in Peter Ghosh and Lawrence Goldman (eds), *Politics and Culture in Victorian Britain: Essays in Memory of Colin Matthew* (Oxford, 2006), pp. 95–117.

19 Windscheffel, *Popular Conservatism in Imperial London*, pp. 8–9.

20 James R. Moore, 'Liberalism and the politics of suburbia: electoral dynamics in late-nineteenth century South Manchester', *Urban History*, 2 (2003), 225–50; Mike Savage, *The Dynamics of Working-Class Politics: The Labour Movement in Preston* (Cambridge, 1987), p. 150; Tim Cooper, 'The politics of Radicalism in suburban Walthamstow, 1870–1914' (PhD dissertation, University of Cambridge, 2004), p. 226; Tom Jeffrey, 'The suburban nation: politics and class in Lewisham', in David Feldman and Gareth Stedman Jones (eds), *Metropolis London* (London, 1989), pp. 189–216.

21 Coetzee, *For Party or Country*, pp. 103, 156.

22 Lawrence Lowell, *The Government of England*, vol. 2, pp. 152–3; Jon Lawrence, 'Review of Sam Davies and Bob Morley ed., *County Borough Election Results in England and Wales 1919–1938: A Comparative Analysis* (Aldershot, 2 vols., 1999–2000)', *English Historical Review*, 118 (2003), 462–4 at 464.

23 Lawrence Lowell, *Government of England*, vol. 2, p. 164.

24 Ibid., p. 151.

25 *The Times*, 25 February 1907, p. 4.

26 Sue Laurence, 'Moderates, municipal reformers, and the issue of tariff reform, 1894–1934', in Andrew Saint (ed.), *Politics and the People of London: The London County Council, 1889–1965* (London, 1989), pp. 93–102 at pp. 97–8.

27 Blewett, *Peers, Parties and People*, p. 70.

28 Martin Daunton, *Trusting Leviathan: The Politics of Taxation in Britain, 1799–1914* (Cambridge, 2001), pp. 363–4.

29 Ernest Morrison-Bell MSS, 2128, leaflet letter from Dorothy Buxton, 22 December 1909.

30 See, for example, 'Tax land not food', *Morning Star* poster from 1909, reprinted in Daunton, *Trusting Leviathan*, p. 340; Amery MSS, AMEL4/5, G.R. Thorne leaflet, December 1910.

31 See, for example, Page Croft MSS, HPC3/1, *Bournemouth Directory*, 8 May 1909, cutting.

32 CPA 1909/10-01 , 'The rewards of the righteous'; CPA 1909/10-03, 'The start – the finish'; CPA 1909/10-09, Unfair preference'; CPA 1909/10-20b, 'The poor man's burden'; CPA 1909/10-36, 'Dearer beer'.

33 CPA 1909/10-16, Budget Protest League poster, 'Less beer, less baccy, less employment'.

34 Green, *Crisis of Conservatism*, pp. 4–5, 242–63, 287.

35 A.K. Russell, *Liberal Landslide: The General Election of 1906* (Newton Abbot, 1973), pp. 87–8.

36 The Unionist Free Food League had counted sixty-five MPs amongst its supporters in autumn 1903 but by 1910 there was only one Unionist free trader left in the Commons, Henry Cecil.

37 Unionists won eight seats at by-elections during 1908, with an average swing against the government of over 10 per cent. Blewett, *Peers, Parties and People*, pp. 26–7, 47.

38 Anthony Howe, *Free Trade and Liberal England, 1846–1946* (Oxford, 1997), pp. 237–8; P.F. Clarke, *Lancashire and the New Liberalism* (Cambridge, 1971), pp. 274–310.

39 TRL, *Monthly Notes*, 13:6 (1910), pp. 378, 397; TRL, *Annual Report* (London, 1913), p. 120.

40 TRL, *Annual Report* (1913), p. 143.

41 Grace A. Jones, 'National and local issues in politics: a study of East Sussex and Lancashire spinning towns, 1906–10' (PhD dissertation, University of Sussex, 1965), p. 224.

42 *Yorkshire Post*, 7 September 1912, p. 11.

43 Churchill College, Cambridge, GLLD16/58, Lloyd MSS, Matthew White Ridley to George Lloyd, 24 September 1912.

44 Clarke, *Lancashire and the New Liberalism*, p. 78.

45 Mike Savage and Andrew Miles, *The Remaking of the British Working Class, 1840– 1940* (London, 1994), p. 64.

46 This was particularly the case in the north-east of England, see Tanner, *Political Change and Labour*, pp. 228–30.

47 Green, *Crisis of Conservatism*, ch. 11.

48 Jarvis, 'Class politics', 64; Windscheffel, *Popular Conservatism in Imperial London*, pp. 75–8.

49 K.M.O. Swaddle, 'Coping with a mass electorate: a study in the evolution of constituency electioneering in Britain, with special emphasis on the periods which followed the Reform Acts of 1884 and 1918' (DPhil dissertation, University of Oxford, 1990), p. 127.

50 Ian Packer, *Lloyd George, Liberalism and the Land: the Land Issue and Party Politics in England, 1906–1914* (Woodbridge, 2001), pp. 126, 130, 137, 157; for a discussion of the problems with Packer's evidence of growing popular support for Lloyd George's land campaign see David Thackeray, 'Rethinking the Edwardian crisis of Conservatism', *Historical Journal*, 54 (2011), 191–213 at 207.

51 Green, *Crisis of Conservatism*, pp. 289–94.

52 Paul Readman, *Land and Nation in England: Patriotism, National Identity, and the Politics of the Land, 1880–1914* (Woodbridge, 2008), pp. 173–6, 180.

53 *Newmarket Journal*, 10 May 1913, p. 5.

54 *Berkshire Chronicle (Reading)*, 17 October 1913, p. 8.

55 Jesse Collings, *The Colonization of Rural Britain: A Complete Scheme for the Regeneration of British Rural Life* (London, 2 vols, 1914), vol. 2, p. 351.

56 *East London Observer*, 14 February 1914, p. 8.

57 *Daily Herald*, 6 January 1914, p. 6; see also 9 January 1914, p. 2; 17 February 1914, p. 5; 20 February 1914, p. 5.

58 *The Times*, 12 February 1914, p. 8; 14 February 1914, p. 9.

59 *The Times*, 13 February 1914, p. 8; 16 February 1914, p. 9.

60 Amery MSS, AMEL2/3/1, Leo Amery to Andrew Bonar Law, 16 December 1910.

61 Lloyd MSS, GLLD18/3, George Lloyd to J.H. Buck, 28 October 1913; GLLD18/5, George Lloyd to Colonel Dobson, 19 May 1913; In January 1910 Sir Mortimer Durand and Waldorf Astor stood as the Unionist candidates for Plymouth. The official return for election expenses put their joint expenditure at £1,375, but Durand's biographer later estimated that he spent £2,000 as a prospective parliamentary candidate, Sir Percy Sykes, *Sir Mortimer Durand* (London, 1926), p. 336.

62   Wolverhampton Archives, Wolverhampton Conservative and Unionist Association MSS, D/SO/27/1, Management Committee minutes, 6 January 1909; Alfred Bird to Charles Marston, 11 May 1909; Jones, *Borough Politics*, pp. 45–7.

63   CPA, Eastern Area of NUCA Executive minutes, ARE7/1/6, annual report, January 1911.

64   Balfour MSS, Add. 49775, fols 150–60, Leo Amery to Robert Sandars, 31 January 1911.

65   Lloyd MSS, GLLD16/58, J. Percy Askew to George Lloyd, 17 September 1912.

66   Ramsden, *Age of Balfour and Baldwin*, p. 105.

67   Michael Pinto-Duschinsky, *British Political Finance, 1830–1980* (Washington, DC, 1981), p. 49.

68   Dawson, 'Politics in Devon and Cornwall', pp. 52–8; Clarke, *Lancashire and the New Liberalism*, pp. 199–200.

69   Churchill College, Cambridge, Chartwell MSS, 2/44/3, James K. Caird to Winston Churchill, 13 December 1909.

70   Ulster Women's Unionist Council Executive Committee minutes, 7 April 1911, in Diane Urquhart (ed.), *Minutes of the Ulster Women's Unionist Council and Executive Committee* (Dublin, 2001), p. 13.

71   For the work of Ebury workers see *Berrow's Worcester Journal*, 3 May 1913, pp. 3, 7; Andrew S. Thompson, *Imperial Britain: The Empire in British Politics, c. 1880–1932* (Harlow, 2000), pp. 56–7.

72   *Southern Weekly News (Brighton)*, 7 March 1914, p. 5; 14 March 1914, p. 11.

73   *Darwen Gazette*, 7 March 1914, p. 4.

74   Alan Sykes, 'Radical Conservatism and the working-classes in Edwardian England: the case of the Workers Defence Union', *English Historical Review*, 113 (1998), 1180–209 at 1186–7, 1204.

75   Amery MSS, AMEL2/3/1, Leo Amery to Arthur Steel-Maitland, 5 March 1909.

76   Alan Sykes, *Tariff Reform in British Politics, 1903–1913* (Oxford, 1979), p. 222; Sykes, 'Radical Conservatism', 185.

4

Cultures of Unionism

As well as encountering divisions based on class and gender, the Edwardian Unionist alliance experienced varying fortunes across the regions of Britain as a result of the uneven reception of tariff reform. Whilst the tariff leagues played a key role in revitalising Unionist activism in southern England and the West Midlands, many Unionists were deeply troubled by the emergence of the tariff reform campaign.[1] It is clear that the controversial nature of Chamberlain's programme impeded attempts to reshape and modernise activist cultures in regions where support for free trade remained widespread.

Given that opposition to Irish home rule provided the cornerstone of the Unionist alliance, it might be expected that the Liberal government's introduction of the Third Irish Home Rule Bill in 1912 would serve to revitalise Unionist fortunes in regions where tariff reform had received a lukewarm or downright hostile reception. Yet historians have come to a variety of conclusions as to the effects that the revival of the home rule issue had on the Unionist cause. Ewen Green argued that opponents of Irish home rule struggled to develop an effective popular campaign in defence of the union. According to Green, the Unionist Party appeared to be drifting towards disaster and possible disintegration on the eve of the First World War.[2] The Irish home rule crisis of 1912–14 has often been seen as exerting a destabilising effect on the Unionist Party as some factions were willing to flout constitutional values and risk civil war to defend the union with Ireland.[3] In Thomas Kennedy's reading, Unionists suppressed 'every positive instinct within the party' during these years.[4]

Other historians have, however, produced more sanguine portrayals of the Unionist party's prospects during the late Edwardian period. John Ramsden argued that popular hostility to the Liberals' Third Home Rule Bill, with its threat to submit Ulster Protestants to the yoke of a Dublin parliament, rebounded to the Conservatives' advantage. As a result, the outbreak of war in 1914 'robbed the Unionist party of a return to power'.[5] Daniel Jackson's more recent work reinforces the claim that the Ulster crisis aided the party's prospects, as defence of the union became a cause that mobilised thousands of political activists across Britain.[6]

Despite all these studies, we still have only a limited understanding of how the issue of opposing Irish home rule affected Unionist activism in the localities. Frans Coetzee has claimed that, during 1913–14, Unionist leaders 'circumscribed the former independence' of the various conservative auxiliary leagues which came to prominence during the Edwardian period.[7] Yet, in making this judgement, Coetzee neglected the activities of the various auxiliary movements that opposed Irish home rule, which have received little historical attention until recently but were vital to the identity of popular Unionism after 1912. The British Covenant organisation, in particular, did much to unite and revitalise grassroots Unionism across the nation during these years, appealing not only to many who had participated in the tariff reform campaign, but also to many who had not. Moreover, auxiliary organisations which had previously focused on the fiscal debate, such as the Women's Unionist and Tariff Reform Association, now devoted their attention to the defence of the union. In the immediate years before the First World War, opposition to Irish home rule galvanised and revitalised Unionist activism across Britain.

The most detailed information we have on the organisation of the Unionist auxiliary forces in the Edwardian years comes from the West Midlands, in the notebook in the Bodleian Library already mentioned in chapter 2.

Table 4.1 *Unionist auxiliary organisations, Midland Union, c. 1913*

Organisation	No. of constituencies in which organisation is active	Details provided	Organisation considered effective (%)	Organisation considered defective (%)
Junior Imperial League	17	12	75	25
National Conservative League	6	6	50	50
Primrose League	25	20	50	50
Women's Unionist Association/ WUTRA	24	20	85	15

Figures based on Midland Union notebook 1907–17, CPA, ARE MU 29/3.

The region surrounded the Chamberlainite fiefdom of Birmingham, and twenty-five of the thirty-three constituencies had a Unionist MP at this time. The Junior Imperial League (JIL), a movement which had been founded in 1906 for men aged sixteen to twenty-one, was active in seventeen of the Midland Union constituencies and underwent a growth spurt nationally after Conservative Central Office provided it with funding and organisational assistance in 1911.[8] In the West Midlands it was widely praised for providing useful help to the Unionist cause in the localities.

The leading auxiliary organisations in the region were WUTRA and the Primrose League. Of the twenty constituencies which commented on the operations of their Women's Unionist Association (WUA)/WUTRA branches, 85 per cent unreservedly presented the women's work as an asset. The organisation was seen as very helpful as it tended to base its activities on polling district boundaries and sought to publicise the Unionist cause both during and between elections. In East Worcestershire, Austen Chamberlain's seat, the Women's Unionist Association had 3,500 members, was self-supporting and had a paid secretary.[9] The Primrose League remained highly active in the region, but its habitations were seen as less of an asset than the women's tariff reform organisation. The twenty constituencies which provided details of habitations' activities were evenly split over whether it was performing effectively as a Unionist auxiliary. The chief cause for dissatisfaction resulted from a sense that the Primrose League was not providing effective assistance in political education outside elections.[10] All the same, it should be remembered that the Primrose League had long played a limited role in West Midlands politics due to Liberal Unionist hostility to this organisation.

West London provides a good example of a region where the Primrose League adopted many elements of the tariff leagues' culture and came to play an important role in revitalising grassroots Unionism. Given the Conservatives' dominance of the alliance in the metropolis, the Primrose League had always been more of a live force here than in areas such as Birmingham.[11] WUTRA developed a few branches in the west of the city, but it struggled to gain a large membership since the Primrose League was able to provide an effective electoral organisation.[12] William Bull, MP for Hammersmith, had close ties with the Primrose League; his wife became the president of a local habitation, which provided at least seven hundred woman helpers during the 1906 election. On being returned for the constituency with a much reduced majority Bull eulogised about the aid he had received from this body: 'If I had not been [supported] splendidly with an organisation that was almost perfect, I should never have withstood the storm.'[13]

Collaboration between the Primrose League and WUTRA was facilitated by the former organisation taking a more serious attitude to political education than it had done during the early 1900s. Linda Walker has claimed that the league 'never evolved beyond the self-imposed boundaries of women's informal, indirect persuasion in politics. The notion that women gained and retained influence not by their talents but by their charms'.[14] Yet this was clearly not the case in areas such as West London, where branches of WUTRA and the Primrose League often shared personnel.[15] In East Marylebone, the Primrose League had suffered from low subscriptions, yet it found a new lease of life when the Irish issue came to the fore in

1912. Members agreed to double their subscriptions and were encouraged to assist in entertainments, thereby cutting the habitation's spending on performers' services. The habitation subsequently had far greater resources to devote to electioneering.[16] Here was the mirror opposite of the frivolous habitations which the tariff leagues' supporters had long criticised.

Whilst the grassroots Unionist organisation was revitalised in party heartlands like West London and the West Midlands during the Edwardian period, it is clear that the controversial nature of Chamberlain's programme divided and demoralised Unionists in other regions where free trade remained strong. This was the case in the Liberal stronghold of North Wales. Following the 1906 election a Unionist conference was held to revive the party in Denbighshire and Flintshire. Chamberlain's supporters, who dominated the North Wales Division of the National Union of Conservative Associations, were at the forefront of calls for a more democratic organisation, with greater working-class and female representation.[17] During subsequent years Denbighshire Unionists implemented significant changes along these lines. The first Unionist women's organisation in the region was formed in Wrexham in 1907, aided by the support of Unionist women like Caroline Bridgeman from neighbouring Shropshire. The following year the West Denbighshire Conservative Association adopted a working man candidate, Sam Thompson, a former Rhondda Valley miner, who had worked for the Tariff Reform League at the 1906 election.[18] However, the Conservative Party leaders in adjoining Flintshire, where Unionism had traditionally been a weaker force, expressed reticence towards Chamberlain's programme. Their disputes with the North Wales Division of the NUCA appear to have undermined attempts at reorganising the party in the county.[19]

In other rural areas where the Liberals remained ascendant, Unionist activists also found it difficult to reorganise along the lines achieved in the West Midlands and Home Counties. The ideal organisation favoured by tariff reformers was self-supporting and based around regular meetings and propaganda drives organised by local activists.[20] Yet this proved unfeasible in much of East Anglia, dominated as it was by disparate farming communities which had a strong Liberal presence due to the popular appeal of free trade and Nonconformity.[21] In Cambridgeshire, Norfolk and Huntingdonshire the tariff leagues' leaders focused chiefly on providing 'missionaries' to constituency associations who distributed leaflets door-to-door and conducted van tours of villages. They appear to have placed significantly less emphasis on developed a locally led branch organisation before Irish home rule returned to the top of the political agenda in 1912.[22]

In northern industrial districts it was the Primrose League, rather than the tariff organisations, which dominated Unionist auxiliary activities at local level. The Primrose League continued to grow significantly in northern England during the Edwardian period, suggesting that in some constituencies it provided a haven for those who resisted the propagandising of Chamberlain's supporters.[23] Whereas Primrose League habitations appear to have largely adopted to the tariff leagues' culture with its focus on political education, in regions where Chamberlain's campaign developed widespread support, this does not appear to have been the case in free trade Lancashire. A Primrose League agency committee report for Lancashire and Cheshire produced in the wake of the January 1910 election presented a picture of stagnation and political apathy. It noted that many Lancashire habitations 'have not had a political address for years, while some complain that they have not been visited by a Provincial Secretary. Many of the Habitations are very poor and often only social clubs without an organisation except for whist drives and dances.' In Lancashire, in particular, tariff reform was 'not understood', given that the cotton industry relied on imports of raw materials and the export market.[24] Preston and Chorley were the only spinning towns where Unionist constituency associations were able to present an effective united front on the issue of tariff reform at the 1910 elections.[25]

In much of Lancashire, tariff reform was a divisive force, which undermined the county's existing standing as a heartland of popular Unionism – a reputation which had been built in the late Victorian period on strong links to the Anglican church and opposition to Irish home rule.[26] The Conservative Party remained strong in Liverpool, but even here the party's residual electoral success in the Edwardian period appears to have owed much to its continued commitment to upholding Anglicanism above other issues. In January 1905 Archibald Salvidge, the leader of the Conservative Party in Liverpool, wrote to F.E. Smith regarding the position of Austin Taylor, a Unionist Free Trader, who sat for East Toxteth:

> I am convinced that it would be a mistake, in present circumstances, for the Tariff Reform League to put you or anyone else up against Austin Taylor...Should the TRL try to displace the acknowledged leader of Protestantism in Parliament it might well end in strengthening Taylor's position and rousing hostility to Tariff Reform in quarters where no such hostility exists.[27]

Clearly, Taylor's position as a bulwark of Anglicanism mattered more to Unionist authorities in Liverpool than his heresy on the fiscal question. In any case the dilemma was solved when Taylor crossed the floor and joined the Liberals in 1907.

The Orange card had played an important role in maintaining the residual strength of the Unionist cause in much of the rest of Lancashire.

Amongst the posters which were prominent in the county during the 1910 elections were images of Redmond leading the Liberal Cabinet by ropes attached to rings in their noses. The Irish Nationalist leader was also depicted trampling on defenceless John Bull, who had no House of Lords to protect him.[28]

Liverpool may have been unusual in the fervour with which religious issues were played out in the city's public life, but denominational identity still played an important role in Edwardian politics, with Nonconformity largely aligned with the Liberal Party and Anglicanism with the Conservatives. Even in Birmingham, the heartland of the tariff reform campaign, political leaders recognised the importance of building relations with religious groups. In 1909, Charles Vince, secretary of the Birmingham Liberal Unionists, wrote a letter to advise Leo Amery on election strategy in the event of his becoming candidate for Bordesley. The elderly incumbent, Jesse Collings was ill at the time and it was unclear whether he would seek election again. If there was a contest, Amery was advised: 'some Church of England clergymen ought to be seen; as the ward has been fought more than once on the Church schools question, the parsons helping'.[29]

As this survey has shown, the prominence of tariff reform in Edwardian politics only served to accentuate the difficulties of reforming Unionist activism in regions where free trade remained a vibrant popular force, especially as Chamberlain's supporters sought to impose their creed in hostile areas. Unionism effectively spoke with two voices in regions such as North Wales, Lancashire and West Yorkshire, undermining its credibility. Nonetheless, the divisions caused by tariff reform proved to be far from insuperable: in the immediate years before the First World War the Unionist Party underwent a revival throughout these hotbeds of free trade, buoyed by its promotion of a more traditional politics, centred around campaigns against Irish home rule and Welsh disestablishment.

In early 1914 a group of Chamberlain's supporters, led by Leo Amery and Lord Milner, organised the British Covenant; a mass petition against Irish home rule. Those who signed the Covenant deemed themselves 'justified in taking or supporting any action that may be effective to prevent [home rule] being put into operation'.[30] The Unionist party leader, Bonar Law, had been consulted in the early stages of the covenant's drafting. Amery noted that he 'was quite sympathetic' and willing to assist the movement with 'the general support of the Party, although the actual organisation would be separate'.[31] That spring, Unionist agents proceeded to work with the newly formed League of British Covenanters in organising anti-home rule meetings across the country.[32]

The rise of the British Covenant campaign has puzzled historians. Green did not mention the movement, claiming that Unionists were unable to generate mass support behind opposition to Irish home rule.[33] Jackson has done much to challenge this viewpoint, demonstrating that popular interest in the cause of defending the Union rapidly gathered momentum in the immediate pre-war years.[34] Nonetheless, like other historians, Jackson does not recognise a difference between the ethos of the British Covenant and the extremist British League for the Support of Ulster and the Union (BLSUU).[35] This latter organisation was founded in 1912 by Willoughby de Broke and developed close links with the Ulster Volunteer Force.[36] By 1914 the BLSUU claimed to have organised ten thousand men ready to fight in the event of an Irish conflict.[37] Figures linked to the BLSUU openly acknowledged that they were ready to take illegal actions to resist home rule. For example, Lord Winterton stated to meetings in Sussex that he was prepared to fund the arming of a militia and fight with it in Ulster.[38]

During the late Edwardian period there was a growing sense amongst some Unionists that the Liberals' actions meant that the constitution was effectively in abeyance. In particular they were alarmed by the 1911 Parliament Act, which undermined the authority of the House of Lords as a constitutional check on government.[39] Asquith's threat to coerce Ulster into a home rule settlement appeared to be the final straw, indicating that his party had abandoned constitutional procedure altogether and was in thrall to the demands of its Irish Nationalist allies. This was potentially dangerous, encouraging Willoughby de Broke and his supporters to believe that extraordinary and extra-constitutional measures were needed to fight the Asquith government.[40]

There was an overlap in the leadership of the British Covenant organisation and the BLSUU. Milner was initially a supporter of Willoughby de Broke's organisation and sat on the executive of the League of British Covenanters. Consequently, historians have portrayed the British Covenant as an outgrowth of the BLSUU.[41] Jeremy Smith, for example, has claimed that 'the Covenant would advertise the strength of popular support for the Union and provide willing recruits who could fight for the cause. Thus it would be a stepping stone to a more military organisation.'[42] Smith accordingly sees Walter Long's claims of around a million men signing the Covenant as 'wildly exaggerated'.[43] Jackson is also sceptical about the Covenant's populist nature, arguing that the members of Conservative auxiliary organisations, such as the Primrose League, would have been placed under considerable aristocratic pressure to sign.[44]

Historians have, however, neglected substantial differences between the BLSUU and the British Covenant, analysis of which reveals that organised opposition to Irish home rule had a greater resonance than has been supposed. Jackson noted that there was growing popular unease with the belligerent ethos of the BLSUU by autumn 1913.[45] At this time, Robert Cecil wrote to Willoughby de Broke, claiming that some of the league's leaflets 'rather frighten me'.[46] Even in the Orange heartland of Liverpool Archibald Salvidge expressed his hostility to the BLSUU holding meetings in the city due to their potential to stoke up sectarian rifts.[47] Nonetheless, Jackson appears to imply that these concerns were submerged during the following months, as opposition to Irish home rule grew increasingly fervent, and popular support for the Ulster cause swelled.

And yet, it seems clear that rather than complementing the BLSUU, the British Covenant emerged from Unionist concerns that the Ulster cause was coming to be dominated by extremists. In drafting the British Covenant, Amery believed that 'the weakness of the League lies in the fact that it is too directly concentrated upon a contingency which the British public as a whole...refuses as yet to contemplate...fighting with a rifle in Ulster...it cannot be said to constitute a really national movement'.[48] Thomas Kennedy has recently claimed that party leaders such as Robert Cecil and Austen Chamberlain had grave reservations about the British Covenant, fearing it might entail a commitment to supporting opposition to home rule through violent means.[49] But it should be emphasised that both men were expressing their concerns with a draft they had received in January 1914, rather than criticising the actual Covenant which was launched in March. In fact, both Cecil and Chamberlain spoke in support of the British Covenant movement.[50] Amery was able to reassure Cecil by stressing that 'what we want is something less immediately bellicose' than Willoughby de Broke's league.[51]

It would have been difficult to avoid the British Covenant during the spring of 1914. Across the country, Unionist activists collected petition signatures through house-to-house canvass, public exhibitions, and even by hawking in pubs.[52] A parallel Women's Covenant petition organised by WUTRA and the Primrose League gained around 750,000 signatures.[53] Far from being an overtly bellicose movement, as the existing historiography maintains, Unionists portrayed the British Covenant as a mass protest against Asquith's defiance of constitutional principles in threatening to coerce Ulster into accepting the authority of a Dublin parliament. The text of the Covenant stated that the government's carrying of the Home Rule Bill into law 'without submitting it to the judgement of the Nation, is contrary to the spirit of our Constitution'.[54] In this desperate situation, the Covenant's supporters claimed that their mass protest was the only hope of awakening the government to the depth of hostility which would result from any attempt to coerce Ulster.[55] Signature of the British Covenant by no means signified a personal commitment to support Ulster by taking up arms. Milner insisted that it was not 'a pledge to offer forcible resistance to the carrying into execution of the Home Rule Bill...it does not bind its signatories to any particular course of action'.[56]

Whereas tariff reform had undermined the Unionist organisation in northern England, the new centrality of the Irish issue after 1913 restored vitality to Conservative activism in regions such as Lancashire and West Yorkshire. Primrose League workers in Darwen, Lancashire, for example, canvassed energetically for the British Covenant, receiving 1,246 signatures within the first month of the campaign and quickly ran out of available forms.[57] Across the Pennines, Bradford Conservatives felt a new spirit of optimism in the spring of 1914. The local party chairman, J.J. Oddy, had been despairing in the weeks before the Unionist Party dropped its commitment to imperial preference in early 1913, imploring Bonar Law to remove the threat of 'food taxes', which had been so injurious to Unionist prospects in the borough.[58] A year later, however, Oddy's mood had brightened considerably, when he informed a meeting of Shipley Unionists that the Liberals knew that, on home rule, 'they have not the country at the back of them…if you will realise the seriousness of the case and take your coats off, we will sweep them out'.[59] Although Oddy was speaking in public, his strident tone was significant, and a fortnight later he reiterated his belief that the Asquith government was living on borrowed time and encouraged Unionists to rally around the British Covenant.[60]

The Irish issue played an important role in Unionist by-election campaigns during autumn 1913 and the winter of 1914.[61] Activists often sought to turn these by-elections into local referenda on the Liberal government's attempts to impose home rule. In November 1913, the *Berkshire Chronicle* implored Reading electors to vote Conservative at the upcoming by-election. The paper claimed that victory for the Liberals would mean that the town had endorsed the government's Irish policy, which in the worst eventuality could end with the Berkshire Regiment being ordered to shoot loyal Ulstermen.[62] The spectre of a potential conflict in Ulster was also raised during the Leith Burghs by-election in February 1914. Speaking in support of the Conservative candidate, the MP for Glasgow Central, Scott Dickson, told an audience that 'it was no longer a question of voting for a man because they liked him or the policy or party to which he belonged. They had got themselves right up against this – were they going to vote for civil war or against it?'[63]

Having already developed a substantial popular appeal, the defence of Ulster gained a new dynamism following the Curragh Mutiny of 20 March 1914. This incident resulted when Sir Arthur Paget, commander of the army base in Curragh, County Kildare, mistook orders from the War Office as an instruction to march north against Ulster. Thinking he was facing this grave undertaking, Paget decided to offer the men under his command the opportunity to resign rather than fight the Ulster Volunteer Force.[64] Outraged by this affair, various Unionist organisations cooperated in organising a mass meeting labelled as 'London's protest against British forces being used to fight Ulster loyalists'.[65] Tens of thousands attended this demonstration in Hyde Park on 4 April, where they could hear a prestigious array of speakers, including Milner, Balfour, Robert Cecil and, in pride of place, Carson. Smaller meetings were staged across the country to celebrate 'Ulster's Day'.[66]

Unlike Irish home rule, the issue of disestablishment of the church in Wales has often been seen as playing a marginal role in the politics of Edwardian Britain, outside the principality itself. Neil Evans has recently suggested that, whilst disestablishment reinforced the vitality of Liberalism in Wales, Unionist-led opposition marches struggled to develop momentum.[67] Nonetheless, Evans neglects the Unionists' ability to transform anti-disestablishment into a populist cause during 1913–14. Liberal attacks on the established church were presented as the latest in a succession of tyrannical assaults on the British constitution, which had started with the undermining of the Lords' veto and reached their apogee in attempts to enact Irish home rule without consulting the electorate. Opponents of the Welsh Church Bill claimed that it would impoverish clergy in the principality, and furthermore undermine the Union's stability, which the established church had played an important role in cementing.[68]

In Wales the issue appears to have trumped opposition to Irish home rule as the leading policy in the Unionist programme. Flint Boroughs had long been a Liberal stronghold, but the party's majority was more than halved at a by-election in January 1913 as Unionists ran a populist campaign in opposition to disestablishment, appealing to the many Anglican communicants in the constituency.[69] The cause also appears to have developed significant support in England; *The Times* estimated that around 120,000 people attended a Hyde Park demonstration held in opposition to the Welsh Church Bill in June 1913.[70] Opposition to Welsh disestablishment augmented the Unionists' populist programme.

In the immediate pre-war years Unionists effectively presented themselves as champions of social justice: supporting rural smallholdings, championing casual workers frustrated by the Liberal National Insurance Act, defending loyal Ulstermen and the position of the established church. Unionists gained six seats at by-elections between November 1913 and May 1914. How the party's success during these months would have affected the outcome of the next general election, had war not intervened, has been debated at length, but the likely outcome of a theoretical 1915 election is unclear.[71] Nonetheless, it should be pointed out that four key factors threatened to stymie Unionist progress at this time: the unstable Irish situation, the differences between voting motives in general and by-elections, the survival of the Liberal–Labour alliance, and possible amendments to plural voting. Whilst the British Covenant campaign dwarfed the militarist BLSUU, the problems of containing belligerent elements across the Irish Sea were very real, not least because Bonar Law had notoriously stated in 1912 that he imagined 'no length of resistance to which Ulster can go in which I would not be prepared to support them'. By the summer of 1914, both the Ulster Volunteers and the Irish Volunteers had become dangerously militarised and the threat of an Irish civil war loomed large.[72] At this time, the Unionist whip, Sir Robert Sanders, was deeply alarmed by the prospect of governing Ireland if his party won the next general election.[73]

Caution is prudent when assessing the Conservatives' by-election successes. The *Conservative Campaign Guide* published in 1914 outlined new policies in agriculture, housing and poor law reform based, in part, on the work of the Unionist Social Reform Committee (USRC). However, there was opposition amongst some Unionists towards the USRC's planned reforms. Even supporters of the committee such as Arthur Steel-Maitland, the Unionist Party chairman, doubted whether it could provide the basis of an effective party programme.[74] Much of the Unionist Party's growth in support during the immediate pre-war years appears to have been based on its ability to lead opposition to unpopular Liberal reforms. In attacking Irish home rule, National Insurance and Lloyd George's land proposals, Unionists sought to render the by-elections referenda on controversial Liberal reforms. Governing parties commonly lose seats in by-elections and rarely gain them. One-off contests provide the electorate with an opportunity to register a high-profile 'protest vote' against unpopular government measures.[75] Furthermore, it should be remembered that Unionists benefited from splits in the left-wing vote at by-elections, which would be unlikely to occur in most constituencies at the next general election.[76] Moreover, Bonar Law's party would have been worst affected by the proposed abolition of plural voting in 1915, given that it attracted much of the business vote.[77]

All the same, the Unionists had largely overcome their earlier malaise by 1914. During the immediate pre-war years , the *Liberal Agent* regularly expressed its alarm at the Unionists' effectiveness in promoting a wide-ranging populist programme. In July 1913, it stressed that, to win the next election, the Liberals would have to 'dam the flowing tide' created by 'the astute and almost superhuman efforts of the Tory organisers' at recent by-elections.[78] By the spring and summer of 1914, with the defence of Ulster growing rapidly as a populist cause through the British Covenant and Curragh Mutiny protests, Unionist Party leaders such as Sanders and Walter Long were increasingly confident that they could break the Liberals' ascendancy. Sanders was impressed by the party's ability to win Leith Burghs, a supposedly safe Liberal seat in March. Victories in north-east Derbyshire and Ipswich in May were likewise 'a great score' for the party. Walter Long was even more ebullient. In July he wrote: 'I believe, and I have been at some pains to obtain accurate information on the subject, that an appeal to the country now would result in a very considerable majority for our Party.'[79]

Over the course of the Edwardian years activists had managed to shape a new culture of Unionism better suited to dealing with the challenges of twentieth-century politics. Unionist politicians were able to develop a more wide-ranging appeal to working-class men through the use of targeted electioneering. The Edwardian years were a crucial period in advancing women's positions within Unionist activism. By placing the housewife at the centre of the fiscal debate, tariff reformers encouraged women to pursue a more assertive role in politics. The consumer-based appeals directed at the housewife, which Unionists began to utilise in the Edwardian period, remained vital to the Conservative Party's appeal to women up to the mid-century and beyond.[80] Organisations such as the League of British Covenanters, the TRL and the WUTRA developed a thriving culture of grassroots activism, beyond the bounds of the Unionist parties' formal structures.[81]

Despite this, it should be stressed that British Unionism remained a loose coalition of sometimes conflicting interest groups. In 1914 the Unionist Party was still far from being truly reconciled to democratic politics. Constituency associations and auxiliary leagues relied on traditional social leaders to finance and organise their activities. Moreover, women's increasing participation in the day-to-day functions of Unionist politics was resisted by some factions within the party. Supporters of Willoughby de Broke's BLSUU provided a precursor to the bellicose culture of the British Workers League (BWL) and British Empire Union (BEU), radical right organisations which were formed during the First World War.

The potential dangers of this division received little attention from contemporaries, given that the moderates who coalesced around the British Covenant were clearly in the ascendant within the Unionist grassroots during 1913–14. All the same, the battle lines were beginning to be drawn for the contest between the two visions of patriotism which would be propounded by the radical right and moderate Unionists during the First World War. The BLSUU's willingness to employ a politics of violence if it perceived that the needs of a crisis justified it laid the basis for the wartime radical right's attacks on pacifist meetings, which threatened to undermine Edwardian Unionists' efforts to fashion an orderly and peaceable politics that could appeal to both sexes.

Notes

1 See in particular Alfred Gollin, *Balfour's Burden: Arthur Balfour and Imperial Preference* (London, 1965); Dilwyn Porter, 'The Unionist tariff reformers, 1903–1914' (PhD dissertation, University of Manchester, 1976), p. 168; Richard Rempel, *Unionists Divided: Arthur Balfour, Joseph Chamberlain and the Unionist Free Traders* (Newton Abbot, 1972), p. 170; Sykes, 'Confederacy and the purge of the Unionist free traders'; Witherell, 'Political cannibalism among Edwardian Conservatives'.

2 Green, *Crisis of Conservatism*, pp. 297–304, 332–3.

3 Searle, 'Critics of Edwardian society'; Alan Sykes, 'The radical right and the crisis of conservatism before the First World War', *Historical Journal*, 26:3 (1983), 661–76.

4 Thomas C. Kennedy, 'Troubled Tories: dissent and confusion concerning the party's Ulster policy, 1910–1914', *Journal of British Studies*, 46:4 (2007), 570–93 at 571–2.

5 Ramsden, *Age of Balfour and Baldwin*, p. 86, see also pp. 68–9, 82–4.

6 Daniel M. Jackson, *Popular Opposition to Irish Home Rule in Edwardian Britain* (Liverpool, 2009), chs 3–5.

7 Coetzee focused chiefly on the TRL, Navy League and NSL. Coetzee, *For Party or Country*, p. 8.

8 Branches had recently been formed in Newcastle-under-Lyme, Southern Herefordshire, West Worcestershire and Wolverhampton East. Midland Union notebook, CPA; following the 1911 Unionist reorganisation, Conservative Central Office provided funds to hire a full-time JIL organiser. Thereafter, the party treasurer, whip and chairman held positions on the JIL council and executive. The JIL estimated its strength at 12,000 members in September 1909; this had risen to over 100,000 by April 1913. McCrillis, *Conservative Party in the Age of Universal Suffrage*, p. 84.

9 Amongst the most widely praised branches were Dudley, East Worcestershire, Stafford and Wolverhampton West; Criticisms were levelled at the women's association in Handsworth and Wolverhampton South. Midland Union Notebook, CPA.

10 Such complaints were voiced in North=West Staffordshire, Southern Shropshire and Stafford. Midland Union Notebook, CPA.

11 Windscheffel, *Conservatism in Imperial London*, pp. 99–101; for the Primrose League's inability to develop an effective foothold in Birmingham see *PLG*, May 1903, 13.

12 *Fulham Chronicle*, 13 February 1914, p. 8; *West London Observer*, 24 April 1914, p. 13.

13 *PLG*, March 1906, p. 6; Bull's Liberal opponent, Blaicklock, also identified the Primrose League as a key reason behind the Unionist victory in Hammersmith. *West London Observer*, 13 April 1906, p. 5.

14 Linda Walker, 'Party political women: a comparative study of Liberal women and the Primrose League, 1890–1914', in Jane Rendall (ed.), *Equal or Different: Women's Politics, 1880–1914* (Oxford, 1987), pp. 165–91 at p. 191.

15 A Mrs Pile, secretary of Fulham WUTRA, was also a Kensington Primrose Dame. *West London Observer*, 3 July 1914, p. 11; Miss Montray Read, honorary secretary of a Kensington habitation, spoke regularly at WUTRA meetings. TRL, *Monthly Notes*, 15:6 (1911), p. 401; 19:6 (1913), p. 386.

16 *Marylebone Mercury*, 30 May 1914, p. 5; for the Primrose League's new professionalism see also Arbuthnot (ed.), *Primrose League Election Guide*.

17 Thomas Wyn Williams, 'The Conservative Party in North-East Wales, 1906–1924' (PhD dissertation, University of Liverpool, 2008), p. 81.

18 Ibid., pp. 72, 77–8.

19 Ibid., pp. 76, 80–2.

20 Amery MSS, AMEL5/10, Leo Amery, 'Women and the National Service League', *Morning Post*, 15 July 1910, cutting; Maxse, foreword to Bagge (ed.), *Unionist Workers Handbook* , p. xxii.

21 Henry Pelling, *Social Geography of British Elections, 1885–1910* (London, 1967), ch. 4; Barry M. Doyle, 'Urban Liberalism and the "lost generation": politics and middle-class culture in Norwich, 1900–1935', *Historical Journal*, 38:3 (1995), 617–34 at 617.

22 Eastern Area of NUCA Executive minutes, annual reports 1911–13, CPA, ARE7/1/6; Upcher of Sheringham MSS, UPC243, North Norfolk Conservative Association minutes, 20 April 1910, 7 November 1910, 28 February 1913.

23 In Lancashire and West Yorkshire over a third of Primrose League habitations extant in 1912 had been founded after 1903, compared to only 13 per cent for Sussex and 11 per cent for London. Primrose League MSS, MS27, Primrose League roll of habitations (1912).

24 Primrose League MSS, MS4, Agency Committee report, letter from Mr Lancaster, 17 February 1910.

25 Jones, 'National and local issues', pp. 239–40.

26 Clarke, *Lancashire and the New Liberalism*, chs 1–2.

27 Quoted in Stanley Salvidge, *Salvidge of Liverpool: Behind the Political Scene, 1890–1928* (London, 1934), pp. 63–4.

28 Jones, 'National and local issues', pp. 19–20.

29 Amery MSS, AMEL4/4, C.A. Vince to Leo Amery, 15 April 1909.

30 Amery, *My Political Life*, vol. 1, p. 441.

31 Amery MSS, AMEL7/12, Amery diary, 13 January 1914.

32 Amery MSS, AMEL1/2/16, memo, statement of objects of the League of British Covenanters, [April] 1914; Walter Long, *Memories* (London, 1923), p. 203.

33 Green, *Crisis of Conservatism*, pp. 303–4.

34 Jackson, *Popular Opposition to Irish Home Rule*, pp. 16, 242.

35 Ibid., pp. 174–5, 182.

36 For Willoughby de Broke see biographical appendix.

37 David Dutton, *'His Majesty's Loyal Opposition': The Unionist Party in Opposition, 1905–1915* (Liverpool, 1992), p. 226; Jeremy Smith, *The Tories and Ireland, 1910–1914: Conservative Party Politics and the Home Rule Crisis* (Dublin, 2000), pp. 79–80.

38 *Southern Weekly News (Brighton)*, 7 March 1914, p. 5; Earl Winterton, *Orders of the Day* (London, 1953), p. 38.

39 Unionist frustrations with the Liberals' ability to 'log roll' reforms because of their alliance with the Irish Nationalists are discussed in Geraint Thomas, 'Constitutional reform and constitutional language in the Conservative Party, c. 1911–1929' (unpublished MS, 2008), pp. 8–10.

40 Gregory D. Phillips, 'Lord Willoughby de Broke: radicalism and conservatism', in J.A. Thompson and Arthur Meija (eds), *Edwardian Conservatism: Five Studies in Adaptation* (London, 1988), pp. 77–104 at pp. 86–7, 91–5.

41 Kennedy, 'Troubled Tories', p. 585; Sykes, 'Radical right and crisis of conservatism', p. 663.

42 Smith, *Tories and Ireland*, p. 173.

43 Long, *Memories*, p. 203; Smith, *Tories and Ireland*, p. 175.

44 Jackson, *Popular Opposition to Irish Home Rule*, p. 182.

45 Ibid., pp. 134–6.

46 Parliamentary Archives, London, Willoughby de Broke MSS, WB6/3, Robert Cecil to Lord Willoughby de Broke, 18 September 1913.

47 Jackson, *Popular Opposition to Irish Home Rule*, p. 134.

48 Amery MSS, AMEL1/2/26, Memo. by L.S. Amery, 18 January 1914, p. 5.

49 Kennedy, 'Troubled Tories', p. 586.

50 *Our Flag*, May 1914, p. 72; *The Times*, 6 April 1914, p. 9.

51 British Library, London, Robert Cecil MSS, Add.51072, fols 219–21, Leo Amery to Robert Cecil, 16 January 1914; for Cecil's whole-hearted support for the Covenant movement's objects see his Hyde Park speech in *Liberal Magazine*, May 1914, p. 240.

52 *Yorkshire Observer (Bradford)*, 13 March 1914, p. 8; *Darwen Gazette*, 21 March 1914, p. 8; *Berrow's Worcester Journal*, 23 May 1914, p. 6; *Hampshire Advertiser (Southampton)*, 7 March 1914, p. 12.

53 Long, *Memories*, p. 203.

54 Amery, *My Political Life*, vol. 1, p. 441; for claims that the Liberal government did not have a popular mandate to enact home rule see *Hampshire Advertiser (Southampton)*, 11 April 1914, p. 7; *Northampton Herald* , 6 March 1914, p. 8; *Evening Star (Ipswich)*, 22 May 1914, p. 1.

55 Amery MSS, AMEL1/2/26, L.S. Amery, '"Sign for Ulster": What the British Covenant stands for', *Manchester Dispatch*, 10 March 1914, cutting; *Shoreditch Observer*, 7 March 1914, p. 5; *Eastern Daily Press (Ipswich)*, 18 May 1914, p. 5.

56 *The Covenanter*, 20 May 1914, p. 4.

57 *Darwen Gazette*, 21 March 1914, p. 8; 18 April 1914, p. 5.

58 Bonar Law MSS, BL82/1/17, J.J. Oddy to Andrew Bonar Law, 11 December 1912.

59 *Yorkshire Observer (Bradford)*, 6 March 1914, p. 8.

60 *Yorkshire Post (Leeds)*, 20 March 1914, p. 4.

61 For discussion of the role of that the Irish issue played in by-election campaigns see also Jackson, *Popular Opposition to Irish Home Rule*, pp. 147–8, 152–3, 210–13.

62 *Berkshire Chronicle (Reading)*, 7 November 1913, p. 5.

63 *The Scotsman*, 20 February 1914, p. 9.

64 See James Fergusson, *The Curragh Incident* (London, 1964); I.F.W. Beckett, *The Army and the Curragh Incident, 1914* (London, 1986).

65 Amongst the organisations which participated were the Union Defence League, the BLSUU, the Primrose League, the Unionist Association of Ireland and the Metropolitan Division of the National Unionist Association, *Our Flag*, May 1914, p. 72; *Shoreditch Observer*, 28 March 1914, p. 5.

66 *The Times*, 6 April 1914, p. 9; *Hampshire Advertiser (Southampton)*, 11 April 1914, p. 7.

67 Neil Evans, '"A nation in a nutshell": the Swansea disestablishment demonstration of 1912 and the political culture of Edwardian Wales', in R.R. Davies and Geraint H. Jenkins (eds), *From Medieval to Modern Wales* (Cardiff, 2004), pp. 214–29.

68 *The Times*, 10 March 1913, p. 6; 2 June 1913, p. 10.

69 Williams, 'Conservative Party in North-East Wales', pp. 103, 133–4, 150–4.

70 *The Times*, 23 June 1913, p. 9.

71 Amongst the most detailed analyses of by-elections in the immediate pre-war years are P.F. Clarke, 'The electoral position of the Liberal and Labour parties, 1910–1914', *English Historical Review*, 90 (1975), 828–36; Tanner, *Political Change and Labour*, ch. 11; Green, *Crisis of Conservatism*, ch. 11.

72 For the speech and its context see Smith, *Tories and Ireland*, pp. 66–8.

73 Sanders diary, 18 June 1914, in Ramsden (ed.), *Real Old Tory Politics: Political Diaries of Sir Robert Sanders, First Lord Bayford, 1910–35* (London, 1984), p. 78; see also Green, *Crisis of Conservatism*, pp. 301–3.

74 For the USRC's activities see Jane Ridley, 'The Unionist Social Reform Committee, 1911–1914: wets before the deluge', *Historical Journal*, 30 (1987), 391–413; Green, *Crisis of Conservatism*, ch. 11.

75 For a perceptive discussion of this trend see Clarke, 'Electoral position of Liberal and Labour parties', p. 829.

76 Tanner, *Political Change and Labour*, pp. 318–37.

77 Ibid., pp. 123, 320.

78 *Liberal Agent*, July 1913, p. 11; see also April 1913, pp. 185–6; July 1913, pp. 23, 26; April 1914, p. 206.

79 For Sanders's increasing confidence in Conservative electoral prospects see his diary entries for 24 February 1914, 5 March 1914, 18 June 1914, in Ramsden (ed.), *Real Old Tory Politics*, pp. 73, 78; British Library, London, Long MSS, Add.62403, fo. 172, Walter Long to Lord Lansdowne, 27 June 1914.

80 Ina Zweiniger-Bargielowska, 'Rationing, austerity and Conservative Party recovery after 1945', *Historical Journal*, 37:1 (1994), 174–97.

81 This is contrary to Frans Coetzee's claim that the popular conservative leagues founded in the 1900s relied on a small core of activists. See Coetzee and Coetzee, 'Rethinking the radical right in Germany and Britain', 524–6 and also Coetzee, *For Party or Country*, ch. 5.

PART II

The First World War

5

Rowdiness and respectability

Across Britain in summer 1917 a series of attacks took place against workers' and soldiers' council meetings. These bodies had been created under the inspiration of the Russian Revolution and provided a fulcrum for supporters of a negotiated peace. Grainy newsreel footage of the most notorious of these attacks, the Brotherhood Church riot in London's East End, survives to this day. Accompanied by a tremulous piano, the film begins with the caption: 'A pacifist meeting held at Kingsland was broken up by the forces of loyalty and patriotism'. The camera focuses on a crowd of people milling around the chapel as its windows are broken; some peace delegates try to repel the invaders but they are struck with missiles or beaten. In the final scene a policeman on horseback passes through the melee but does not intervene.[1] Having gained admission to the chapel, the crowd systematically destroyed the interior of an adjoining schoolroom and hunted down those delegates who had offered forcible resistance to their entry.[2]

According to the liberal *Daily News* this was possibly the most serious riot London had witnessed during the war.[3] By contrast, the conservative press played down the violence. Brutal attacks made against the many peace delegates were either neglected by right-wing papers or blamed on the recklessness of those who scorned police help.[4] Speeches by the patriot ringleaders were also selectively reported. The address by a Canadian corporal which brought the meeting to a close reads like a plea for calm in the *Morning Post*'s telling.[5] However, a local paper claimed that the corporal had referred to the delegates as 'a set of rotten skunks' and stated that 'we don't want a lot of dirty pro-Germans using our name in order to work their own dirty ends'.[6] Rather than pacifying the crowd, the speech immediately preceded the high point of violence, when the peace delegates dispersed and were at the mercy of a baying crowd outside the chapel.[7]

Although a wartime electoral truce existed in Britain between 1914 and 1918, it did not mean that politics was in abeyance. In fact, the emergence of radical right politics during these years indicated that it excited more furious passions than ever. The wartime radical right was essentially a loose coalition of ultra-patriots, which presented two faces to the public. On the one hand, demagogues such as Horatio Bottomley and Noel Pemberton-Billing called for more aggressive war leadership and insinuated that Britain's failure to break Germany was the result of disloyal elements at home.[8] Their style of activism found its voice in by-elections, press campaigns and anti-alien petitions. The activities of organisations such as the British Workers League and British Empire Union were related to this movement, but distinct in the sense that their agitators encouraged the breaking up of meetings held in support of a negotiated peace, such as that at the Brotherhood Church.[9] Those scholars who have provided the most substantial studies of the wartime radical right tend to argue that it played a major role in shaping public opinion and influencing government policy.[10] Brock Millman has claimed that the government-sponsored National War Aims Committee (NWAC) colluded with organisations such as the BWL and National Federation of Discharged Sailors and Soldiers (NFDSS) to rally the nation around the war effort, employing black propaganda, and encouraging violence against pacifists.[11]

Instead, radical right groups may have initially attracted widespread support for their attempts to break up pacifist meetings by force, but mainstream Unionists increasingly came to see violent forms of street politics as a hindrance to both the war effort and their own attempts to adapt to democratic politics. Instead of fuelling patriot violence, organisations like the NWAC provided a platform for activists to promote an alternative, peaceable politics.

Grassroots Unionism had flourished in Edwardian Britain, attracting a wide range of activists of both sexes. And yet, the hyper-masculine culture of the wartime radical right threatened to set back Unionist efforts to widen the appeal of their politics. Such concerns were made all the more important as the female activist became increasingly important to grassroots politics during the war. Male-led Unionist organisations lost many of their members to the armed forces. In particular, the Junior Imperial League was devastated, with six-tenths of members going into khaki during the early stages of the conflict.[12] Unionist Party constituency associations also lost many of their supporters to the war effort and met rarely during the conflict.[13] By contrast, female Unionism remained a relatively coherent force; women formed the backbone of many patriotic voluntary organisations established to aid the war effort.

The First World War played an important role in remoulding the identity of British Unionism and enabling it to develop a wider appeal than it had experienced before 1914. Unionists increasingly came to distance themselves from violent street politics after 1917; in doing so they built on Edwardian efforts to encourage a restrained politics that could appeal to both sexes. This strategy laid the basis for the Conservatives' post-war efforts to present themselves as the party of orderliness and the family interest, in opposition to the supposedly rowdy masculinist culture of organised labour.[14]

★

The radical right's belligerent street politics was far removed from the orderly culture of the Edwardian tariff leagues. From the BWL's London reports we see that theirs was an altogether more plebeian world of demonstrations at dock gates and pitches outside pubs. One Catford meeting was enlivened by a woman who had paid numerous visits to the nearby Black Horse ale house accusing the BWL speaker of being the Kaiser in disguise![15] Such seedy locales were distant from the decorous culture of summer fetes and smoking concerts which had been the hallmark of the tariff leagues' culture.

If the demotic politics of the radical right appeared to risk pandering to mob instincts, why was patriot violence initially condoned, or even supported, by Unionists? The most obvious explanation is that groups like the BWL and BEU provided a means to express popular frustrations with the stalemate on the Western Front, frustrations which found few other outlets during the early years of the war. But the success of radical right groups also owed much to the sophistication of their discursive strategies. Groups like the BWL drew on traditions of public politics to justify their violence, claiming to represent the patriotic concerns of the serviceman and promoting a hierarchy of masculinity, which denigrated the manliness of pacifists.

The BWL portrayed public politics as a competition to represent popular opinion by contesting civic space, a long-standing concept which was widely accepted at the time.[16] In consequence, the BWL regularly argued that its meetings were held in response to demonstrations in support of a negotiated peace; patriot gatherings provided local residents with the opportunity to demonstrate that peace supporters did not represent popular opinion within their localities.[17] As such, disruption of peace meetings was justified by the similar treatment that patriot gatherings had received from pacifist opponents in areas such as Glasgow.[18] By and large, the conservative national press concurred with these sentiments, as is indicated by their coverage of the breaking up of a peace meeting which was to have been addressed by Ramsay MacDonald at Cory Hall in Cardiff during November 1916. According to the *Morning Post*: 'the battle of Cory Hall…was won in a fair fight by the working people of Cardiff, with, for the most part, the police – civil and military – looking on as more or less passive spectators'. By its actions the city had supposedly 'vindicated its own fair fame as the great industrial and loyal capital of Wales'.[19]

The enthusiastic tone with which patriot violence was initially reported by the conservative press also owed much to the radical right's claims to speak for the serviceman. The radical right's emergence as a popular force owed much to its attacks on the working of the Military Service Act, introduced in January 1916. An organisation called the National Union of Attested Married Men ran a series of candidates at by-elections that year, with the support of Horatio Bottomley, editor of *John Bull*, and Lord Northcliffe, proprietor of *The Times* and the *Daily Mail*. Their candidates condemned the Military Service Act's lack of preferential treatment for married men who had previously attested for military service. In Hyde in Cheshire attacks were made against unmarried 'slackers' and 'shirkers', feeding on popular hostility to workers who 'had stolen into the munitions factories out of the danger zone', avoiding military service by working in protected trades.[20] Although Pemberton-Billing was the only independent MP elected in 1916, several radical right candidates polled respectably, especially those associated with the attested married men.

Table 5.1 *Radical right candidates at by-elections, January–September 1916*

Date	Constituency	Candidate	Vote (%)	Winner
10/01	W. Newington	Terrett	22.9	Liberal
25/01	Mile End	Pemberton-Billing	44.8	Conservative
09/03	Hertford	Pemberton-Billing	56.3	Independent
23/03	Harborough	Gibson Bowles+	32.1	Liberal
29/03	Hyde	Davies+	44.0	Liberal
19/04	Wimbledon	Kennedy-Jones+	44.4	Conservative
16/05	Tewkesbury	Boosey	16.8	Conservative
16/08	Berwick	Turnbull	14.1	Liberal
20/09	Mansfield	Turnbull	37.0	Liberal

Figures based on F.W.S. Craig (ed.), *British Parliamentary Election Results, 1885–1918* (Chichester, 1974).
All two-way contests + candidate of National Union of Attested Married Men.

The electoral truce meant that there was officially a united front of Liberals and Conservatives in support of Coalition candidates. Nonetheless, it was widely felt that men with Conservative loyalties were willing to ignore their leaders and support radical right candidates as a protest vote. One paper estimated that of the 3,711 who voted for the Attested Married Men candidate in Harborough, Leicestershire around 3,000 were disgruntled Conservatives.[21] Arguably, the independent candidates would have achieved even greater success had their Coalition opponents not also promised to take up the cause of the attested married men.[22] The achievements of independent candidates at by-elections in early 1916 galvanised radical right activism. In March the BWL was created and the Anti-German Union relaunched itself as the BEU.[23]

Representations of soldiers and sailors during the early decades of the twentieth century commonly lauded their self-control, courage and attachment to nation and family.[24] Servicemen's disciplined values were also perceived to act as a check on the excessive and irrational conduct of crowds.[25] The BWL took pains to argue that it stood for the interests of this group, commonly seen as the most patriotic of Britons. At times, the BWL journal portrayed its leaders as temporary colonels channelling the emotions of military men. For instance, when the league leader Victor Fisher was faced with pacifist interruptions at a Walthamstow meeting in 1917 he asked 'are fifty men ready to come with me to turn these reptiles out?' The *British Citizen* continued: 'Fisher leapt from the platform to the accompaniment of a prolonged cheer, a small battalion, in which there were some sturdy lads in khaki, followed him amid tense excitement, and such a sympathetic tumult as was itself an inspiration to a wise intolerance'.[26]

Conservative newspapers colluded with the radical right in legitimating patriot violence by claiming that it was supported, but also controlled, by servicemen. In their coverage of the Brotherhood Church riot, the right-wing press stressed the ability of soldiers to curb the unruly excesses of the inflamed crowd. The *Morning Post*'s highly selective report of proceedings emphasised that the soldiers were willing to listen to the dissenting voice of a convalescing serviceman who had been admitted as a peace delegate, and pleaded for the crowd to be quiet whilst he spoke. A Canadian corporal eventually brought proceedings to a close with a plea for calm: '"For God's sake", he said "don't break up the House of God. We have come to break up a Pacifist meeting…having attained our object do not let us go further"'.[27] Meanwhile, the *Daily Express* focused on the gallantry of the soldiers in quelling violence. When a woman threatened to drag a female peace delegate into the street, the paper observed that she was persuaded to leave by another Canadian soldier. On exiting the hall the Canadians also 'sprung to the rescue' of a young woman whom the crowd threatened: '"Back, back!" they shouted. "Be Britons, not Huns!" Each took the arm of the trembling young woman. A woman struck her from behind. "Mother" said one of the soldiers, "that's not good enough, don't do it again".'[28]

The BWL's rhetoric promoted a hierarchical reading of masculinity based around war service with the soldier and sailor as hegemon.[29] Pacifists were their antithesis and not true men. A group of interrupters at a Walthamstow BWL meeting are described by the *British Citizen* as 'stunted degenerates' who whimpered many 'a teardrawn sob' when they were hustled out of the hall.[30] Pacifists were also commonly represented as ridiculous, effete and long-haired.[31] In the BWL's logic, refusal to serve in the war excluded men from the rights of citizenship. The fact that conscientious objectors were allowed to retain the vote whilst young men on military service were effectively disenfranchised because of residency requirements seemed a blatant injustice in this reading.[32] By promoting a politics of machismo, the radical right failed to integrate women into its street politics; only a handful of women appear to have spoken at BWL meetings.[33] This is not to say that women did not participate in the violence of patriot crowds. However, they were not portrayed by newspapers or periodicals as the crowd's leaders or figures who controlled its excesses.

Historians have focused on the feminised representation of male pacifists by their opponents, but there has been a neglect of the different ways in which male and female peace supporters were portrayed by the patriot media.[34] Unlike their male counterparts, there was no sense that female pacifists were behaving in a fashion that deviated from expected gender roles: their actions were instead the product of misplaced feminine virtues. For example, Irene Fisher, wife of the BWL chairman, wrote in the *British Citizen* criticising the Women's International League's concerns for the welfare of German prisoners of war: 'All the British women must feel sadly humiliated by the foolish behaviour of the women who are associated with the many Leagues and fellowships for the purpose of "comforting" the enemy and protecting him against the punishment earned by his misdeeds'.[35]

The conservative press portrayed women pacifists as dignified persons who had gone astray and needed to be protected by male authority figures from the excesses of patriot crowds. In its coverage of the Brotherhood Church riot the *Daily Express* observed that 'most of the [peace] delegates, many of whom were women, sat quietly in their seats in the church'. The relative dignity of the female pacifists is reinforced by the description of a tall young woman who was shaking with fear; having been rescued by chivalrous soldiers, she was threatened by 'hatless' patriot women.[36] Likewise, a local paper claimed that the civility of a patriot crowd which forced the abandonment of a workers' and soldiers' council meeting in Swansea was demonstrated by their treatment of women peace delegates. It was observed that a few of the women fainted but that no attempt was made to 'molest or interfere' with them, contrasting implicitly with the overtly sexual attacks that suffragettes had sometimes been subjected to during the Edwardian period.[37] Such coverage tended to undermine female participation in wartime street politics. Men were portrayed as the authority figures who controlled civic space. The supposed meekness and emotionalism of women diminished their authority to contest public politics in the fraught atmosphere of wartime.

The limited involvement of women within the leadership of patriot violence arguably reflected wider contemporary anxieties about the ways in which the social upheavals of war were supposedly threatening traditional gender roles. Noel Pemberton-Billing's fantastical accusations of widespread homosexuality within Britain's governing circles may well have explained the popular fascination with his libel trial in 1918, as it suggested a crisis in the gender order. The sexual climate of the war supposedly threatened British values and risked polluting the country with 'German perversions', to borrow a contemporary phrase.[38] Concerns to maintain 'appropriate' female behaviour were widespread during the war. As Susan Grayzel notes, women's voluntary organisations went to considerable lengths to insist that their members remained feminine, despite doing what had been considered men's work.[39] Philippa Levine's study of policewomen during the Great War also demonstrates that there was widespread concern with maintaining female decorum. Most of the new women patrols' duties consisted of the moral policing of public activities of women, in response to alarm at rising sexual promiscuity and prostitution.[40] These examples indicate that the war was generally a time of conservatism in terms of gender relations. Whilst some women participated in the radical right's disruptive politics, they failed to establish a sense that they were engaging in normative female behaviour. Indeed, their violence could be seen as one of the many potential threats to the gender order that were thrown up by the war.

Clashes between pacifists and patriots had been a prominent feature of British politics since 1915.[41] They gained a new resonance in spring 1917, as peace supporters grew in confidence. The Women's Peace Crusade, which had previously confined its activities to Clydeside, launched its first national campaign, beginning with a rally in July which attracted a crowd of over ten thousand to Glasgow Green. During the following months similar mass meetings were held across Britain, often in provocative locations on public land such as Birmingham's Bull Ring and Victoria Park in Nelson, Lancashire.[42]

Nonetheless, despite the initial support that it had received from conservative papers, rowdy street politics increasingly came to be seen as a threat to patriotic unity as summer 1917 progressed. At this time, liberal newspapers widely criticised patriot violence, presenting the Brotherhood Church riot as bedlam incarnate.[43] Under the headline 'Soldiers lead an angry mob. Fight in a pulpit', the *Daily Chronicle* depicted a wild scene: 'Hatless women screamed like furies, and attacked male and female delegates indiscriminately...one woman was only got into a passing bus after much of her clothing had been torn off and her face was streaming with blood'.[44]

The *Manchester Guardian* was similarly critical of the apparent growth in patriot violence. It printed a picture of an 'emissary' from the BWL chalking an invitation for the people of Stockport to 'roll up' and wreck a 'traitors meeting' of the workers' and soldiers' council.[45] Those patriots who subsequently attempted to force their way into the conference were dismissively referred to as 'a few Stockport idlers', hardly representative of respectable local opinion.[46] The paper was unstinting in its criticisms of the attacks that occurred following the dispersal of delegates: Women were 'badly knocked about' in cowardly street brawls, which had been 'deliberately worked up' by the BWL. In a plea to Lloyd George to take action, it noted: 'This sort of thing has only to develop and we shall be back in the days of the later Roman Republic, when the streets of Rome were terrorised by the gangs of one or other political bully. The Government is not so weak that its functions need to be usurped by a mob.'[47]

Unionists grew uncomfortable with violent street politics, in part, as a result of the left-wing National Federation of Discharged Sailors and Soldiers' use of this form of activism to protest at existing provision for ex-servicemen. At the Abercromby by-election in Liverpool in June 1917 a federation candidate stood in opposition to the Unionist, Lord Stanley, who won the seat *in absentia*. Stanley was the son of Lord Derby, the secretary of state for war. The federation campaign attacked Derby's record and stressed that there should be no recall of discharged soldiers until all men registered as Class A under the Military Service Act had been called up.[48] Groups like the BWL and BEU had claimed to represent the soldiers' interest, but they were now being outflanked by an organisation which was significantly more representative of servicemen. Having been created in April 1917, the federation grew rapidly, claiming a hundred thousand members by July.[49]

The conduct of federation supporters during the Abercromby campaign led local Unionist leaders to conclude that rowdy street politics, if it was harnessed against the war leadership, could hamper the British effort. Ian Macpherson, under-secretary of state for war, was vigorously heckled by federation supporters when he spoke for Stanley in Liverpool.[50] Archibald Salvidge, the leader of the Unionists in the city, noted in his diary that Derby was troubled by the federation campaign. Salvidge felt that, 'at some of the meetings there was a nasty, strident, undisciplined note amongst the opposition that in a lifetime of British politics I have not heard before. It made one think of the disturbing things that are beginning to leak through about Russia. If the hysteria spreads, politics after the war are going to be dangerous.'[51] Derby's alarm about the character of the servicemen's political movement led him to form the Comrades of the Great War as an alternative in July.[52] Even though this movement was led by Unionists who had been fellow travellers of the BWL, and suffered from sporadic attacks at its meetings by federation supporters, it does not appear to have engaged in a politics of violence.[53] Salvidge was reluctant to confront pacifists with force, believing that the formation of local war aims committees was the best means to challenge anti-war orators.[54] By the end of 1917 there were only two constituencies in the Liverpool area which had no war aims committee.[55]

Formed in August 1917, the government-sponsored NWAC played a central role in encouraging the public to mobilise peacefully in support of Britain's democratic war aims.[56] It emerged chiefly as a result of growing government concern with industrial unrest and a sense that a greater public understanding of the nation's war aims was needed.[57] Unionists were at the forefront of the NWAC's campaigning. Over the course of the organisation's existence, 313 local war aims committees were formed. Only eighteen of the local WACs had no Unionist involvement, and Unionists formed the largest group of speakers whose political affiliation is known.[58]

The NWAC managed to develop a highly effective public campaign, dwarfing the radical right's efforts to claim public space. From August to November 1917 the NWAC held forty-five demonstrations with an attendance of over two thousand, and 680 smaller meetings.[59] The NWAC strove to undermine violent street politics by downplaying the threat of the pacifist agitation, which it claimed was of little significance in many districts. Presiding at a conference of the West Riding War Aims Committee in September 1917, F.E. Guest, the NWAC's chairman, remarked, 'the chief enemy we have to defeat…is not so much the pacifist – we are proud to say in England that they are few and far between – our chief enemy is war weariness'.[60]

It has been claimed by Brock Millman that the NWAC was an attempt by the state to organise violent street politics, that the organisation had close ties with the BWL, and even acted as 'Lloyd George's stormtroopers'.[61] This judgement appears to be partly based on a misunderstanding which emerged from Scally's work regarding the relationship between Lloyd George and Milner, who was a close sympathiser with the BWL, Scally suggests that Milner's entrance into Lloyd George's war cabinet in December 1916 meant that the BWL, which was supposedly at his bidding, became closely linked to the Coalition.[62] This ignores the fact that Milner apparently never explicitly mentioned his formal links to the BWL in public and that Lloyd George did not appear to know about them.[63]

War aims committee meetings were sometimes characterised by heckling and scuffles, but there appears to have been only one major instance of serious crowd violence perpetrated by patriots at a NWAC demonstration, when, on May Day 1918 a crowd from a war aims gathering in Leicester broke up a rival peace meeting held across the Market Square by Ramsay MacDonald. Even so, the BWL appears to have had some culpability in this incident, with its local organiser informing the Leicester War Aims Committee that the MacDonald meeting would be broken up.[64] Local newspaper reports also suggest that the crowd was provoked by the chairman, who referred to their 'ugly mugs', which could be interpreted as a particularly insulting remark given that several had been disfigured whilst fighting in France.[65] In the troubled days of spring 1918 Special Branch was grateful for all patriotic efforts to challenge the 'pacifist spirit' and in its state of growing alarm with public morale had started the surveillance of ex-servicemen's groups. Basil Thompson, the head of MI5, praised the work that the BWL was doing in Glasgow and Newcastle – both areas that the NWAC was also working.[66] Yet, in general, the government appears to have held the BWL at arm's length; the NWAC even went to the trouble of refuting a claim in the *British Citizen* that this organisation had borrowed a van from one of its local committees to stage 'patriotic anti-Henderson demonstrations'.[67]

Following the violent scenes at aborted workers' and soldiers' councillors' meetings in summer 1917, supporters of a negotiated peace increasingly struggled to find rooms to hold meetings in the provinces. Moreover, as Julia Bush has noted, many pacifists moderated their views during the final year of the war, shifting from calls for an immediate end to the war to support for early negotiations over peace.[68] All of these factors diminished the public profile of the violent factions within patriotic organisations such as the BWL.[69]

Even in circumstances where the BWL did participate in capturing pacifist platforms in autumn 1917, it tended to play a subsidiary role in organising the patriot forces. When an Independent Labour Party (ILP) meeting in Todmorden, West Yorkshire, was abandoned in November the local press focused solely on the role that the National Association of Discharged Soldiers had played in disrupting the meeting.[70] This was a left-wing servicemen's organisation whose ideological outlook had similarities with the NFDSS.[71] The local servicemen's organisation drew around 150 people to a protest meeting before the Todmorden ILP gathering.[72] By contrast, the BWL struggled to gain support in this part of Yorkshire. When it held its first gathering in Todmorden, a fortnight before Snowden's abandoned meeting, fewer than twenty people, including a couple of press representatives, attended.[73]

The volatile politics of the war challenged traditional ideas about 'manly' politics which legitimated unruly and rowdy behaviour at public meetings. Military defeat seemed a possibility for a time following the German spring offensive of 1918.[74] By that summer government expectations that public meetings could be self-policing in London had been undermined. Special powers granted under the Defence of the Realm Act were used to ban a series of meetings by supporters of a negotiated peace, which had been threatened by radical right groups who were generating widespread support for their campaign to intern all enemy aliens.[75] Although a British military victory seemed assured by late summer, the threat of revolutionary activity spreading from Europe appeared a real possibility to leading politicians in the months following the Armistice.[76]

Concerns about the threat of masculine political violence were by no means the preserve of the Right at this time. In his *Aims of Labour* (1918), Arthur Henderson, the former Labour Party leader, expressed his concerns for the new democracy born out of the Representation of the People Bill.

Henderson voiced his alarm at the many men who had 'become habituated to thoughts of violence' as a result of their military service. In the difficult early days of the peace many men of 'unstable temperament' would see extra-parliamentary force as the most effective means to achieve their aims.[77] Even more alarmingly, following demobilisation, thousands of men would return to Britain who were 'skilled in the use of arms, inured to danger and accustomed to act together under orders'. These men would be 'capable of assuming leadership again if insurrectionary movements come into existence'.[78]

In the run-up to the 1918 general election, members of the NFDSS persistently interrupted a meeting held by William Bridgeman, a Unionist whip and MP for Oswestry. Frustrated by the difficulties he had apparently encountered in gaining a hearing, and forgetting the rough treatment which supporters of a negotiated peace had received at public meetings, Bridgeman wrote to his wife, recounting the mood of the crowd: 'The majority present were disgusted – and it will be a good object lesson for them to see what a Labour Government would be like'.[79] Here Bridgeman was promoting an idea that became integral to post-war Conservative politics, namely that violence at political meetings was the disreputable preserve of trade union militants and other Labour 'rowdies'.

Intriguingly, Bridgeman had met with BWL leaders in June 1916 and had been keen to accept their offer of a post-war working agreement.[80] As we shall see, the Unionist Party did not formally sever its electoral ties with the BWL during the war for a variety of reasons. Nonetheless, it adopted a cooler relationship with this organisation as the war progressed, not least as a result of growing Unionist hostility to violent street politics after 1917. Rather than support the divisive and hyper-masculine politics of the radical right, most Unionists preferred to participate in peaceable and non-sectarian forms of activism, such as the work of the NWAC.

Male rowdiness at public meetings had been tolerated during peacetime as this forum was seen as providing a vital opportunity for political engagement, especially for the non-voter. But as the war progressed there was a growing sense across the political mainstream that the demotic politics of the street had been pushed too far and would pose a threat to the stability of Britain's post-war democracy, which already appeared vulnerable as a result of the influx of new voters and the threat of revolutionary dissent spreading from Europe in the wake of the Russian Revolution. After the war all parties responded to their alarms at the challenges posed by Britain's new democracy by seeking to fashion new appeals to gendered identities. In the process, they sought to distance themselves from the belligerent street politics of the war and endeavoured to appeal to voters of both sexes.

Notes

1   Topical Film Co. 310-1, 'Pacifists routed in Brotherhood Church' (1917), www.
    screenonline.org.uk/film/id/583515/index.html, accessed on 14 March 2011.

2   *Worker's Dreadnought*, 4 August 1917, p. 819; *Manchester Guardian*, 30 July 1917,
    pp. 5–6.

3   *Daily News and Leader*, 30 July 1917, p. 2.

4   *Morning Post*, 30 July 1917, p. 9; the account in *The Times*, 30 July 1917, p. 3 was
    unusual amongst conservative papers in its ambivalent attitude to patriot violence.
    It claimed that some Dominion soldiers had participated in beating up peace
    delegates. Local Unionist papers appear to have understated the violent excesses
    that occurred when peace meetings were broken up. Compare, for example, the
    graphic depiction of excessive patriot violence in the liberal *Birmingham Post*,
    30 July 1917, p. 2 with the more orderly scenes presented in the conservative
    Birmingham Daily Mail, 30 July 1917, p. 2.

5   *Morning Post*, 30 July 1917, p. 9.

6   *Islington News and Hornsey Gazette*, 3 August 1917, p. 5.

7   *Worker's Dreadnought*, 4 August 1917, p. 5.

8   For Bottomley and Billing see biographical appendix.

9   W.C. Anderson, Labour MP for Sheffield, Attercliffe, who chaired the Brother-
    hood Church meeting accused BWL organisers of coordinating the violence.
    Manchester Guardian, 13 August 1917, p. 8; for the BEU's involvement see Panikos
    Panayi, 'The British Empire Union in the First World War', in Tony Kushner and
    Kenneth Lunn (eds), *The Politics of Marginality: Race, the Radical Right and Minorities
    in Twentieth Century Britain* (London, 1990), pp. 113–28 at p. 122.

10 Panikos Panayi, *The Enemy in our Midst: Germans in Britain during the First World
    War* (Oxford, 1991), p. 287; Brock Millman, *Managing Domestic Dissent in First
    World War Britain* (London, 2000), p. 118.

11 Ibid., pp. 230–48; this claim is also made in Keohane, *Party of Patriotism*, p. 109.

12 CPA, CCO506/5/5, Junior Imperial and Constitutional League, *Handbook for
    Organisers and Workers* (n.d. [c. 1930]), pp. 6–7.

13 J.W.B. Bates, 'The Conservative Party in the constituencies, 1918–39' (DPhil
    dissertation, University of Oxford, 1994), p. 8.

14 This work builds on that of Jon Lawrence, who noted the widespread hostility
    to violent public politics which existed in Britain during the 1920s. See his
    'Transformation of public politics'.

15 *British Citizen and Empire Worker* (hereafter *British Citizen*), 15 September 1916,
    p. 78; see also 25 August 1916, p. 18.

16 Lawrence, 'Transformation of British public politics', 188–92.

17 *British Citizen*, 15 September 1916, p. 78 and 2 December 1916, p. 252.

18 *Parliamentary Debates*, 87 H.C. Deb. 5s, 14 November 1916, col. 721; *British
    Citizen*, 18 November 1916, p. 216; 9 December 1916, p. 269.

19 *Morning Post*, 13 November 1916, p. 6; see also *Daily Express*, 13 November 1916,
    p. 4; *Scotsman*, 13 November 1916, p. 6.

20 *Hyde Reporter*, 1 April 1916, pp. 3–4; *The Times*, 20 March 1916, p. 7.

21 *Midland Mail (Market Harborough)*, 31 March 1916, p. 4; see also *Wimbledon Herald*,
    28 April 1916, p. 4; *D.P.'s Daily Paper*, 20 March 1916, p. 3; 25 March 1916, p. 2;
    Liberal Agent, July 1916, p. 33.

22 *Midland Mail (Market Harborough)*, 17 March 1916, pp. 4, 8; *Morning Post*, 17
    March 1916, p. 6.

23 *Morning Post*, 17 March 1916, p. 9; 23 March 1916, p. 2.

24 Graham Dawson, *Soldier Heroes: British Adventure, Empire, and the Imagining of Masculinities* (London, 1994), p. 1; Mary A. Conley, *From Jack Tar to Union Jack: Representing Naval Manhood in the British Empire, 1870–1918* (Manchester, 2009), p. 3.

25 Jon Lawrence, 'Forging a peaceable kingdom: war, violence and the fear of brutalization in post-First World War Britain', *Journal of Modern History*, 75:3 (2003), 557–89 at 567.

26 For Fisher see biographical appendix; *British Citizen*, 1 September 1916, p. 38; for other descriptions of BWL leaders as ultra-masculine figures see 15 September 1916, p. 79; 10 March 1917, p. 138.

27 *Morning Post*, 30 July 1917, p. 9.

28 *Daily Express*, 30 July 1917, p. 3.

29 For the concept of hegemonic masculinity see R.W. Connell, *Masculinities* (Cambridge, 1995), ch. 3; R.W. Connell and J.W. Messerschmidt, 'Hegemonic masculinity: rethinking the concept', *Gender and Society*, 19:6 (2005), 829–59.

30 *British Citizen*, 10 March 1917, p. 138.

31 Ibid., 20 September 1916, p. 103; see also 2 December 1916, p. 253; 23 June 1917, p. 340.

32 Ibid., 25 August 1916, p. 11.

33 Only one female BWL speaker was identified as a member of WUTRA by the league's journal, Elizabeth Collum the secretary of the Chelsea branch. Ibid., 16 February 1918, p. 82.

34 Lois Bibbings, 'Images of manliness: the portrayal of soldiers and conscientious objectors in the Great War', *Social and Legal Studies*, 12:3 (2003), 335–58 at 337; Nicoletta Gullace, *'The Blood of our Sons': Men, Women and the Renegotiation of British Citizenship during the Great War* (Basingstoke, 2002), p. 182.

35 *British Citizen*, 29 September 1917, p. 201; see also 24 November 1917, p. 323.

36 *Daily Express*, 30 July 1917, pp. 1, 3.

37 *Swansea and Glamorgan Herald*, 4 August 1917, p. 5; Jon Lawrence, 'Contesting the male polity: the suffragettes and the politics of disruption in Edwardian Britain', in Amanda Vicery (ed.), *Women, Privilege and Power: British Politics, 1750 to the Present* (Stanford, CA, 2001), pp. 201–26 at 212.

38 For the Pemberton-Billing trial see Philip Hoare, *Wilde's Last Stand: Decadence, Conspiracy and the First World War* (London, 1997).

39 Susan R. Grayzel, '"The outward and visible sign of her patriotism": women, uniforms and National Service during the First World War', *Twentieth Century British History*, 8 (1997), 145–64 at 160.

40 Philippa Levine, '"Walking the streets in a way no decent women should": women police in World War One', *Journal of Modern History*, 66 (1994), 34–78 at 42–5, 57–8; the Primrose League also claimed that older women should encourage girls to attend church regularly and act as moral guardians to them, due to the threat to their sexual morals under wartime conditions. *PLG*, June 1915, p. 10.

41 See Millman, *Managing Domestic Dissent*, chs 1, 5–6; Jon Lawrence, 'Public space/political space', in Jay Winter and Jean Louis-Robert (eds), *Capital Cities at War. Paris, London, Berlin, 1914–1919. Vol. 2: A Cultural History* (Cambridge, 2007), pp. 280–312 at pp. 293–7.

42 James Smyth, 'Rents, peace, votes: working-class women and political activity in the First World War', in Esther Breitenbach and Eleanor Gordon (eds), *Out of Bounds: Women in Scottish Society, 1800–1945* (Edinburgh, 1992), pp. 174–96 at

p. 182; Women's Peace Crusade, *The New Crusader*, 13 July 1917, p. 1; 21 July 1917, p. 3; 26 October 1917, p. 3; *Colne and Nelson Times*, 3 August 1917, p. 4; *Birmingham Daily Mail*, 30 July 1917, p. 2.

43 *Daily News and Leader*, 30 July 1917, pp. 2–3; *Daily Chronicle*, 30 July 1917, p. 3; *Manchester Guardian*, 13 August 1917, pp. 3, 8.

44 *Daily Chronicle*, 30 July 1917, p. 3.

45 *Manchester Guardian*, 13 August 1917, p. 3.

46 Ibid., pp. 3, 8.

47 Ibid., p. 4.

48 For Derby see biographical appendix; *The Times*, 25 June 1917, p. 3.

49 *Cheshire Daily Echo*, 30 July 1917, p. 2.

50 *Scotsman*, 27 June 1917, p. 4.

51 Archibald Salvidge diary notes for July 1917, in Salvidge, *Salvidge of Liverpool*, pp. 158–9.

52 Stephen R. Ward, 'Intelligence surveillance of British ex-servicemen, 1918–1920', *Historical Journal*, 16:1 (1973), 179–88 at 181.

53 Norton-Griffiths and Wilfrid Ashley, two Unionist sympathisers with the BWL, were amongst the comrades' founders. Meetings between BWL and Unionist Party representatives were held at Norton-Griffths's office, Amery MSS, AMEL7/13, Amery diary, 4 July 1917, 2 August 1917, 15 August 1917, 26 September 1917; for examples of federation disruption at comrades meetings see *Scotsman*, 14 November 1917, p. 10; *Manchester Guardian*, 24 January 1918, p. 8.

54 *Liverpool Courier*, 12 October 1917, cited in David Monger, 'The National War Aims Committee and British patriotism during the First World War' (hereafter 'NWAC and British patriotism' (PhD dissertation, University of London, 2009), p. 100.

55 Ibid., p. 100.

56 This section owes much to David Monger's work. For a detailed analysis of this organisation see his *Patriotism and Propaganda in First World War Britain: The National War Aims Committee and Civilian Morale* (Liverpool, 2012).

57 John Horne, 'Remobilizing for "total war": France and Britain, 1917–18', in John Horne (ed.), *State, Society and Mobilization in Europe during the First World War* (Cambridge, 1997), pp. 195–211 at p. 199; Turner, *British Politics and the Great War*, pp. 192–3.

58 Of the 116 MPs and War Cabinet members who spoke at NWAC meetings, fifty-eight were Unionists, Monger, 'NWAC and British patriotism', ch. 2.

59 *Scotsman*, 15 December 1917, p. 10.

60 *Yorkshire Post*, 27 September 1917, p. 7.

61 Millman, *Managing Domestic Dissent*, pp. 232, 245, 248.

62 R.J. Scally, *The Origins of the Lloyd George Coalition: The Politics of Social-Imperialism, 1900–1918* (Princeton, NJ, 1975), pp. 366–7; Millman states that Milner had 'ideological predominance' within the BWL, Millman, *Managing Domestic Dissent*, p. 115.

63 Despite ongoing talks with the BWL, the deputy chairman of the Unionist Party appeared to be unfamiliar with Milner's direct involvement in this organisation. Bayford diary, 3 March 1918, in Ramsden (ed.), *Real Old Tory Politics*, p. 101; Milner also did not mention his role within the BWL when writing to Lloyd George about the organisation. John Stubbs, 'Lord Milner and patriotic labour, 1914–1918', *English Historical Review*, 87 (1972), 717–54 at 737.

64 For a wider discussion of this subject see David Monger, 'Transcending the nation: domestic propaganda and supranational patriotism in Britain, 1917–1918', in Tony Paddock (ed.), *Propaganda and the First World War* (forthcoming).

65 *Leicester Daily Mercury*, 8 May 1918, p. 6.

66 National Archives, London, CAB24/52, GT4624, Basil Thompson, Pacifism and revolutionary organisations in the United Kingdom, 23 May 1918, cited in Monger, 'NWAC and British patriotism', p. 319; Ward, 'Intelligence surveillance of ex-servicemen', 182.

67 National Archives, London, T102/9, NWAC to Alderman G. Naylor, 30 April 1918 and 4 May 1918; Stubbs has claimed that there was a working relationship between the BWL and NWAC, see 'Milner and patriotic labour', p. 740.

68 Bush, *Behind the Lines*, p. 69.

69 Significantly fewer pacifist–patriot clashes were mentioned in the *British Citizen* and the Women's Peace Crusade journal *The New Crusader* between November 1917 and March 1918 than in previous months.

70 *Hebden Bridge Times and Calder Vale Gazette*, 30 November 1917, p. 4; a book produced to commemorate the town's war effort also portrayed the disruption of the meeting as solely the work of discharged soldiers. John A. Lee, *Todmorden and the Great War, 1914–1918* (Todmorden, 1922), p. 196.

71 Graham Wootton, *The Politics of Influence: British Ex-servicemen, Cabinet Decisions and Cultural Change (1917–57)* (Cambridge, MA, 1963), pp. 96–7.

72 *Hebden Bridge and Calder Vale Gazette*, 30 November 1917, p. 4.

73 *Todmorden and District News*, 14 December 1917, p. 3.

74 Turner, *British Politics and the Great War*, ch. 8.

75 Lawrence, 'Public space/political space', pp. 297–9.

76 Chris Wrigley, *Lloyd George and the Challenge of Labour: The Post-war Coalition, 1918–1922* (London, 1990), chs 2–6.

77 Arthur Henderson, *Aims of Labour* (London, 1918), p. 58.

78 Ibid., p. 59.

79 William Bridgeman MSS, 4629/1/1918/106, William Bridgeman to Caroline Bridgeman, 9 December 1918.

80 Bridgeman diary, 23 June 1916, cited in Philip Williamson (ed.), *The Modernisation of Conservative Politics: The Diaries and Letters of William Bridgeman, 1904–1935* (London, 1988), p. 104.

6

Labour, civic associations and the new democracy

During the 1918 general election campaign the Labour Party published a leaflet in the form of a fictitious letter from a wife to her husband serving abroad in the army. He, and by extension the voter, were asked to remember the indignities that workers faced during the war and the important concessions which the labour movement had won for them. Attention was drawn to 'the dreadful tales of soldiers' wives who were threatened with ejection' which circulated before the Labour-championed Rent Restrictions Act was introduced. The wife recounts waiting for hours in food queues during the bitter winter of 1918: 'It wasn't as bad as the trenches, but oh dear, how cold and dismal it was! Sometimes I waited hours and then I got nothing. It was the Labour party with their policy of controlling the food profiteers and giving us rations that helped us out.'[1] By developing a variety of practical solutions to everyday problems such as these, the labour movement widened its support base significantly during the war. Most importantly of all, the membership of trade unions expanded significantly from four million supporters in 1914 to more than 6.5 million at the end of the conflict.[2] Although inflation led to a decline in real income for wage-earners over the course of much of the war, trade unions managed to win pay increases for their members, which meant that real wages rose sharply in 1918.[3]

For Unionists the strides that Labour made in developing its appeal within working-class communities during the war were made all the more alarming because they occurred at a time when the electoral franchise was being dramatically expanded. The 1918 Representation of the People Act increased the electorate from seven million to over twenty million.[4] Reports from Unionist constituency associations compiled in May 1917 showed that 259 expressed opposition to the original bill, 32 were in support, whilst 83 were against a change in wartime.[5] We should be cautious in our use of such figures. It is hard to gauge underlying attitudes towards franchise expansion amongst Unionists in the localities, and there is little to indicate widespread hostility to universal male suffrage.[6] All the same, anxiety about the character of the new electorate was widespread. Indeed, the Conservative Party's willingness to extend Lloyd George's coalition into peacetime has often been seen as a defensive measure designed to halt Labour's advance.[7]

Nonetheless, Unionists began to make significant attempts to widen the appeal of their politics during the war. In the existing historical literature produced on the progress of Unionist politics during the First World War much attention has focused on the party's efforts to develop an appeal to 'patriotic labour' by establishing an alliance with the British Workers League.[8] Although the BWL engaged in violent street politics, several of the league's leaders did not participate in the breaking up of pacifist meetings and presented a more respectable face. For example, Eldred Hallas received the support of Neville Chamberlain and was celebrated by the conservative *Birmingham Daily Mail* for the work he did for army recruitment, war savings and prisoner-of-war welfare.[9]

Yet, despite the attention it has received, the 'patriotic labour' alliance with the BWL became increasingly marginal to the Unionist Party as the war progressed and barely limped through the 1918 election. Far more significant in shaping the long-term identity of Conservative politics was activists' reaction to the expansion of non-party and cross-party organisations that occurred during the war. Unionist activists, and women in particular, threw themselves into various forms of patriotic war work in civic organisations such as the Women's Institutes (WIs), which were less hierarchical than the pre-war tariff leagues and party constituency associations. After the war, these experiences meant that activists were better able to forge a Conservative Party with a more truly cross-class appeal.

In June 1916 William Bridgeman, a Unionist whip, met with leaders of the BWL. Discussions appear to have progressed amicably; Bridgeman felt that this party should accept the BWL's offer of a post-war working agreement, for it was 'the only way to fight Syndicalism and ultra-socialism, which are bound to be dangerous after the war'.[10] Like the league's other fellow-travellers, Bridgeman was deeply alarmed at the industrial unrest which heavily affected the South Wales coalfields and Clydeside munitions industry during 1915–16.[11] Such anxieties only intensified the Unionists' existing desire to develop a 'patriotic labour' movement which could provide a counter-force to stymie the growing influence of the Labour Party and trade union movement.

Concerns about the inability of existing conservative organisations to deal with wartime industrial conditions were expressed most explicitly by the National Service League's leadership, whose chief organiser and secretary chose to work for the BWL.[12] A memorandum produced by the NSL's secretary in 1916 candidly admitted that 'one of the greatest difficulties with which the League, throughout the whole period of its existence, has had to contend, has been the apathy or hostility of the working-classes, and especially organised labour'.[13] As the BWL had the support of several Labour MPs and trade unionists, including Stephen Walsh, George Barnes and Charles Stanton, it appeared to provide a more effective means to appeal to the industrial working class than existing conservative organisations.[14] Following talks, the Unionist Party sealed an electoral agreement with the BWL in February 1917, signifying that it would not run candidates against the league in ten seats.[15]

Propaganda by radical right groups such as the BWL sought to rationalise frustrations with the ongoing stalemate on the Western Front, encouraging the idea that Britain's prolonged struggle was the result of enemy influences within the country, which acted as a 'Hidden Hand' doing the Kaiser's bidding. Victor Fisher, the BWL's leader, engaged in unpleasant anti-Semitic attacks on what he referred to as the 'uncleanly pest-houses' of London's East End, and claimed that 'dirty German money' was being spent in London to fuel pacifist activities.[16] Similarly, in May 1917 the British Empire Union journal claimed that, had all enemy aliens been interned, a recent air raid on Folkestone would have been averted, implying that it relied on intelligence from spies.[17]

Much like the NSL, the Women's Unionist and Tariff Reform Association had experienced difficulties in appealing to working-class women before the war. Therefore it is perhaps unsurprising that its chairman, Mary Maxse, was initially an enthusiast for the BWL. Writing to WUTRA members in June 1917 she noted that pacifist 'agitation has lain at the root of many of the industrial troubles which have hindered the output of war material; it is spreading at a deplorable rate'. In response, she recommended that her supporters should try and get in touch with working women in their neighbourhoods: 'It would be a great help to study Labour's point of view as put forward in their best news organs…the paper of the British Workers League should be carefully studied'.[18]

That month a WUTRA delegation, led by Maxse and Beatrice Chamberlain, met separately with the BWL and Sir George Younger of Unionist Central Office. Irene Fisher, wife of the BWL leader, had publicly called for the creation of a women's branch of that organisation the day before their meeting with WUTRA was finalised.[19] Maxse felt that throughout the Younger meeting 'the discussion breathed no spirit of hope'; there was a risk of WUTRA 'falling to pieces unless it is given something to bite on. The whole meeting gave me at any rate the feeling that they despair of Bonar Law [and] that they see no hope of even fighting while he is head of affairs.' Conversely, Maxse wrote effusively to her husband about the meeting with the BWL: 'there, at any rate, something is being done', in contrast to the Conservatives' apparent neglect of the working classes.[20] The BWL's anti-syndicalist policies struck her as 'thoroughly sound' and she hoped her association might 'help them without giving it them away'.[21]

Bonar Law's leadership was a common cause for complaint amongst Unionists in 1916–17.[22] During the same month that WUTRA's delegation met with the party leader, Leo Amery recorded his impressions of a Commons lunch with Alfred Milner, Edward Carson and F.S. Oliver: 'there was a general agreement…that Bonar Law's leadership in the Commons was fatal and ought somehow or other to be got rid of, though nobody has any positive suggestions as to how it was to be done'.[23] All the same, it is important to emphasise that institutional loyalty towards the Unionist Party remained strong despite such frustrations. WUTRA's leaders repeatedly implored Bonar Law to give them a programme to rally behind. They were very reluctant to sever their relations with Unionism or the Coalition. Concerns to remain loyal to the Conservative Party were reinforced by the context of the war, the need to avoid factional conflicts which might undermine patriotic unity, and uncertainty about the electoral future, given that plans for a significant expansion of the franchise were currently being debated. On the occasion Maxse presented a reform programme to her members in June 1917 she felt the need to insist that 'there is nothing in all this antagonistic to our position as a party Unionist Association'.[24] Radical right organisations such as the BWL could act as a ginger group for those frustrated with the war effort, but they never posed a serious threat to the authority of the mainstream political parties, as was demonstrated by the enthusiastic response when the government launched the National War Aims Committee as a measure to rally patriots.

Up until the spring of 1917 the government had remained confident that patriots could self-mobilise in support of the war effort. Such assumptions came under strain due to growing labour unrest.[25] During May over two hundred thousand men were involved in stoppages when there was an engineering strike on the Clyde.[26] Following these disturbances, a series of regional commissions on industrial unrest conducted reports on the situation of organised labour. Their summary findings were published in the national press during late July, with the reports appearing shortly afterwards.[27] The government had already been planning to launch a war aims campaign, but the commissions' findings gave these plans a new resonance.[28] Faced with the conclusions of the industrial commissions, the BWL and BEU's wild claims about a German 'Hidden Hand' appeared an especially crude way to explain the recent upsurge in industrial unrest. The reports demonstrated that strike action was based on material issues and working-class perceptions that the people were being called upon to make undue sacrifices compared with the rest of the community. High food prices were singled out as the most important cause behind recent disturbances.[29]

By launching the NWAC the Lloyd George Coalition government was attempting to establish a space for a moderate, centrist politics to thrive, counteracting the polarisation of public politics which had occurred as a result of clashes between pacifists and patriots.[30] As part of this strategy,

Lloyd George developed his own claim to represent patriotic labour. Responding to the discontent noted by the commissions on industrial unrest, the government granted a 12.5 per cent wage bonus to skilled workers on hourly rates in October 1917. The bonus was subsequently extended to other groups of time-workers over the following months.[31] NWAC literature promoted Britain's humane and peaceable values, contrasting them with the 'Hunnish' behaviour of the German governing elite. In *If the Kaiser Governed Britain* (1918) the positions of the British and German working man are compared. The latter was supposedly viewed by his Prussian rulers as merely 'cannon fodder' or 'factory fodder'. Whereas the British workman enjoyed 'a high level of freedom' and opportunities to better himself, the German suffered from 'the conditions and outlook of a serf'.[32] In another pamphlet it was claimed that one of the key reasons for the Prussian elite plunging the world into war was its desire to prevent the development of a democratic labour movement in Germany, such as Britain enjoyed.[33] In effect, these publications argued that whilst the position of the British labour movement was not perfect, a German victory would be calamitous for it. The true 'patriotic labour' policy was to support the Coalition, thereby avoiding damaging political dissension and risking losing the war to an adversary determined to crush the freedoms of organised labour. Whilst Unionist anxieties about the violent street politics conducted by groups such as the BWL were already beginning to be apparent by summer 1917, Lloyd George's initiatives further weakened the appeal of Victor Fisher's 'patriotic labour' project. WUTRA cuts its ties with the BWL during the autumn, resisting calls from that body for all 'patriotic women's organisations' to band together and combat the pacifist Women's Peace Crusade.[34]

The BWL's claims to act as a rallying point for 'patriotic labour' were further undermined at the Labour Party's conference of January 1918. In a circular letter to national newspapers at this time, Victor Fisher claimed that the BWL's policy 'voices the sentiments and opinions of nine-tenths of the rank-and-file of the trade unionists of the country'.[35] This was clearly wishful thinking: the BWL came under attack at the conference for its plans to oppose Labour Party candidates at the next election, with the result that seven MPs resigned from Fisher's movement. The BWL was now represented by a paltry three Labour MPs.[36] Neville Chamberlain, who had initially been sympathetic to the BWL, was left in no doubt about the result of the January conference.[37] Noting that John Boraston, the Unionist Party's joint chief agent, shared his misgivings, he confided to one of his sisters that 'the BWL's tactics in dissociating itself so completely from the Labour party has destroyed its usefulness' to Unionists.[38] Lloyd George's war aims statement, delivered to trade unionists the previous month, had stressed that Britain was not fighting a war of aggression against the German people for imperialist concerns. The statement was widely welcomed at the Labour Party conference, Robert Smillie, an opponent of the war, received keen applause when he insisted that postponing the memorandum would only prolong the war further. A motion opposing Lloyd George's war aims statement received only a dozen votes.[39]

By March 1918 relations between the Unionist Party and the BWL were distinctly cool. A central office memorandum produced by Robert Sanders, deputy chairman of the party, that month stated:

> It is very hard to ascertain what support the BWL has in the country…in some places where they claim to be strong, their existence has not come to the notice of leading Conservatives. Our Agents and those representatives of Conservative Associations who have been to [Unionist Central] Office do not look on them as of any value to our Party.[40]

According to Sanders, it was widely felt that the BWL relied on men who would vote Unionist rather than on erstwhile Labour supporters. The memorandum did not call for an end to the electoral alliance, given that 'Conservative MPs are generally in favour of an agreement with the BWL'.[41] But even then, over the following months signs began to emerge that local parties were unhappy with the imposition of BWL candidates in their constituencies.

Perhaps unsurprisingly, it was the candidature of the BWL firebrand, Victor Fisher, in Stourbridge, Worcestershire, which sparked one of the main revolts. Fisher's campaign was distinguished by his tactless attacks on Lloyd George's supporters; he even absurdly labelled the sitting Liberal MP, J.W. Wilson, as a pacifist for supporting the prime minister's January 1918 statement of war aims to Labour leaders.[42] In late June Neville Chamberlain, the leader of the Unionist organisation in nearby Birmingham, criticised the 'confoundedly aggressive' tactics of the BWL, which will 'alienate everyone and particularly the very Labour section we want to attract'.[43] A week later Robert Sanders observed that 'agreement with [the] BWL is getting more and more difficult. Our people won't have them in many places.'[44] Matters came to a head in Stourbridge in July when the Unionist constituency association passed a resolution requesting that the decision to support Fisher's candidature be reconsidered. Fisher subsequently blamed Unionist opposition for his position at the bottom of the poll.[45]

Although the BWL was able to win nine seats at the 1918 general election, this success relied on an ability to present its candidates as supporters of the Coalition and the patriotic labour experiment was largely dead by this time. Up until a few weeks before polling it was expected that the election would be a wartime contest.[46] It was therefore unlikely that Unionist supporters of the Coalition would attempt to excise the

BWL from their existing electoral agreement, as this might damage the much-needed impression of patriotic unity in a 'khaki' election.[47] The BWL's campaign in November 1918 depended heavily on presenting its candidates as supporters of Lloyd George's coalition, a somewhat peculiar position given Victor Fisher's recent behaviour. Its electoral organisation went under the name of the 'National Democratic Party', and readers of local newspapers would have been hard pressed to find out that the candidates of this organisation were actually members of the BWL. BWL men who received the coupon usually presented themselves as 'Coalition Labour' candidates.[48] Rather than focusing on the features of their

Figure 6.1: Joint advertisement by Bradford Coalition candidates, 1918 general election

league's programme, BWL candidates stressed the importance of voting for them as Lloyd George's couponed men. In Consett, electors were implored to 'vote for Captain Gee who supports Mr. Lloyd George in his endeavour to make a better Britain for the British!'[49] Electors in Walthamstow were likewise asked to 'vote for Jesson and Lloyd George'; an advert in the local press stated, 'we want West Walthamstow for Lloyd George'.[50] Coalition adverts in other papers, such as the *Bradford Daily Argus*, made no differentiation between Unionists, Lloyd George Liberals and BWL candidates, merely imploring voters to choose whoever was the couponed man, thereby demonstrating that their district was behind the man who won the war – Lloyd George.

Whilst the 'patriotic labour' experiment appealed to many Unionists during the early years of the war, it gradually became clear that the BWL did not command a significant following amongst the organised working class. However, this does not mean that Unionists abandoned hope of forging a party culture with a cross-class appeal. Helen McCarthy's recent work has highlighted the importance that non-party organisations played in civic life in inter-war Britain, encouraging a centrist politics.[51] McCarthy has challenged Ross McKibbin's claim that non-party associations encouraged a form of supposedly 'apolitical' sociability which integrated the suburban middle class into a political culture of Conservatism. Rather, non-party organisations were keen to establish a space in British political life where issues could be discussed, free from acrimonious party debates.[52]

Even so, our understanding of the parties' response to the emergence of this competing form of associational culture remains unsatisfactory. For sure, some Unionists expressed anxieties that the emergence of non-party (and cross-party) organisations would hamper their own efforts to organise new voters, although in the immediate post-war years these fears appear to have been mainly voiced by senior party agents.[53] But we should not overlook the fact that Unionists also valued non-party movements, precisely because they appeared to break down traditional social barriers which had inhibited the tariff leagues' growth before 1914. Several of the leading non-party organisations, such as the Mothers' Union and Girls' Friendly Society, were based on denominational rather than class lines and promoted a conservative, Anglican ethos.[54]

Unionist women played a vital role in supporting the development of a variety of voluntary organisations to aid the war effort. Work to care for Belgian refugees provided the leading subject for patriotic voluntary service during the early years of the war.[55] The 'Help the Ulster Women' committee, which WUTRA founded, provided much of the original basis for this effort. Those who had pledged to provide shelter for Ulster refugees in the event of an Irish civil war were asked to offer hospitality to Belgians.[56] The women's tariff association also played a leading part in promoting the need for household economy and an avoidance of waste. Caroline Bridgeman raised this issue in print as early as 1915, and WUTRA convened a conference on household economy with delegates from the women's Liberal associations the following year.[57] Several female Unionists subsequently became involved in the government-supported Voluntary Food Economy Campaign.[58] By 1917 schemes for female labour on the land and the nascent WI movement provided the widest opportunities for civilians to engage in patriotic voluntary service. The administration of both movements fell under the direction of the Women's Branch of the Board of Agriculture, of which Edith Lyttelton was deputy director.[59] Female Unionists were prominent in the work of county agricultural committees, which met regularly to organise the local administration of women's work on the land. These organisations sought to present women's war work as complementing that of men. A Women's Land Army handbook claimed that female agricultural workers were 'serving [their] country just like the soldiers, though in a different way. You grow the food for them and for the whole Country and your work is quite as important as theirs.'[60] Yet, far from promoting militant values, civilian war service was fostering women's retreat from the disruptive forms of politics in which they had previously participated. Two photos in the *Bystander* during 1915 contrasted suffragette and Women's Volunteer Reserve 'militancy'. As Susan Grayzel observes, the implication was that political violence had been redirected into 'militant' service in support of the war effort.[61]

Mary Maxse, the leader of WUTRA, saw war work organisations as providing a platform to combat the development of a divisive class politics, which she felt would aid extreme socialist doctrines. In a memorandum produced for a WUTRA delegation's meeting with Bonar Law in July 1917 the women's association stressed its concern to 'work steadily among our own followers, and spread [our political] doctrine quietly through our work for women generally during the war'.[62] Significantly, when Maxse wrote to WUTRA members in June 1917, advising them how they could best combat the spread of pacifist propaganda, she focused on her members' war work in organisations like the Infant Welfare Centres, [National] Baby Week, Girls Clubs for Munitions and War Workers, and Soldiers' Wives Clubs. Such activities gave the largely middle-class membership of WUTRA new opportunities to get in touch with working women in their neighbourhoods.[63] The Duchess of Atholl, a leading figure in Scottish women's Unionist activism, was similarly enthusiastic in her support for war work organisations. Recording her impressions in one of the several notebooks she kept in relation to women's war work activities, Atholl observed that those women who volunteered to work for war pensions committees came from 'all sorts and classes...most useful in drawing

Labour and others together. Labour formerly all against vol[untary] workers and suspicious – now very friendly.'[64]

Perhaps more than any other organisation, the WIs symbolised the peaceable and consensual ethos of grassroots activism which war work activists sought to mould during the war. Visitors to the WIs' first exhibition in 1918 could watch their organisation's secretary, Alice Williams, starring as Britannia in her play *Life's a Game o' See-saw*. We are introduced to the 'cliquey' village of Redstone, presided over by the 'deadly superior' Lady Alexandra Brown-Jones, a fierce opponent of the WIs. Undeterred by the village's matriarch, a working-class woman defies the traditional rural hierarchy to set up a WI in Redstone. Consequently, she is able to break down the village's traditional divisions and win Lady Alexandra over to this movement where rich and poor 'work together to raise the standard of social life'.[65] Alice Williams's play indicates the desire of women involved in the land movement to create better, healthier communities in the rural heartland of Britain and subvert traditional barriers. All the same, in practice the rural revival tended to rely on the paternalism of traditional social leaders. Leaders of the Land Army hoped to recruit educated middle-class girls who could provide ideal role models for village women and eventually help revitalise country festivals after the war.[66] Similarly, whilst the WIs were praised for the opportunities they provided for the mingling of classes, it remained common practice for the 'lady of the manor' to lead the local WI in many regions, particularly in southern England.[67]

Therefore it should perhaps not come as a surprise to learn that the WIs flourished in Unionist strongholds such as Sussex, which had eighty-four branches by late 1918. Unionist women also had a large presence on the executives of WI county federations like Worcestershire.[68] Mary Maxse was a keen supporter of the WIs. On becoming president of a village branch, she wrote a letter explaining the workings of the institute movement to her husband serving in France. Maxse noted that the WIs, with their professedly democratic structure, had 'caught on like wildfire' in her native Sussex: 'It is managed by the women themselves, a committee is formed representing all classes, and they run it, everyone is alike…It is supposed when started to settle all the female energies of the village.'[69] By settling energies and providing a forum for all classes to discuss domestic subjects, the WIs' expansion appeared to offer a bulwark against the spread of extreme social-ist doctrines. After 1918, the Unionist women's organisation attempted to follow the WIs' ideal and appeal to women of all classes, challenging the traditional stereotype of the 'Lady Bountiful'.

At the time of the Armistice far more people identified with the organised labour movement than had been the case before the war. But it should be emphasised that the Unionist Party's response to the challenge of widening its appeal had never been monolithic. Already, before the war, attempts had been made to develop stratified electioneering techniques, breaking voters down into multiple interest groups rather than addressing them along straightforward class lines. Unionist hopes that a viable 'patriotic labour' movement could be developed to challenge the Labour Party were dashed by the failure of the BWL. This only served to enhance further the attraction of developing a pluralistic appeal in which class identities would play a circumscribed role.

As a result of the proliferation of patriotic voluntary organisations, the influence of non-party and cross-party activism within civic life expanded significantly during the war. Such was the appeal of these organisations that Caroline Bridgeman, WUTRA's vice-chairman, expressed her concern that unless Bonar Law offered more active leadership, women from her association would 'drift away to…patriotic organisations, which are formed almost daily for some fresh purpose'.[70] In retrospect, it is clear that Unionist activists' engagement with these new forms of civic association helped lay the basis for the party to expand the appeal of its politics to new voters after the First World War. Men did play a significant role in cross-party civic activism, most notably through the voluntary enlistment campaign of 1914–15 and the activities of the NWAC, whose leadership was male dominated and reliant on Liberal and Unionist constituency party agents for its local administration.[71] But it was chiefly women who participated as volunteers in war work organisations and saw the expansion of non-party movements as a means to undermine the appeal of socialism. After the war, Conservatives would argue that charitable and voluntary organisations could supplement the activities of the state in areas such as the relief of the unemployed, and thereby sought to present Labour's schemes for higher government spending as reckless and based on class interests rather than those of the wider public. Moreover, they consciously sought to imitate the demotic social culture promoted by non-party organisations, thereby widening the appeal of Conservative politics to the new electorate.

Notes

1 Labour Party MSS (microfiche), 1919/36, 'Why I shall vote Labour. A working woman's letter from "Blighty"'.
2 Turner, *British Politics and the Great War*, p. 369.
3 Adrian Gregory, *The Last Great War: British Society and the First World War* (Cambridge, 2008), p. 206.
4 For a good analysis of Conservative supporters' alarm regarding their long-term electoral future at this time see David Jarvis, 'The shaping of Conservative electoral hegemony, 1918–39', in Jon Lawrence and Miles Taylor (eds), *Party, State and Society: Electoral Behaviour in Britain since 1820* (Aldershot, 1997), pp. 131–52 at p. 144.

5 CPA, National Union of Conservative Associations, NUA3/1/1, Central Council minutes, 8 June 1917.

6 Keohane, *Party of Patriotism*, pp. 132–3.

7 Turner, *British Politics and the Great War*, p. 191; for tensions in the constituencies see E.H.H. Green, 'Conservatism, Anti-Socialism, and the end of the Lloyd George Coalition', in his *Ideologies of Conservatism*, pp. 114–34 at pp. 118–19; Bates, 'Conservative Party in the constituencies', pp. 14–18.

8 Stubbs, 'Milner and patriotic labour'; Roy Douglas, 'The National Democratic Party and the British Workers' League', *Historical Journal*, 15:3 (1972), 533–52; Scally, *Origins of the Lloyd George Coalition*, pp. 342–8.

9 Neville Chamberlain to Ida Chamberlain, 2 June 1918, in Robert Self (ed.), *Neville Chamberlain Diary Letters* (Aldershot, 4 vols, 2000–5), vol. 1, p. 270; *Birmingham Daily Mail*, 5 December 1918, p. 2.

10 Bridgeman diary, 23 June 1916, cited in Williamson (ed.), *Diaries and Letters of William Bridgeman*, p. 104.

11 Chris Wrigley, *David Lloyd George and the British Labour Movement* (Hassocks, 1976), p. 184.

12 Stubbs, 'Milner and patriotic labour', p. 718.

13 Parliamentary Archives, London, Hannon MSS, HNN5/2, appendix, R.H. MacLeod to Patrick Hannon, 12 June 1916, 'Memorandum on the proposed amalgamation of the National Service League and the Royal Colonial Institute'.

14 Paul Ward, *Red Flag and Union Jack: Englishness, Patriotism and the British Left, 1881–1924* (Woodbridge, 1998), p. 124.

15 Steel-Maitland MSS, GD193/99/2/18-32, 'Memorandum on Unionist Party–BWL relations with regard to future election candidates', 3 February 1917.

16 *British Citizen*, 10 March 1917, p. 138; 6 October 1917, p. 213.

17 *British Empire Union [BEU] Monthly Record*, May 1917, p. 60.

18 Shropshire Archives, Shrewsbury, Caroline Bridgeman MSS, 4629/2/1917/4, Mary Maxse duplicated letter, n.d. [May 1917].

19 *British Citizen*, 16 June 1917, p. 318; Irene Fisher was writing under the *nom-de-plume* 'Mitera', as indicated by 14 December 1918, p. 203.

20 William Bridgeman MSS, 4629/1/1917/46, Mary Maxse to Caroline Bridgeman, 24 June 1917.

21 Maxse family MSS, C. Uncatalogued 181, Mary Maxse to Ivor Maxse, 24 June 1917.

22 John M. McEwen, 'The press and the fall of Asquith', *Historical Journal*, 21:4 (1978), 863–83; Turner, *British Politics and the Great War*, p. 102.

23 After the word 'fatal', Amery wrote a handwritten note in the margin: '? Too pessimistic'. It is not clear when this note was added. Amery MSS, AMEL7/12, Amery diary, 25 June 1917.

24 Caroline Bridgeman MSS, 4629/2/1917/4, Mary Maxse circular letter to WUTRA members, June 1917.

25 Wrigley, *Lloyd George and the Labour Movement*, p. 184; Horne, 'Remobilizing for "total war"', pp. 199–200.

26 Wrigley, *Lloyd George and the Labour Movement*, p. 184.

27 *The Times*, 1 August 1917, p. 4.

28 Monger, 'NWAC and British patriotism', ch. 1.

29 Sir William Chance, *Industrial Unrest: The Reports of the Commissioners (July 1917) Collated and Epitomised* (London, 1917), p. 12.

30 For Lloyd George's interest in establishing a 'centrist' politics see Scally, *Origins of the Lloyd George Coalition.*

31 Wrigley, *Lloyd George and the Labour Movement*, pp. 219–20.

32 War Reserve Collection, Cambridge University Library, WRC35a.314, series 44, reel 6, Wm. Stephen Sanders, *If the Kaiser Governed Britain: The Lesson of Germany* (1918).

33 Harry Gosling, *Peace: How to Get it and Keep it* (London, n.d. [c. 1917–18]).

34 On launching the Women's Patriotic Crusade, Irene Fisher noted her differences with the WUTRA leaders, Lady Ilchester and Beatrice Chamberlain, who she claimed wished to work in a separate sphere of activism. *British Citizen*, 10 November 1917, p. 301; for the BWL's pleas asking 'patriotic women's associations' to cooperate in a campaign against pacifists see 15 September 1917, p. 170; 29 September 1917, p. 201; for BEU involvement in the campaign see *BEU Monthly Record*, December 1917, p. 10.

35 *Manchester Guardian*, 26 January 1918, p. 6.

36 Abraham, Crooks, Duncan, O' Grady, Toothill, Wadsworth, Walsh and Wilkie resigned from the BWL following the conference debacle. Hancock, Hodge and Stanton were the league's remaining MPs. Stubbs, 'Milner and patriotic labour', pp. 745–6.

37 Neville Chamberlain to Hilda Chamberlain, 17 November 1917, in Self (ed.), *Neville Chamberlain Diary Letters*, vol. 1, p. 234.

38 Neville Chamberlain to Ida Chamberlain, 16 February 1918, cited in Self (ed.), *Neville Chamberlain Diary Letters*, vol. 1, p. 255.

39 *County Express for Worcestershire and Staffordshire (Stourbridge)*, 12 January 1918, p. 6.

40 Bonar Law MSS, BL83/1/15, memorandum on BWL enclosed in Robert Sanders to Andrew Bonar Law, 18 March 1918.

41 Ibid.

42 *Labour Leader*, 10 January 1918, p. 6; *County Express for Worcestershire and Staffordshire (Stourbridge)*, 5 January 1918, p. 4; 12 January 1918, p. 6.

43 Neville Chamberlain to Ida Chamberlain, 29 June 1918, cited in Self (ed.), *Neville Chamberlain Diary Letters*, vol. 1, pp. 274–5; see also CPA, ARE MU2/5, Midland Union minutes, Executive Committee, 28 June 1918, pp. 30–1.

44 Sanders diary, 14 July 1918, cited in Ramsden (ed.), *Real Old Tory Politics*, p. 107.

45 Bonar Law MSS, BL83/5/14, Robert Sanders to Andrew Bonar Law, 15 July 1918; Steel-Maitland MSS, GD193/274/57, Victor Fisher to Arthur Steel-Maitland, 13 January 1919.

46 Martin Pugh, *Electoral Reform in War and Peace, 1906–18* (London, 1978), p. 171; Turner, *British Politics and the Great War*, p. 434; Roy Douglas, 'The background to the "Coupon" Election arrangements', *English Historical Review*, 86 (1971), 318–36 at 328.

47 A Coalition pamphlet produced for the Clapham by-election of June 1918 had gone as far as declaring that no contest should be held, claiming that Pemberton-Billing's decision to run an alternative candidate was undermining patriotic unity: 'A Billing candidature will create feelings of distrust and discontent amongst people, thereby causing confusion and weakness and opening the road to ruin. It would cheer the heart of Berlin'. *The Times*, 19 June 1918, p. 3.

48 *Consett and Stanley Chronicle*, 6 December 1918, p. 2; *Walthamstow, Leyton and Chingford Guardian*, 6 December 1918, p. 4.

49 *Consett and Stanley Chronicle*, 13 December 1918, p. 2.

50 *Walthamstow, Leyton and Chingford Guardian*, 29 November 1918, p. 4.

51 McCarthy, 'Parties, voluntary associations and democratic politics'.

52 Ibid., 910; Ross McKibbin, *Classes and Cultures. England, 1918–1951* (Oxford, 1998), p. 96.

53 For agents' criticisms see the various pieces that appeared in the *Conservative Agent's Journal* during 1919–20, particularly July 1919, p. 19; August 1919, p. 5; June 1920, p. 6; April 1922, p. 6; for a rare example of female criticism of non-party organisations in *Home and Politics* see 'Women's conference', November 1920, p. 4.

54 Brian Harrison, 'For church, queen and family: the Girls' Friendly Society, 1874–1920', *Past and Present*, 61:1 (1973), 107–38; Caitriona Beaumont, 'Moral dilemmas and women's rights: the attitude of the Mothers' Union and Catholic Women's League to divorce, birth control and abortion in England, 1928–1939', *Women's History Review*, 16:4 (2007), 463–85.

55 Pamela McIsaac, '"To suffer and to serve": British military dependents, patriotism and gender in the Great War' (PhD dissertation, MacMaster University, 1997), pp. 34–5.

56 Women at work collection (microfilm), BEL2/2/14, reel 4, Edith Lyttelton, 'Some personal experiences and accounts of individual Belgian refugees', p. 5; Barbara McLaren, *Women of the War* (New York, 1918), pp. 141–2.

57 William Bridgeman MSS, 4629/1/1915/2, WUTRA [Caroline Bridgeman], *Economy: A National and Personal Duty* (1915); Women's Library, London, Fawcett Society MSS, 2/LSW/I/D/4/6/45, WUTRA file, memorandum – National Economy: War Savings Propaganda campaign (1916).

58 Mrs C.S. Peel, *A Year in Public Life* (London, 1919), pp. 47–8.

59 For Lyttelton see biographical appendix.

60 D. Ferrar, *Women's Land Army Handbook*, Imperial War Museum, London, Department of Documents, 92/30/1, cited in Janet S.K. Watson, *Fighting Different Wars: Experience, Memory and the First World War in Britain* (Cambridge, 2004), p. 119.

61 *Bystander*, 17 February 1915 cited in Grayzel, 'Outward and visible sign', p. 155.

62 William Bridgeman MSS, 4629/1/1917/111, Caroline Bridgeman memorandum, n.d. [July 1917].

63 Caroline Bridgeman MSS, 4629/2/1917/4, Mary Maxse duplicated letter to WUTRA members, n.d. [June 1917].

64 Blair Castle, Perthshire, Duchess of Atholl MSS, NRAS980, file 57, Women's services notebook 2.

65 Women's Library, London, Alice Williams MSS, 7AHW/E15, Alice Williams, *Life's a Game o' See-saw: A Comedy in Three Acts*, n.d. [c. 1918].

66 Susan Grayzel, 'Nostalgia, gender and the countryside: placing the "Land Girl" in First World War Britain', *Rural History*, 10:2 (1999), 155–70.

67 James Hinton, *Women, Social Leadership, and the Second World War: Continuities of Class* (Oxford, 2002), pp. 142–4.

68 Women's Library, London, National Federation of Women's Institutes (hereafter NFWI) MSS, 5FWI/A/2/2/01-02, NFWI annual report, list of County Federations (1917); NFWI annual report (1918), p. 11.

69 Maxse family MSS, C. uncatalogued 222, Mary Maxse to Ivor Maxse, 24 May 1918.

70 William Bridgeman MSS, 4629/1/1917/111, Caroline Bridgeman, memorandum, n.d. [July 1917].

71 For the 1914–15 recruitment campaigns see Kit Good, 'England goes to war, 1914–15' (PhD dissertation, University of Liverpool, 2002), ch. 4; party agents were usually appointed as joint honorary secretaries of the local NWAC committees, Monger, 'NWAC and British patriotism', pp. 41–2.

7

'Country before party'

In November 1917 the House of Commons discussed a clause in the Representation of the People Bill which would reconfigure the landscape of public politics. In Edwardian Britain auxiliary leagues had played a vital role in electioneering. The proliferation of such leagues amongst supporters of the Unionist and Liberal parties, and their ability to spend unlimited sums during elections without contributing to a candidate's election expenses, had given them an advantage against less generously funded Labour candidates.[1] Moreover, auxiliary leagues had been at the heart of the Unionist organisation's Edwardian modernisation; the tariff leagues, in particular, often proved more dynamic than constituency party organisations. Yet under the new election law persons would be forbidden from promoting the election of a candidate without being included in their election expenses.

Given that auxiliary leagues had proven so important to the culture of Edwardian politics, it may seem surprising that MPs spent little time on debating a clause which threatened to curtail their activities severely. This reticence may have resulted, in part, from a sense that the clause was not watertight and could be flouted.[2] But the debates also reveal a general assumption that, having put 'country before party' during the war, people would, by and large, respect the spirit of the law and distance themselves from the acrimonious partisanship that had been a feature of Edwardian politics. These concerns were widely expressed on the Liberal benches. For instance, Percy Harris stressed the need for a more orderly political discourse: 'the public and electors are desirous that an election should be made as calm and clear as possible'. Harris felt that this would be facilitated by only allowing the parties standing for election to distribute propaganda within the constituency.[3] Sir Hamar Greenwood, a fellow Liberal, felt that the clause was not watertight, but he stated that it acted as 'a warning to all kinds of agencies not to come into the constituency and not to spend money furthering the cause of a candidate without authorisation…In that way we may do something to stop a practice which is to all of us most objectionable'.[4]

Unionists likewise attacked the old ways of electoral politics. Auxiliary political leagues, officially independent from party control, had been responsible for much of the more sensationalist and scurrilous election literature which had blighted Edwardian election contests.[5] Herbert Nield, a prominent tariff reformer, reminded the Commons of some of the more infamous aspects of the Free Trade Union's campaigning before 1914: 'the model of a Chinaman in chains, in slavery', 'the notorious North Paddington shop where black bread and offal were exhibited as the food of the Germans'.[6] Sir William Hayes Fisher, whilst aware of the weaknesses of the clause on expenses, stated that it would act as 'a kind of warning to outside organisations not to spend money in supporting a particular candidate', and could be strengthened at a later date if necessary.[7] Fisher had good reason to believe that the clause could be flouted. Newspapers such as the *Daily Mail* and *Daily Mirror* ignored the legislation, spending large sums intervening in by-elections, until an amending measure was introduced in 1922, making corporate bodies liable for prosecution if they broke the law on outside election expenditure.[8]

All the same, the Commons' debate on election expenditure is significant as it demonstrates that politicians were reluctant to return to pre-war patterns of politics. When the Armistice was signed in November the future shape and identity of parties remained uncertain. Speaking in November 1918 Edward Goulding, former chairman of the Tariff Reform League, told his constituents that the old political parties could never exist again in the forms they had taken before the war.[9] Such attempts at playing down the importance of party appear to have been in line with contemporary popular opinion. Following the 1918 election, executive members of the Birmingham Conservative Association noted that when the issue of party was raised in campaign meetings it was greeted with dissatisfaction.[10] In 1919 the *Conservative Agent's Journal* was regularly filled with correspondence expressing concern with popular animosities and apathy towards party politics. 'An anxious agent' felt that 'there are many former supporters who now disavow Party politics, and decline to remain [party] members or support a purely Conservative Association'.[11] During the same year the Primrose League scrapped its 1913 Declaration, by which new members pledged to support the Unionist Party. Explaining his support for the measure, Grand Master Viscount Curzon stated: 'There is no party which can be correctly or exclusively described as the Unionist Party. Parties are being reshaped and their future nomenclature is unknown...I personally think that a greater future lies before the Primrose League if it is not too closely identified with this or that Party organisation.'[12]

The late Edwardian period had been newly demonised as an era of damaging partisanship in politics, characterised by an ineffective government which had failed to recognise the threat posed by Germany. F.S. Oliver's *Ordeal by Battle* was a seminal work in this regard. It claimed that party politicians had lost their sense of long-term priorities during the immediate pre-war years and had unfairly neglected the vital issue of compulsory military service.[13] Reflecting the *zeitgeist*, Leo Amery told his adoption meeting that during those years 'we were making progress with nothing, except the business of wrangling with each other', culminating in Ireland being brought to the brink of a civil war.[14]

It is important to emphasise that Unionists in 1918 remained uncertain about their party's future identity, and of how party politics would function in peacetime. Although the policies of the Lloyd George government were broadly sympathetic to Unionism and Bonar Law's party came to dominate the Coalition, it is by no means clear that it faced the end of the war with much confidence. The 1918 election should be seen as a victory for Lloyd George and the achievements of coalition government rather than the Unionist Party. In the immediate years before the First World War opposition to Irish home rule had helped to heal the divisions caused by Joseph Chamberlain's tariff reform campaign. Yet as early as May 1917 the leaders of conservative auxiliary leagues were concerned that these two policies, which had been the main planks of Edwardian Unionist politics, would be enacted in some form and were no longer effective policies which could provide the basis for a post-war programme.[15]

Opposition to Irish home rule had led to creation of the Unionist alliance in 1886 and provided its *raison d'être*. Nevertheless, events during the First World War led to a rethinking and narrowing of the Conservative Party's unionist identity. Following the Easter Rising in 1916, when republicans had organised a short-lived armed insurrection against the British administration in Dublin, the Cabinet met to discuss the position of Ireland. The fraught position of Britain's war effort in summer 1916 makes it easier to comprehend why the Conservative Party was willing to compromise its commitment to the union at this time. Unprecedented manpower resources had been devoted to the Somme campaign. However, the British army suffered its worst one-day combat losses on the first day of the offensive and struggled to make meaningful advances. Diverting men to deal with unrest in Ireland at this time would have only exacerbated the problems which the army faced in trying to make a breakthrough on the Western Front. A survey of the Unionist provincial press by Conservative Central Office in June 1916 had concluded that the majority favoured an Irish settlement rather than a continuation of martial law.[16] The following month the government decided that Ulster would be excluded from the operation of the Home Rule Act of 1914. Thereafter, Conservatives focused chiefly on defending Ulster's right to separation, effectively dropping their commitment to the union with Ireland.[17]

Many Unionists became exasperated by Ireland's apparent unwillingness to make the same level of sacrifices as Britons had made during the conflict. With the collapse of the Russian war effort in autumn 1917 fears grew that Germany would be able to overwhelm allied forces on the Western Front.

The issue of Irish conscription gained a new prominence following the Ludendorff spring offensive, which began on 21 March 1918, and rocked the British government's confidence in its war prospects. Milner wrote a gloomy letter to Lloyd George that week: 'If the plague is stayed, we are in for a long and dragging fight. It must be at least a year before the Americans can make their weight felt. We and the French can at best <u>hold</u> the Germans. We are not strong enough to do more.'[18]

In response to the offensive, Lloyd George's government quickly rushed Irish conscription through parliament, even though it made dubious military sense, would be difficult to enforce and ultimately destabilised the British administration in southern Ireland, enabling Sinn Féin to develop a hegemony in rural areas.[19] As Adrian Gregory demonstrates, Lloyd George's decision to enact Irish conscription was motivated chiefly by his concern to pacify critics on the Right.[20] Writing in April 1918 Victor Fisher, of the British Worker's League, sensed that the Irish conscription clause in the Military Service Bill might be 'a piece of high political *camouflage* for the special consumption of the extreme right wing of the Unionist Party'.[21] During the debates on the Military Service Bill, Irish conscription received keen support from Unionist MPs and the right-wing press. Ireland was portrayed as a nation of shirkers who had remained free from the imposition of rationing.[22]

Ultimately, Irish conscription gained few men for the British army but recruited many to the cause of republicanism. With the authority of British rule becoming increasingly nebulous in many parts of southern Ireland by summer 1918, some Conservative constituency associations pondered dropping the word 'Unionist' from their titles.[23] It should be remembered that events in Ireland could still excite keen passions amongst Conservative activists after the war. The Lloyd George government's handling of the Anglo-Irish war of 1919–21 and subsequent negotiations with Sinn Féin returned the Irish problem to the centre of British politics and provided one of the main reasons for post-war Conservative opposition to the continuation of the Coalition. But popular support for the union appears to have been strained by the experience of the war.

The Unionist Party's response to the changing Irish situation during the First World War demonstrated that it was willing to compromise key ideological tenets in the interests of being seen to preserve patriotic unity. Nonetheless, it also undermined the cause of defending the union, the key issue which had galvanised Unionist activists before the war. Responses to the creation of a breakaway 'National Party' further demonstrated the strong institutional loyalty that existed within the Unionist Party, and its supporters' reluctance to engage in actions which might appear to undermine patriotic unity. Even so, this episode caused deep ruptures within the TRL, fatally undermining an organisation which had been at the heart of the Unionist revival in Edwardian Britain.

Henry Page Croft's decision to launch the National Party in August 1917 resulted from his frustrations with Bonar Law and Lloyd George's leadership.[24] Before the war Page Croft had played a prominent role within the TRL, becoming chairman of its organising committee and president of the league's Lancashire and North-West Counties Division in 1913. He was at the forefront of the TRL's wartime revival; over one hundred branches were resuscitated in the year after July 1916 alone, and celebrations were held on Chamberlain's birthday in several towns.[25] It was Page Croft who introduced the league's new journal, the *Tariff Reformer and Empire Monthly*, in March 1917.[26] The National Party is often lightly dismissed since it only returned two MPs at the 1918 general election, but it should be remembered that the movement did receive some sympathy from prominent tariff reformers. Shortly before the National Party's launch, Page Croft wrote to Mary Maxse, chairman of WUTRA, asking for her support. Although frustrated by the lack of influential supporters, Maxse thought the National Party could 'serve as a rallying point' and privately considered the prospect of joining if her association's ongoing negotiations with Bonar Law proved unsatisfactory:

I see nothing for it but for our association to split!…It is quite impossible for me to go on working for the Unionist Party just because it is the Unionist Party!…I am sure there is a lot of dirty intrigue going on in the political world…If the National Party can win support in the country it will help to stiffen the politics – I believe Winston-Smith-Guest are starting a 'Lloyd George' party – what chaos we shall be in![27]

And yet, the National Party's challenge was destroyed by its botched attempts to amalgamate with the TRL at that organisation's annual conference in Manchester on 15 September.[28] Page Croft's ill-advised attempts to rush through the amalgamation by loading the conference with his supporters and announcing the resolution at short notice drew widespread criticism. In a private TRL meeting, Halford Mackinder later claimed that there was 'written evidence that branches were formed in Lancashire' surreptitiously before the conference to gain more delegates to support Page Croft.[29] Writing in the *Morning Post*, Sir Joseph Lawrence, a long-standing member of the TRL executive, registered his disgust with Page Croft's behaviour, noting, 'we are in the midst of a great and appalling war, and must all support the King's Government'.[30] The TRL conference became a farce when Lawrence threw his report on the floor and claimed that 90 per cent of the executive committee had never seen it. As a result of persistent heckling he was unable to continue his speech.[31] On the day of the conference Bonar Law had announced that National Party supporters would be opposed by Unionists at the next election – a decision which was subsequently highlighted by Page Croft's opponents at Manchester.[32] Major Hamilton referred to Page Croft's actions as an act of 'treason to Mr. Bonar Law', claiming that whilst the Unionist Party leader was prepared to work with his political enemy, Lloyd George, in the interests of patriotic unity, the National Party had the potential to undermine the war effort.[33] Hamilton claimed that that the development of the National Party threatened to destabilise the war effort and 'would not be a help, but a hindrance to the Government at the present critical time'.[34]

Stanley Baldwin, MP for West Worcestershire, perhaps best summed up the reasons why most Conservatives were reluctant to support Page Croft's party. A week after the Manchester conference debacle, he told the annual meeting of his constituency association that the National Party was 'unconsciously weakening the executive powers of government'.[35] Baldwin believed that the first step to a better post-war world was 'to win the war in the right spirit, and the best way to do that is to close ranks as much as possible'. If the Unionists had rejected the party truce and formed a government they would be faced by 'a stronger anti-war agitation and obstruction of war measures'. While they might well be frustrated by the Lloyd George Coalition, active opposition towards it meant they ran the risk of destabilising the war effort, enabling the extreme Left to gain in influence.[36] The fact that the Representation of the People Bill was under consideration in parliament around this time added to Unionists' sense that their position was in danger, leading most of them to reject Page Croft's breakaway movement.[37]

While the creation of the National Party helped to rally Unionists around Bonar Law, the TRL had effectively been undermined in Manchester, the traditional citadel of free trade. Several members of the TRL executive committee left in the months between the Manchester conference and its next meeting in March 1918. Significantly, this group included both opponents and supporters of the National Party.[38] The TRL also lost support in the localities. During 1918 there was 'a marked falling off of subscriptions and donations', leading Halford Mackinder to suggest that the league be closed down.[39] A 1919 report noted the nominal existence of fifty branches in the West Country, although 'little has been heard of these since 1917'. Similarly, the Hertfordshire federation was 'still in existence, though at present inactive'. Letters from local secretaries, which were included as an appendix to the report, indicated that there was confusion as to whether the TRL was still operating.[40] Certainly, this atrophying of tariff reform activism reflected the weakness of the organised free trade movement following the introduction of limited tariff duties by Reginald McKenna in 1915 and their extension into peacetime. The FTU did not resume publication of its journal until 1920, and a survey of opinion in Midland constituencies conducted during the previous year had highlighted division within the Liberal and Labour ranks over fiscal issues and a widespread sense that free trade was no longer a key fighting policy.[41]

As has been well documented, elements of the Conservative grassroots were frustrated with the compromises required from Coalition government. For some, the maintenance of the Coalition experiment into peacetime was expedient and relied on a desire to exploit Lloyd George's popular image as 'the man who won the war'.[42] Ewen Green memorably characterised the coalition agreement as a state of 'armed truce'.[43] Yet, whilst discontent with the Coalition was already beginning to manifest itself before the Armistice, cross-party initiatives such as the National War Aims Committee had a widespread appeal at this time, and we should be careful not to exaggerate the level of right-wing dissent which existed towards the Lloyd George Coalition in its early years.

Aside from placing Irish conscription on the statute book, Lloyd George made a number of important concessions in 1918 which helped to placate dissent from his critics on the right. From 1916 onwards, radical right leagues devoted much of their attention to campaigns in support of interning enemy aliens. This was always one of the chief goals of the British Empire Union (originally titled as the Anti-German Union), and the cause was taken up by the National Party, which claimed that only British subjects could join its organisation.[44] The growth of the anti-alien movement helped to effectively unite the radical right for the first time through the activities of the British Commonwealth Union (BCU). The BCU was established as an umbrella organisation in June 1918, under the leadership of Patrick Hannon, bankrolling the Pankhurst's Women's Party, BEU and National Party with the contributions of industrialists.[45] From 1919 it also funded the BWL.[46]

The initial success of the German spring offensive of 1918 gave a new impetus to those who claimed that a foreign 'Hidden Hand' was undermining the British war effort. This was manifested most notoriously in Pemberton-Billing's bizarre libel trial during summer 1918, which enabled him to make lurid and fantastical allegations, labelling large sections of the governing classes as sexual perverts and asserting that Britain's state secrets had been betrayed to Germany 'in the throes of lesbian ecstasy'.[47] As Gregory argues, the theme of British racial degeneration and the supposed alien threat ran throughout this trial; Pemberton-Billing's witnesses included staunch anti-Semites.[48]

Lloyd George responded to the growing demand for civilian enemy internment by appointing an Aliens Committee in July 1918 with an extremist bias, consisting of five MPs, led by his confidant Sir Henry Dalziel and including Sir Richard Cooper of the National Party and Joynson-Hicks, an MP on the Conservative right. Sir George Cave, the home secretary, accepted most of the committee's punitive recommendations, which included a call for all enemy alien women to be interned and a review of British naturalisation certificates issued since January 1914.[49] Many appear to have felt that these proposals did not go far enough. A series of rallies calling for the internment of all enemy aliens was held across the country, culminating in a demonstration in Hyde Park promoted by the BEU in August. Seventy thousand protestors marched to Downing Street in support of a petition claiming to have over a million signatures in favour of the internment of all enemy aliens.[50] But Lloyd George's reforms headed off a more serious revolt. Two Pemberton-Billing candidates contested by-elections at Clapham and East Finsbury in London during summer 1918, but they lost to Coalition men who supported the internment of enemy aliens.[51] After East Finsbury in mid-July, radical right organisations did not contest any more by-elections for the duration of the war, despite being provided with twelve more opportunities for contests. The enemy aliens issue remained prominent in patriot rhetoric, and Unionist candidates regularly expressed hostility to aliens during the November general election. For example, the line taken by Alfred Bird, MP for West Wolverhampton, was indistinguishable from the radical right's vindictive policies. He called for all Germans to be expelled and not be allowed to enter Britain for at least ten years.[52] The Coalition had effectively co-opted the cause, which meant that it was no longer a trump card for the radical right to play.

John Ramsden has suggested that the Conservatives' inter-war electoral success was aided significantly by the new electoral system created by the war. There is much to commend this argument. Most obviously, the post-war party was assisted by the collapse of the Irish Nationalist Party and Sinn Féin's refusal to participate at Westminster after 1918. This resulted in the removal of a block of seventy to eighty anti-Unionist Irish MPs. The Conservative Party was also the main beneficiary of an expansion of plural voting, and the redistribution of seats which occurred in 1918. Unionism had been a strong force in the outer London suburbs of Kent, Surrey, Essex and Middlesex before the war. This region, which experienced a significant population expansion during the early decades of the twentieth century, accounted for fifteen MPs at the 1910 elections but forty MPs in 1918. As a result of these combined changes, Ramsden estimates that the Conservative position improved by a hundred seats.[53]

Nonetheless, we should be careful not to exaggerate the effect that these electoral changes had on the Conservative Party's position. Ramsden claimed that the Representation of the People Act of 1918, and the Government of Ireland Act of 1921, which ended southern Ireland's representation at Westminster, transformed the Conservatives into 'a natural majority party'.[54] Under the new system the Conservatives could consistently rely on success in two hundred seats with 'a substantial middle-class element' between the wars, according to Ramsden.[55] However, this approach risks assuming a straightforward relationship between middle-class identity and support for the Conservative Party. As we shall see in subsequent chapters, class identity was far from hegemonic in shaping the politics of the 1920s, and rival parties sought to develop their own appeals to 'brainworkers' and blackcoats, dividing them into a variety of interest groups. In any case, the new electorate created by the Representation of the People Act was largely working class. The Conservative Party would have to develop new appeals which could win the support many of these new voters, if it was to establish itself as a governing party in post-1918 Britain. As Philip Williamson has noted, 'the high number of constituencies described by some historians as safely Conservative is obtained by a definition of "middle class" which in some cases falls as low as 20 percent of voters...nor were those seats decisive, because the party had to win 100 seats with even larger working-class compositions [to form a government]'.[56] In the aftermath of the First World War it was widely assumed that much of the new electorate, and women voters in particular, lacked settled political convictions and were liable to change their party allegiances.[57]

Importantly, the Conservative Party co-opted perhaps the most significant of the auxiliary leagues formed during the Edwardian period, the Women's Unionist and Tariff Association, in January 1918. The amalgamation was formally sealed by a vote at WUTRA's final conference in May, and several Primrose League habitations decided to convert to branches of the newly formed Conservative Party Women's Unionist Organisation (WUO) from summer 1918 onwards.[58] Nonetheless, the task of integrating women into the party would not be straightforward by any means. Mary Maxse, who was retiring from her position as leader of WUTRA, greeted the decision to amalgamate with the Conservative Party sombrely, feeling that they had 'amalgamated like lambs with the official Unionist men'.[59] She was saddened to see 'the women handed over to a body so completely dead as Unionist Central Office' and felt that colleagues such as Caroline Bridgeman were 'now as miserable' as her.[60] Indeed, when Bridgeman became the first chairman of the WUO in May she dallied with calling it the 'Imperial and National Party'.[61] This demonstrates how she was still uncomfortable with her organisation becoming an official party auxiliary and was keen to maintain some independence in its identity. Archival records indicate that the leaders of WUTRA had devoted more time to the Women's Institutes and Land Army during the later years of the war than party activism.[62] Female Unionists were by no means keen to revert to partisan politics at the end of the conflict. Speaking at the WIs' October 1918 conference, Mary Maxse praised the movement: 'We have been so gloriously happy for four years without politics'. As the Women's Institutes functioned on a non-party basis, she claimed that their discussions could be conducted 'on the highest possible level'.[63]

At the end of the war, the Conservatives had established their position as the leading partner in the Lloyd George Coalition which scored a triumph at the 1918 election. The Conservative Party's concern with being seen as maintaining patriotic unity and fighting the war to the finish meant that it did not suffer the divisions experienced by its rivals. By contrast, Labour's leaders were divided over the conduct of the war. Ramsay MacDonald and other prominent Labour leaders were widely vilified as a result of their support for a negotiated peace, several meetings which were to be addressed by MacDonald were broken up, and he paid for his stance on the war by losing his Leicester seat at the 1918 election. Labour's parliamentary ranks were depleted by the creation of the ultra-patriot BWL in 1916, although most of these MPs left the BWL following the Labour Party conference in January 1918. Of more serious long-term consequence was the wartime division and demoralisation of the Liberal Party. During the 1918 general election one faction fought in support of Lloyd George, whilst a rump under the leadership of Asquith, who also lost his seat, stood outside the Coalition. The Conservatives ultimately proved more willing to accept the wartime encroachments of the state and the introduction of measures such as military conscription, which sat uneasily with the ideological tenets of Liberalism.[64]

Nonetheless, despite the Conservatives' domination of the Coalition, pressing challenges to the party's authority and uncertainty about its future identity remained. The great issues of Edwardian Unionist politics, tariff reform and Irish home rule, had been transformed by the war and no longer appeared to be policies which could stand at the forefront of the Conservative Party's programme. Furthermore, there was a widespread desire amongst politicians at this time to distance themselves from aspects of the demotic electioneering of the pre-war years. Unruliness at public meetings had previously been tolerated as it was seen as a means for the public – non-electors in particular – to demonstrate their support or opposition towards political candidates. The orchestrated violence of patriot and pacifist groups during the war and the threat of revolution spreading from Europe undermined these assumptions and led politicians to place an increasing emphasis on promoting 'peaceableness'. As well as avoiding violence at meetings, politicians sought to create a more sober electoral culture, confining election campaigns to official party organisations, and thereby avoiding the sensationalism which had previously been encouraged by auxiliary leagues. In November 1918 going to the country on a Coalition ticket seemed to be common sense and it was by no means clear that the old political parties would regain their former influence, given that non-party and cross-party activism had gained a new prominence during the war.

All of these changes posed challenges to politicians, but the Conservative Party's existing attempts to adapt to democratic politics put it in a good position to respond to the new environment shaped by the war. Edwardian Unionists had created a vibrant women's organisation and sought to develop a 'peaceable' culture which could appeal to activists of both sexes. By the end of the First World War, the party had distanced itself from the radical right, with its more exclusive and masculinist culture.

Before 1914 Unionists had developed targeted electioneering techniques, lessening its reliance on single-issue national programmes. If the Conservative Party was to succeed in post-war politics it would have to build a new auxiliary culture, recognising the growing appeal of non-party movements. But here too it was aided by Conservative activists' widespread experience of working in non-party organisations during the war. After 1918 popular Conservatism would take on new forms, but ones rooted in the cultural changes which had occurred within the Unionist ranks since the beginning of the century.

Notes

1   Clarke, *Lancashire and the New Liberalism*, pp. 200–1; Ross McKibbin, *The Evolution of the Labour Party, 1910–1924* (Oxford, 1974), pp. 17–18.

2   99.H.C. Deb. 5s., 26 November 1917, col. 1757 (Sir Hamar Greenwood); col. 1758 (Herbert Samuel); col. 1762 (William Anderson); col. 1764 (James Gilbert), col. 1765 (Sir George Younger).

3   99 H.C. Deb. 5s., 26 November 1917, col.1754.

4   99.H.C. Deb. 5s., 26 November 1917, col. 1757; James Gilbert, Liberal MP for Newington West referred to the intervention of outside organisations in recent by-elections as 'practically a public scandal', col. 1764.

5   Lawrence, *Electing Our Masters*, pp. 80–1; for examples of contemporary complaints regarding the use of scurrilous propaganda by auxiliary leagues see *Scotsman*, 19 May 1914, p. 8; *Evening Star (Ipswich)*, 19 May 1914, p. 4; *Conservative Agent's Journal*, July 1914, p. 77.

6   99.H.C. Deb. 5s., 26 November 1917, col. 1760.

7   99.H.C. Deb. 5s., 26 November 1917, col. 1768.

8   *Conservative Agent's Journal*, September 1922, p. 5; *Liberal Agent*, April 1922, pp. 105–8.

9   *Berrow's Worcester Journal*, 2 November 1918, p. 7.

10 Birmingham Central Library, Birmingham Conservative and Unionist Association (hereafter BCUA) MSS, Alderman David Davis and Mr Walthall, memorandum, 29 January 1919.

11 *Conservative Agent's Journal*, July 1919, p. 19; see also August 1919, pp. 5–7, 32; October 1919, p. 1; November 1919, pp. 5, 13–14.

12 Primrose League MSS, MS6/1, Grand Council, 22 January 1919.

13 F.S. Oliver, *Ordeal by Battle* (London, 1915), pp. 210–13; See also J.O.P. Bland, 'The people versus the party machine', *Nineteenth Century and After* (March 1917), pp. 528–39.

14 Amery MSS, AMEL4/8, Leo Amery, speech notes for 1918 general election adoption meeting; see also the criticisms of party government in Birmingham University, Mosley MSS, OMN/C/2/1, *Hanwell Gazette*, 17 August 1918; *Observer*, 13 December 1918, cuttings.

15 Caroline Bridgeman MSS, 4629/2/1917/5, Mary Talbot to Caroline Bridgeman, 3 May 1917.

16 Bonar Law MSS, BL63/c/65, memorandum, 'Ireland, Mr Lloyd George's proposals. Summary of views of provincial papers', n.d. [June 1916], cited in Stubbs, 'Impact of the Great War on the Conservative Party', p. 31.

17 Stephen Evans, 'The Conservatives and the redefinition of Unionism, 1912–21', *Twentieth Century British History*, 9:1 (1998), 1–27 at 21; Keohane, *Party of Patriotism*, p. 92.

18 Parliamentary Archives, London, Lloyd George MSS, LG/F/38/3/22, Alfred Milner to David Lloyd George, 27 March 1918.

19 Adrian Gregory, '"You might as well recruit Germans": British public opinion and the decision to conscript the Irish in 1918', in Adrian Gregory and Senia Pašeta (eds), *Ireland and the Great War: 'A War to Unite us All?'* (Manchester, 2002), pp. 113–32 at p. 128; David Fitzpatrick, *Politics and Irish Life, 1913–1921: Provincial Experience of War and Revolution* (Cork, 1977), pp. 126, 132–3, 233.

20 Gregory, *The Last Great War*, pp. 242–3.

21 *British Citizen*, 13 April 1918, p. 173.

22 Gregory, 'You might as well recruit Germans', pp. 123–7; Keohane, *Party of Patriotism*, pp. 87–8; *John Bull*, 13 April 1918, pp. 6–7; Perth and Kinross Council Archive, Perth, West Perthshire Unionist Association MSS, MS152/2/1/1, letter from Lord Stirling, 10 May 1918.

23 Keohane, *Party of Patriotism*, pp. 93–4.

24 Robert Sanders, deputy Unionist chairman, claimed that the National Party 'started earlier than intended owing to the rumour that Lloyd George meant to start a party under that name'. Sanders diary, 3 October 1917, cited in Ramsden (ed.), *Real Old Tory Politics*, p. 89; Sanders' observation is confirmed by Page Croft's autobiography, Henry Page Croft, *My Life of Strife* (London, 1948), p. 130.

25 *Tariff Reformer and Empire Monthly*, 6 (August 1917), p. 171.

26 Ibid., 1 (March 1917), pp. 5–6.

27 Maxse family MSS, C. uncatalogued 182, Mary Maxse to Ivor Maxse, 31 August 1917, Maxse was referring to a rumour that Lloyd George's main Liberal backers, Winston Churchill, F.E. Smith and Frederick Guest were planning to start a party to rally the prime minister's supporters.

28 For contemporary observations about the effects that the conference had on the National Party's standing see Amery MSS, AMEL7/13, Amery diary, 7 September 1917 (misdated); Bonar Law MSS, BL82/4/22, Edmund Talbot to Sir George Younger, 16 September 1917, enclosed in Sir George Younger to J.C.C. Davidson, 29 September 1917.

29 London School of Economics, Tariff Commission MSS, TC11/1/3, TRL general

purposes committee file, Halford Mackinder to TRL special committee, 12 December 1917, p. 1.

30 Page Croft MSS, CRFT3/4, *Morning Post*, 14 September 1917, cutting.

31 *Manchester Weekly Times*, 22 September 1917, p. 4.

32 McCrillis, *Conservative Party in the Age of Universal Suffrage*, p. 29; for Bonar Law's hostility to the National Party see Bonar Law MSS, BL84/6/123, Andrew Bonar Law to Edmund Talbot, 11 September 1917.

33 *The Times*, 17 September 1917, p. 6; the idea that the National Party leaders were traitors to the Unionist Party was also expressed in *Conservative Agent's Journal*, October 1917, p. 119.

34 *Manchester Weekly Times*, 22 September 1917, p. 4.

35 Worcestershire Record Office, Worcester, BA956, West Worcestershire Conservative Association minutes, 22 September 1917.

36 *Berrow's Worcester Journal*, 22 September 1917, p. 2.

37 Unionist leaders refused even to discuss a working agreement with the National Party in autumn 1918, Hannon MSS, HNN12/1, Henry Page Croft to Patrick Hannon, 30 November 1918.

38 Tariff Commission MSS, TC11/1/1, TRL Executive Committee minutes, March 1918, June 1919.

39 Tariff Commission MSS, TC11/1/2, TRL Special Committee minutes, 18 February 1919.

40 Tariff Commission MSS, TC11/1/3, TRL general purposes committee file, appendices C and D of 12 November 1919 entry.

41 Churchill College, Cambridge, McKenna MSS, MCKN9/8, Charles Alec Fellowes to Reginald McKenna, 30 June 1919.

42 Green, *Ideologies of Conservatism*, 'End of the Lloyd George Coalition', p. 119; Bates, 'Conservative Party in the constituencies', pp. 14–18; Turner, *British Politics and the Great War*, p. 51; Ramsden, *Age of Balfour and Baldwin*, pp. 115, 138; Keohane, *Party of Patriotism*, ch. 2.

43 Green, *Ideologies of Conservatism*, pp. 118–19.

44 Panayi, 'British Empire Union in the First World War', p. 117; Bodleian Library, Oxford, National Party MSS, MS. Eng. Hist. C.2359, Provisional Council minutes, 20 September 1917.

45 For Hannon see biographical appendix. In 1919 £10,000 was spent in subsidising the Women's Party. The National Party received £2,000. Hannon MSS, HNN11/1, [British Commonwealth Union] National Propaganda Committee. memo. on purposes, aims and policy, n.d. [1919].

46 From March 1919 the BCU had a secret arrangement to transfer £300 a month to maintain the propaganda work of the BWL, which lapsed in January 1920, see Hannon MSS, HNN11/2, Patrick Hannon to R. MacLeod, 28 March 1919 and Patrick Hannon to R. Crossfield, 24 January 1920; for the BCU's sympathies towards the BWL in 1918 see John A. Turner, 'The British Commonwealth Union and the General Election of 1918', *English Historical Review*, 93 (1978), pp. 528–59 at p. 541.

47 *The Imperialist*, 26 January 1918, p. 3.

48 Gregory, *Last Great War*, pp. 241–2.

49 The other MPs were Sir Henry Dalziel, Kennedy Jones and C.W. Bowerman. *The Times*, 2 July 1918, p. 7; 13 July 1918, p. 7; 17 July 1918, p. 6; Cate Haste, *Keep the Home Fires Burning: Propaganda in the First World War* (London, 1977), pp. 135, 137.

50 *The Times*, 6 July 1918, p. 3; 15 July 1918, p. 3; 29 July 1918, p. 3, 12 August 1918, p. 3; Lawrence, 'Public space/political space', p. 297.
51 See *The Times*, 21 June 1918, p. 6; *Finsbury Weekly News*, 19 July 1918, p. 3.
52 Wolverhampton Conservative and Unionist Association MSS, D/SO/27/9, *Express and Star*, 4 December 1918, cutting; see also the examples in McCrillis, *Conservative Party in the Age of Universal Suffrage*, p. 39.
53 Ramsden, *Age of Balfour and Baldwin*, pp. 121–3.
54 Ibid., p. 123.
55 Ibid.
56 Williamson, 'The Conservative Party, 1900–1939', p. 15.
57 *Conservative Agent's Journal*, January 1921, p. 1; *Liberal Agent*, October 1920, p. 7; July 1926, pp. 93–4; *Labour Organiser*, January 1922, pp. 7–9; Cambray, *Game of Politics*, p. 8.
58 Primrose League MSS, MS6/1, memo by H. Crowe, 'The Halifax habitation', 19 June 1918; General Purposes Committee minutes, 3 October 1918.
59 Maxse family MSS, C. uncatalogued 222, Mary Maxse to Ivor Maxse, 14 May 1918.
60 Maxse family MSS, C. uncatalogued 222, Mary Maxse to Ivor Maxse, 25 May 1918.
61 William Bridgeman MSS, 4629/1/1918/18, draft reply to S.L. Ancaster to Caroline Bridgeman, 10 August 1918.
62 For Mary Maxse's reluctance to continue working for the Conservative party see Maxse family MSS, C. uncatalogued 185, Mary Maxse to Ivor Maxse, 11 May 1917; C. uncatalogued 221, Mary Maxse to Ivor Maxse, 22 October 1918; Maxse's enthusiasm for the Land Army and Women's Institutes is indicated in C. uncatalogued 222, Mary Maxse to Ivor Maxse; C. uncatalogued 198, Mary Maxse to Ivor Maxse, 17 February 1916; for Caroline Bridgeman's support for the women on the land movement see William Bridgeman MSS, 4629/1/1915/1, 'Notes for a lecture on the war its causes and conduct', n.d. [1915].
63 NFWI MSS, 5FWI/A/2/3/01, report of Women's Institute conference, 24 October 1918, p. 134.
64 Trevor Wilson, *The Downfall of the Liberal Party, 1914–1935* (London, 1966), part 1; McKibbin, *Parties and People*, p. 24.

PART III

From the Armistice to Baldwin

8

The peaceable man and the prudent housewife

In the fortnight leading up to the 1922 general election Jessie Stephen, a Labour organiser, was sent to work in Wakefield, Yorkshire. Hastily recruiting a band of female canvassers, Stephen held 280 meetings over the course of eight days, using a technique called 'mass canvassing'. This involved holding open-air meetings in the terraced streets of working-class neighbourhoods. Canvassers knocked on doors to inform the women of the upcoming meeting, and those who could not attend, due to housework or childcare duties, were given literature to read.[1] Writing in the *Labour Woman*, Jessie Stephen noted that 'only such points as were likely to appeal to the women in the home were given [by speakers]' and that the most valuable part of the exercise was the 'little informal chats' with individual women which followed the meeting. It was claimed that mass canvassing could reach many women who were confined to the home and would never otherwise attend a political meeting. Stephen singled out 'women who are so poverty stricken that they have not the necessary clothes to go out in. Their pride is such that if they cannot go out respectably dressed, they will not go out at all. This group is much larger than many suppose.'[2] Labour's promotion of mass canvassing during the early 1920s was emblematic of its vigorous attempts to engage with the daily life of working families. Its approach to political activism relied on evangelical grassroots effort, an understanding of locality, and a knowledge of working-class community.

How did the Conservatives respond to Labour's initiatives and develop their own appeals to gendered identities? We now know a great deal about how Conservative literature represented women during the 1920s.[3] Despite this, little attention has been given to how Conservative women developed their own activist cultures in the localities. Even less is known of how the Conservative Party engaged in a competitive dialogue with Labour in its attempts to appeal to the female voter following the enfranchisement of most women aged thirty or over in 1918.[4]

The expansion of the Women's Unionist Organisation played an important part in the Conservative Party's adaptation to the new electoral environment created by the 1918 Representation of the People Act. Whereas Unionist leaders had previously struggled to reach out to working-class women, they now sought to compete on the same terrain as Labour activists such as Jessie Stephen by developing new forms of organisation which would appeal to the social cultures of women in industrial areas.

Aside from the work of David Jarvis, the existing literature largely neglects the key question of how the Conservative Party developed new appeals towards masculine identities after 1918. Jarvis has shown that masculine identities remained integral to politics in the 1920s and it was common for male Conservative candidates to highlight their war service and wear military dress in election literature.[5]

Building on this work, the following chapter demonstrates that the Conservatives' claim to represent ex-servicemen's interests played an important role in refashioning the party's identity. Two hundred Conservative MPs who won seats at the 1924 election had undertaken uniformed service during the First World War, and the party always returned ex-servicemen MPs in significantly larger numbers than its rivals managed to achieve between the wars.[6] Building on the culture of the Edwardian tariff leagues, post-war Conservatives sought to present themselves as the party of orderliness. In turn, they claimed that the rowdiness of Labour militants was an affront to the patriotism and discipline of servicemen and demonstrated that Labour was unfit to govern. The politics of the serviceman provided the Conservatives with a cause that appealed widely to both men and women. By focusing on improving the quality of domestic life and presenting its values as being under attack from the Labour Party, the Conservative Party was responding effectively to the new climate created by the First World War. As cultural historians have demonstrated, domesticity had a strong resonance for both sexes during the early 1920s as they sought stability and security following the traumas of recent years.[7]

It was the Labour Party that made most of the running in shaping a new appeal to masculine interests in the early months after the Armistice. Laura Beers has persuasively demonstrated that trade unions were able to counteract claims that industrial action was inspired by unruly Bolshevik elements. When a rail strike was called in autumn 1919 the National Union of Railwaymen launched a major publicity campaign to educate the public on the reasons behind their action. Whereas papers such as the *Daily Mail*, *Daily Express* and *The Times* initially presented the workers' action in hostile terms, their line moderated over the course of the strike due to the effectiveness of the trade union campaign. The most successful poster produced during the strike, 'Is this man an anarchist?', presented an image of a dignified man and his poverty-stricken family. It was argued that, far from being an unpatriotic plot, the strike was forced by the worker's need to secure a living wage for his family.[8] In the months after the strike ended Labour made a series of breakthroughs in the first municipal elections held since the end of the war.

However, the worsening economic climate during 1920–21 meant that trade union attempts to secure higher wages for their members through industrial action increasingly came to be resented by the Right. An 'anti-waste' agitation, supported by the Northcliffe and Rothermere press, called for a significant reduction in government expenditure and attacked trade union demands for wage increases.[9] Conservatives presented trade union 'direct action' as a threat to the authority of parliamentary government.[10] In 1922 Caroline Bridgeman, the leader of the WUO, warned the readers of the women's Conservative magazine that 'democracy or government by the people is on trial'.[11] Conservative publications aimed at women often portrayed industrial action as inimical to the housewife's interests. Lady Talbot told *Home and Politics* readers that 'women dislike strikes because they know that the home and the children suffer first, that strikes are an appeal to brute force and not to reason'.[12]

As part of its wider anti-socialist strategy, the Conservative Party sought to refashion its appeal to masculine identities by asserting that it represented the serviceman and the values he had traditionally embodied: patriotism, order and self-restraint, in opposition to the unruliness of trade union militants. In doing so, the Conservative Party sought to build on the Edwardian tariff leagues' attempts to craft a peaceable culture which could appeal to activists of both sexes. Recent cultural histories have demonstrated that the ex-serviceman's war experience was lauded in Britain during the early years of the peace and increasingly became privileged over that of women and male non-combatants.[13] Martial and domestic ideals of manly behaviour elided in the influential cultural stereotype of the soldier who acted as a breadwinner and good husband.[14] Throughout the early 1920s ex-servicemen made up the majority of the long-term unemployed, so by questioning Labour's claim to represent this group, the Conservatives also challenged its wider claim to protect the interests of poor working families. Whereas the trade unions had won the publicity battle over the railway strike in 1919, they were criticised during the following year for their apparent reluctance to loosen demarcation procedures and permit the employment of non-unionised ex-servicemen, particularly if they had a disability.[15] However, it was the dispute over 'Poplarism' during 1921 which did more than anything else to energise Conservative attacks on Labour's claims to represent the serviceman's interest.

Poplarism was presented by its opponents as a fiscally reckless challenge to constitutional government, which indicated that Labour was not fit to rule. Furthermore, supporters of the jailed Labour councillors were presented as upholding an unruly and violent street politics, antagonistic to the true values of the ex-serviceman. The term Poplarism is used to refer to the policy of boards of guardians giving out-relief on an illegal scale. In March 1921 Poplar's Labour-dominated council, led by George Lansbury, decided

to levy an illegal rate to cover the costs of providing relief to the district's
many unemployed and under-employed families. Poplarism became a *cause
célèbre* with the arrest of thirty Poplar councillors, who were imprisoned for
up to six weeks in September and October 1921.

Around the time of the imprisonments, the Lansbury-edited *Daily
Herald* sought to present the Poplar movement as the true representative
of unemployed ex-servicemen's interests. For instance, the paper made
the following reference to a procession of eight thousand unemployed
Shoreditch workers who supported the Poplar councillors: 'The men
marched. [I]t may not have been in the orderly fours of their route
marches in Flanders, but nevertheless with the same determination.
There was no cheering en route.'[16] Poplar's Labour councillors built on
the theme, portraying their imprisonment as a sacrifice made on behalf of
ex-servicemen's interests. One councillor, Chris Williams, was attending
a meeting of a war pensions committee when arrested. The night before,
he had told the *Daily Herald*: 'I should be a traitor to those left behind on
the battlefield if I did not stand against the attempt to overburden soldiers'
widows with tiny rates'.[17]

Nonetheless, anti-socialist papers were able effectively to challenge the
legitimacy of the Poplar councillors' movement from a variety of angles,
portraying it as a 'Bolshevik' threat to the power of democratic government.
On the first day of the arrests the *Daily Mail* stated that the councillors'
apparent prodigal spending was 'the outcome of a definite policy of redis-
tributing the national wealth. Since the country has prudently refused to
return a Communist majority to Parliament, the Communists and the com-
munistically inclined are attempting to attain their objects through local
administration.'[18] The paper stated that such actions 'may – intentionally or
otherwise – wreck the whole machinery of local government'.[19] London's
Labour guardians supposedly provided over-generous relief whilst 'thousands of poor but employed ratepayers are struggling to keep a roof over
their heads'.[20]

Lansbury was accused of harnessing a dangerous form of demotic politics
by the national press, who highlighted the violence which accompanied
demonstrations by the London Labour guardians' supporters. The day
after the Poplar arrests began, guardians in nearby Woolwich were met
by a deputation of the unemployed, who refused to leave until substantial
rises in the relief rate had been conceded. When these demands were not
granted, the leader of the deputation was alleged to have shouted that he
was 'prepared to smash every window in the High Street'.[21] Furthermore,
an unemployed march on Trafalgar Square shortly before the release of the
Poplar councillors, where demonstrators broke through a police cordon,
was portrayed as unrepresentative of the mass of unemployed workers.[22]
The *Daily Mail* claimed that 'lawless Communist elements' had infiltrated

the movement and large numbers of London guardians were receiving police protection following the receipt of threatening letters.[23]

For *The Times*, the Trafalgar Square riot demonstrated that the Poplar councillors' values were the antithesis of the ex-serviceman's movement, which was committed to patriotic, community-building activities. The paper observed of the demonstrators: 'The preservation of a rough semblance of military formation aided the impression which the agitators are always trying to convey, that the ex-serviceman is the main object of their commiseration, but the British Legion could have organised something much more convincing in that respect'.[24] The British Legion was created in summer 1921 as a result of the amalgamation of the leading ex-servicemen's organisations. In the months before the legion's formation, these groups had come together to organise relief efforts for their unemployed members. Amongst the most substantial of these efforts was that of the Manchester and Salford relief committee, which raised £35,000 in ten weeks. The committee was able to provide 235,000 meals for distressed families in one month, as well as offering clothing and shelter in appropriate cases.[25] Fundraising campaigns were also promoted on a national level, most notably through the selling of poppies in the run-up to Remembrance Sunday. In 1922 the British Legion raised £321,000 (around £8 million in current prices) to support benevolent work.[26]

The Conservative Party periodical, *Popular View*, argued that the creation of the British Legion demonstrated that 'ex-servicemen know no politics', and that it was now impossible for their activities to be exploited 'for mere party purposes'.[27] Subsequently, the Poplar councillors were accused of using the ex-serviceman to push their own extremist and sectarian agenda. The British Legion's activities built on earlier initiatives to supplement the state's efforts to provide for the unemployed through charity and voluntary work. During the First World War over one thousand local pensions committees had been founded to solicit donations for war victims, drawing widespread support from political leaders and activists. One hundred thousand voluntary workers participated in the local committees' work between 1916 and 1919.[28] As Deborah Cohen has demonstrated, ex-servicemen's organisations were keen supporters of such voluntary efforts, given that they demonstrated the gratitude of the public towards the sacrifices they made.[29] In effect, *The Times*' coverage of the Trafalgar Square riot was suggesting that the rowdy demonstrators' conduct did not represent ex-soldiers as a whole or the spirit which had been promoted by the British Legion. The divisive policies of the London Labour guardians appeared to be endangering efforts to bring servicemen to work together in a spirit of non-partisanship. Moreover, Poplar's guardians could be seen as undermining efforts at reconciling the serviceman and society, dividing communities and classes through a violent and unconstitutional politics.

★

In the months following the Poplar imprisonments Conservatives regularly argued that ex-serviceman's interests would be best served by keeping Labour out of power. *Popular View* ran a series of cartoons depicting the life of 'Demobilised Democrat', a decorated ex-serviceman whose attempts to join a trade union are thwarted by his unwillingness to 'come under the Red Flag'.[30] Other cartoons in the series depicted Labour leaders as wild-haired men who had opposed the First World War, but now advocated Communism and 'Red' revolution.[31] Socialism was portrayed as an unruly, foreign force, particularly in the depiction of a meeting where a rabble tear down the Union Jack from a platform and hurl missiles at the speaker (see figure 8.1).

Throughout the early 1920s Conservative politicians contrasted their records as soldiers with pacifist Labour candidates, who were portrayed as lacking in courage and unable to control trade union militants.[32] For example, Captain Erskine-Bolst, Coalition candidate for South Hackney at the August 1922 by-election, played up his heroic war record and attacked the claims of his Labour opponent, Holford Knight, who had been a conscientious objector, to have local support from the British Legion.[33] Erskine-Bolst made much of the apparent rowdyism at Holford Knight's meetings, some of which were broken up to the strains of the 'Red Flag'.[34] Sensationalising the disturbances, one election poster carried the blunt statement: 'Constitution or Revolution? Moderate men vote for Erskine-Bolst'.[35]

Alarmed by the disturbances at public meetings, Holford Knight subsequently sent his opponent a telegram, strongly repudiating disorder

Figure 8.1: Demobilised Democrat cartoon, *Popular View*, December 1921

and inviting him onto a common platform where they could denounce the violence. Despite this plea, Erskine-Bolst told a local paper that he could not see what purpose would be served by their holding a joint meeting: 'I can control my people,' the captain said, 'but I cannot possibly control his; that is up to him'.[36] Erskine-Bolst was implying that his war record made him a natural leader of men, unlike his conscientious objector opponent. The disturbances were used to suggest that Holford Knight was supported by sinister, unpatriotic forces. In a notorious handbill, electors were instructed to 'Vote for Erskine-Bolst and keep the Bolshie out' (see figure 8.2).[37]

Erskine-Bolst put his narrow victory down to his constituents' disgust with 'the rowdy tactics of imported ruffians, who gave them a practical illustration of the mentality of Communism'.[38] One of the more colourful of Conservative MPs, Erskine-Bolst was condemning Ramsay MacDonald's

Figure 8.2: 'Vote for Erskine-Bolst' handbill, Blackpool election, November 1922

war record as late as 1931 and praising the golf club that had expelled him in 1916![39]

Intriguingly, Conservative publications aimed at women were particularly keen to highlight instances of apparent unruliness and violence by Labour supporters, especially if they were directed against female politicians – implicitly contrasting their behaviour with the restrained masculinity of Conservative leaders.[40] In Leeds the *Conservative Woman* made much of the violence by young men at public meetings in the run-up to the 1924 election, publishing an appeal from the wife of Charles Wilson, Conservative MP for Leeds Central. She called the 'Bolshevik' methods of Labour rowdies 'a disgrace to our city'. Their conduct was contrasted with the Conservative politician, a man who was not be 'easily turned aside from his settled convictions'.[41]

All this criticism of Labour rowdyism did not necessarily mean that Conservatives became fully reconciled to new demands for orderly politics. Jarvis has highlighted male activists' ambivalence towards the growing influence of women within the Conservative Party during the 1920s. Whilst it was common for activists to celebrate the organisational vitality of women's constituency associations, men were also alarmed by the increasing feminisation of the party's grassroots organisation and sought to maintain a 'male space' in politics. Concerns were raised that young men might be attracted from Conservative associations to the Fascist movement due to its manly culture and greater opportunities for lively incidents at meetings.[42]

Nonetheless, it is important to emphasise that many of the complaints about growing female influence within the party came from conservative organisations with a strong tradition of homosocial association such as the Junior Imperial League and Conservative Club movement.[43] Women's encroachment into party club life became a less pressing issue over the course of the 1920s as new Conservative organisations emerged, such as the Unionist Women's Institutes and Fuchsia Clubs, which flourished across the country and sought to provide working women with a social outlet. Furthermore, the WUO was brought into the party organisation in 1926, resulting in increased cooperation with Conservative Central Office and a clearer demarcation of women agents' responsibilities, which had previously tended to clash with those of constituency agents.[44]

After the war, the old ways of manly politics survived in some urban, industrial constituencies where Conservative politicians tolerated retaliatory violence against troublemakers at public meetings.[45] But on the whole, official party authorities recognised the value of presenting a more orderly and peaceable face to the electorate. During the mid-1920s the *Conservative Agent's Journal* criticised a letter which suggested that Baldwin should have been supported by Fascist stewards at a recent public meeting in London's

East End and cautioned against the use of the old 'prize fighting type' of steward.[46]

The Conservatives' claim to represent ex-servicemen's interests may have played an important role in their attempts to appeal to the male voter in the immediate years after the war, although it should be emphasised that the cultural purchase of this discourse had weakened by the mid-1920s after Labour had successfully campaigned for civilian widows' pensions to be given on the same terms as those given to soldiers' widows.[47] The development of new gendered appeals to the male voter was vital given that party organisations were struggling to recruit men in large numbers. Conservative leaders regularly expressed concerns that Conservative Clubs were politically apathetic, and that their Labour rivals were more effective in recruiting young men, due to their trade union ties.[48] The Conservatives' problems in recruiting men were also part of a wider problem which voluntary organisations faced at this time. Men's leisure was dominated by the pub, gambling and working men's clubs, whereas there were a significant number of women's organisations which focused on political education. A Pilgrim Trust survey of the Becontree estate on the outskirts of London, conducted in the early 1930s, found that the only active presence which the Conservative Party held on the estate was in the form of its women's associations.[49] The Pilgrim Trust estimated that no more than seven hundred men on the estate were attached to voluntary associations, and these were 'almost entirely social clubs'. By contrast, around 2,500 women were members of religious organisations, many of which met in the afternoons to suit housewives' schedules, and a further 1,100 or so belonged to other voluntary associations 'partly educational and partly social'.[50]

After the First World War the Labour Party sought to reach out to the new woman voter through targeted campaigning. Canvassers were encouraged to fit their talks to the concerns of the particular woman they were addressing:

> If she is suffering from unemployment, tell her about the Labour Party and the right to work or maintenance. If she is a housewife, tell her how much money she pays for tea or sugar is a tax which the Labour Party wants to do away with. If she has a little baby, tell her about the Labour Party's fight for free or cheap milk.[51]

During the early 1920s, Labour pamphlets rarely focused on women wage workers, but tended regularly to address women as consumers, perhaps reflecting an assumption that most women voters in parliamentary contests were housewives. This approach was a particular feature of the

1924 election, where attention was focused on the Labour government's promotion of 'the free breakfast table'. Philip Snowden, the chancellor of the exchequer, claimed to have introduced a 'housewife's budget', reducing food duties by £30 million.[52] Labour presented Conservative plans for economy as being opposed to the interests of the working mother. Voters were instructed to remember that 'a well spent rate is the truest economy', and that Labour would create a more efficient and healthier society through housing reform, improved schooling and better infant welfare services.[53]

The Conservative Party responded by promoting a variety of appeals, which focused on women's roles as housewives, much as they had done during the Edwardian tariff reform campaign. Henry Houston, who acted as election agent for several anti-waste candidates in 1921, claimed that bread-and-butter issues were the key to the woman's vote: 'Never mind about the Treaty of Sevres. It is very important, no doubt, but seventy five percent of electors have never heard of it. What they do understand – especially the women – is the purchasing power of the pound and the problem of unemployment. Tell them how your policy will affect those.'[54] A Conservative magazine, *Home and Politics*, was introduced, which originally appeared as a special edition of an existing party publication, *Popular View*, in 1921. Notes on party organisation sat together with features typical of a contemporary women's lifestyle magazine, including advice on cookery and dress. Occasional tips on household economy were published under titles such as 'The anti-waster at home'.[55] Circulation of the publication grew rapidly, and by 1929 it was selling two hundred thousand copies a month.[56] Part of the growing appeal of Conservative magazines may have been the ostensibly non-political character of much of their content. The successor magazine, *Home and Empire*, introduced in 1930 regularly including features on sport, film and celebrities.

In an important move, the WUO encouraged constituency associations to develop localised versions of *Home and Politics*. By 1926 there were thirty-nine local editions of the publication, often covering multiple constituencies. Inserts varied from four to sixteen pages and local editions often contained a page relating to the work being undertaken by the prospective Conservative candidate.[57] Henry Houston's election manual encouraged politicians to refer to locality when addressing the female electorate, as they were 'more likely to be influenced by the personal or local questions which they understand, or are brought more to their notice than the great national questions of the day'.[58] Such an approach also made sense given that municipal politics provided an introduction to electoral politics for young women as female tenants or owner-occupiers aged twenty-one or over could vote in local elections, whereas they remained disenfranchised in parliamentary contests until they reached the age of thirty.[59] Most importantly of all, it provided Conservative women with an opportunity to mould their appeals to suit a variety of working women's social cultures, something which the Women's Unionist and Tariff Reform Association and the Primrose League had struggled to do when promoting the national programmes of tariff reform and opposition to Irish home rule in the Edwardian period.

The *Conservative Woman*, which began publication in Leeds in 1921, provides a good example of party efforts to develop localised appeals. As well as the usual branch news relating to local women's associations, this publication attempted to foster a wider female Conservative world-view, including sections on lifestyle and the home. The *Conservative Woman* also paid particular attention to the work of the party's female members on the board of guardians, who were instrumental in forming a women's advisory committee.[60] A regular feature offered household hints, providing advice on economical cookery and domestic management to the hard-pressed housewife.[61] The *Conservative Woman* attempted to demonstrate that the party was attuned to local interests, committed to the advancement of able women in municipal administration and concerned with the welfare of all classes.

The publication may well have aided the Conservatives' post-war advances in the industrial areas of Leeds. Before 1914, Conservative women's associations in the city had thrived in affluent suburbs such as Headingley and Roundhay. However, after the war there was significant organisational growth in older urban districts like Hunslet and Chapel-Allerton.[62] This new support was important as women canvassers in Yorkshire were noting the increasing apathy of voters in middle-class districts by the mid-1920s. In such areas it was becoming increasingly difficult to get women to work for the party before elections. According to the *Yorkshire Post*, this was a particular problem in the business districts of Leeds Central.[63] Yet, over two thousand activists worked for the victorious Conservative candidate, Charles Wilson, during the July 1923 by-election, including many women canvassers.[64]

The Conservatives also widened their appeal to women after the war by interacting with the cultures of non-party movements. Annie Chamberlain, wife of future prime minster, Neville Chamberlain, decided to launch the 'Unionist Women's Institute' movement in her husband's deprived constituency, Ladywood, Birmingham in 1919.[65] Based on the model of the Women's Institutes, of which the Chamberlain family were keen supporters, these bodies aimed to provide a social centre for women along with talks on citizenship, although, unlike the WIs, they had an explicit party bias.[66] Whereas pre-war party associations had devoted much of their energies towards training women who were keen to be of practical service at elections as canvassers, helpers and speakers, it was now understood that simpler meetings were necessary to appeal to the female voter who may previously have had little interest in party politics. Annie Chamberlain's institutes offered an opportunity for working women to congregate in an informal setting quite different from the drawing-room meetings in the home of a well-to-do local lady, which had been a common feature of WUTRA's social culture during the Edwardian period. Indeed, when Neville Chamberlain gave a talk to a Ladywood institute, he felt that the scene 'seemed more like an infant welfare centre than a political gathering'.[67]

The institutes' relaxed style, with their afternoon meetings based around the housewife's leisure time, resembled the cottage meetings which all of the main political parties were experimenting with at this time in rural areas. Such meetings were designed to cater for mothers who may have been reluctant to leave their children at home to attend a conventional meeting, but were willing to take them along to an informal political discussion at a neighbour's home.[68] As well as providing their babies with a hearty dose of Conservative politics, Birmingham women could participate in sewing clubs and see demonstrations on topics such as economical hay-box cookery. In Ladywood, simple political talks were given on subjects like 'The A.B.C. of Unionism', the Conservative-led council's attempts to improve housing and 'What the city is doing for the children'.[69] The Unionist Women's Institutes spread rapidly throughout the industrial centre of the city and were also promoted in the surrounding region by Annie Chamberlain in her capacity as head of the West Midlands WUO.[70] Whereas the strength of the Unionist women's movement in the West Midlands had been concentrated in counties such as Worcestershire and Staffordshire before 1914, Chamberlain's institutes meant that working women from Birmingham's city-centre districts began to play an important role in the party's electoral activities. At least 115 members of the Ladywood organisation canvassed for the Conservatives during the 1923 election.[71]

As we have seen, Conservative women threw themselves into work for non-party patriotic associations during the war. Therefore, it seems unsurprising that the Conservative Party was keen to attract women with experience in such movements after 1918, for example the WUO South Eastern Section employed a woman who had previously been involved in the development of village institutes.[72] Writing in 1922, Henry Houston recommended that: 'If the co-operation can be secured of some popular woman who is active in such organisations as the local Women's Institutes, the Women's Co-operative Guilds, or other women's organisations, it is of inestimable value to the agent'.[73]

Annie Chamberlain's Unionist Women's Institutes provide the leading example of how female Conservatives were able to learn from the wartime success of non-party associations and imitate their democratic style of activism.[74] Chamberlain's model was not merely influential in the West

Midlands, but also promoted nationally in Conservative publications as a form of organisation to be imitated.[75] Similar movements emerged across the country such as the Fuschia Clubs, and rival parties also sought to imitate Chamberlain's mixture of simple educative talks and apolitical socialising which provided a break from the monotonous routine of housework.[76] Annie Townley, the Labour woman organiser for south-west England, wrote in 1922:

> Obviously, the method is not to try and teach these women the particular Party programme, but first to attract the women to cheerful meetings, as bright as possible – with always a cup of tea. So dull and dreary becomes the life of the average working-class mother, so over-worked is she, that only be providing some relaxation and real change can we gain her interest.[77]

It should be emphasised that the Unionist Women's Institutes were still not truly meritocratic compared to organisations such as the Women's Co-operative Guild.[78] Educated social workers were encouraged to provide help in launching the institutes in poor districts and the cooperation of traditional social leaders was encouraged in such ventures. All the same, Annie Chamberlain was clearly no 'Lady Bountiful', briefly lecturing the workers before returning to the comforts of suburbia. Institutes usually became self-supporting and all members paid the same reasonable fees of 2s. a year.[79]

Chamberlain's institutes were part of a wider attempt amongst Conservative women to distance themselves from the exclusivity of their pre-war social culture. References to gaining the support of well-to-do local 'ladies' were notably absent from the advice that *Home and Politics* gave on forming and running branches, being replaced by a new emphasis on enlisting professional help. A 1923 piece recommended that the local WUO district agent should be invited to the first meeting of new branches; if she could not attend, the agent would send a suitable woman speaker.[80] This new professionalism was aided by the WUO's ability to draw on the Conservative Party's financial resources, which meant it could employ salaried workers. Before the war, WUTRA had few agents and they could claim only limited expenses from a fund set up by Lord Ebury, meaning that the positions tended to be filled by well-to-do women.[81] The female relations of male constituency leaders remained prominent within the women's Conservative organisation, as they had done during the days of WUTRA, but after 1918 the role of woman agent became less the preserve of 'ladies'.[82]

After 1918 the Liberals struggled to match their opponents' experiments with targeted appeals to the woman's voter. Perhaps this should not come as a surprise, given the problems which racked British Liberalism after

1918. Ideological divisions had developed between the Lloyd George Liberals and Asquithian Liberals during the First World War over issues such as military conscription, and they effectively acted as separate parties from late 1916 until 1923.[83] The issue of the conduct of the war effort also led to defections to rival parties. Several Liberals who supported a negotiated peace during the war such as Charles Trevelyan, Arthur Ponsonby and E.D. Morel played influential roles in the Union of Democratic Control and subsequently joined Labour.[84]

Given that the parliamentary Liberal Party remained under the leadership of Asquith, who had been a convinced opponent of women's suffrage, it was poorly placed to develop an effective programme of appeals to the new female voter. The Liberal Party lacked an effective women's magazine to compete with *Home and Politics* and *Labour Woman* until 1925. The *Women's Liberal Magazine* restricted itself to a weekly digest of branch news and the activities of the national organisation, harking back to the format of Edwardian party magazines. By late 1920 the publication was making a substantial loss, with only 104 out of 815 Women's Liberal Associations bothering to subscribe; subsequently it was cut back to a four-page monthly and relaunched as the *Federation News*.[85] Yet this name change had little effect on the magazine's content. Whereas rival party magazines for women gave regular advice on innovative ways to run constituency branches, it was only after the 1923 election that the *Federation News* began to pay serious attention to offering advice on organisation.[86]

Prior to the party reunification in 1923 the Asquith and Lloyd George Liberals appear to have taken somewhat different approaches to the question of appealing to women, with the latter being the more progressive. The Asquithian Liberals appear to have been hesitant to embrace the need to develop targeted appeals directed towards different sections of voters. Remarkably, a record of the discussion of election methods at the Liberal agents' annual meeting in 1920 stated that 'special appeals for the votes of ex-service men is pure waste. There is no solid Women's Vote as such. As evidence secured by special tests proves that 90 per cent of the women vote the same way as their husbands do.'[87] Some Asquithian Liberal agents appear to have supported the production of specialist literature for interest groups, but overall the evidence suggests that they struggled to match their rivals' targeted electioneering techniques.[88] Asquithian Liberals made few effective interventions in the debates on the welfare of ex-servicemen's families, which were dominated by arguments between the Lloyd George Coalition and the Labour Party.

Finally, in January 1925 the Liberal Party launched two popular magazines, the *Liberal Women's News* and *Liberal Pioneer*. The latter heavily imitated the style of *Home and Politics*, addressing party policies in a simple fashion, and including household hints and competitions pages. This change in approach brought some belated success: whereas *Federation News* had three thousand subscribers at the time of its demise, the relaunched *Liberal Women's News* reached a circulation of ten thousand by May 1925. But even so, fewer than 10 per cent of Women's Liberal Association members were subscribing to the magazine two years later.[89]

Clearly, the Conservative Party's ascendancy in inter-war British politics was built, in part, on its ability to develop a substantial women's movement, dwarfing its rivals. By 1928 the WUO claimed nearly one million supporters – over three times the size of WUTRA's pre-war membership. Its membership at this point was around four times the size of its Labour rival.[90] The Conservatives' achievement was all the more impressive given the problems which the Liberal women's organisation faced. Whereas the Women's Liberal Federation had a paper membership of 115,000 the membership of the successor organisation fell from 95,000 in 1920 to 66,000 in 1923, before making a partial recovery to 88,000 in 1926.[91]

When assessing the Conservative Party's appeals to gendered identities in the early post-war years what is most striking is its adaptability. Conservatives responded to the new environment created by the war, seeking to represent ex-servicemen, responding to the growing appeal of non-party movements and localising party literature to address new electorates. The claim to represent the ex-serviceman held an important function in Conservative efforts to challenge the advances that Labour had made in the months after the end of the First World War. The serviceman was supposed to embody patriotism, self-restraint and discipline. By implying that Labour endangered the serviceman's interests and could not control unruly militants, Conservatives challenged trade union claims to uphold the just demands of working families. Violence by 'socialist rowdies' at public meetings was used to suggest that Labour hampered female political participation and remained a refuge for disreputable, masculine street politics.

It should be emphasised that that there were limits to the post-war Conservative Party's ability to develop constituencies of support through discursive strategies. In developing appeals to gendered identities they always had to compete with alternative Labour and Liberal appeals. Annie Chamberlain did more than anyone to develop a culture of female Conservatism, which adapted to working women's social cultures and responded to the appeal of non-party movements. Yet the Conservatives still struggled to overcome the onslaught of Labour in parts of urban Britain during the early 1920s. Ladywood nearly fell from the Conservative grasp in 1924 despite the missionary zeal of Annie Chamberlain.

All the same, there is much to suggest that gendered appeals helped the Conservatives to widen the appeal of their politics after 1918, particularly amongst women, who were already playing an important role in Unionist activism before 1914. Women's roles as workers was rarely mentioned by the WUO, far more often they were addressed as consumers and housewives, much as they had been in Edwardian Unionist literature. Even in publications aimed at young 'flapper' voters in 1928, images of home, family and consumption predominated.[92] Much of this literature also had an ostensibly non-political character, which may have widened its appeal at a time when overtly political papers such as the *Daily Mail* were beginning to lose readers to papers such as the *Daily Express*, which paid more attention to non-political human interest stories.[93] In 1928 employees of Conservative Central Office held a conference to discuss their plans for *Women of Today and Tommorow*, a pamphlet which was aimed at new voters and published in a print run of five million copies in 1928. Recording his observations of the meeting, A.R. Linforth noted that 'it was agreed that generally speaking pamphlets and leaflets, obviously political in character, and dealing with political matters in a political manner, were liable to be disregarded by the millions of women of [the working and lower middle] classes'.[94] The wider significance of the Conservatives' gendered appeals was that they formed part of a wider anti-socialist strategy developed after 1918 which drew strength from its multiple discourses that could be fashioned to address a variety of audiences.

Notes

1 *Labour Woman*, 1 November 1922, pp. 171, 174; for a further description of mass canvassing see Marion Phillips and Grace Tavener, *Women's Work in the Labour Party: Notes for Speakers' and Workers' Classes* (London, 1923), p. 12.

2 Ruskin College, Oxford, MSS31, Jessie Stephen, 'Submission is for slaves', unpublished MS autobiography, p. 106; Jessie Stephen, 'Some lessons of the election', *Labour Woman*, 1 January 1923, p. 7; Elizabeth Andrews, the Labour Party woman organiser for Wales, was another keen exponent of 'mass canvassing'. Canvassers lent clothes and shoes to the poorest women to go out and vote, and looked after their babies. Elizabeth Andrews, 'Wales – then and now: 1919–1947', *Labour Woman*, February 1948, reproduced in Elizabeth Andrews, *A Woman's Work Is Never Done*, ed. Ursula Masson (Dinas Powys, 2006, originally published 1957), p. 114.

3 Jarvis, 'Mrs. Maggs and Betty'; Adrian Bingham, '"Stop the flapper vote folly": Lord Rothermere, the *Daily Mail*, and the equalization of the franchise, 1927–28', *Twentieth Century British History*, 13:1 (2002), 17–37.

4 The Labour women's organisation has received less attention than its Conservative counterpart. The main study remains Pamela M. Graves, *Labour Women: Women in British Working-class Politics, 1918–1939* (Cambridge, 1994), which is largely concerned with internal party dynamics.

5 David Jarvis, 'The Conservative Party and the politics of gender, 1900–1939', in Martin Francis and Ina Zweiniger-Bargielowska (eds), *The Conservatives and British Society, 1880–1990* (Cardiff, 1996), pp. 172–93 at p. 184.

6 Only thirteen Liberal MPs and fourteen Labour MPs returned at the 1924

election had seen military service during the First World War. The figure for the Conservatives was 200 MPs. Richard Carr, 'The phoenix generation at Westminster: Great War veterans turned Tory MPs, democratic political culture, and the path of British Conservatism from the Armistice to the Welfare State' (PhD dissertation, University of East Anglia, 2010), p. 88.

7 Joanna Bourke, *Dismembering the Male: Men's Bodies, Britain and the Great War* (London, 1996), pp. 20–4, 70–5, 167–70, 252; Alison Light, *Forever England: Femininity, Literature and Conservatism between the Wars* (London, 1991); Susan Kingsley Kent, *Making Peace: The Reconstruction of Gender in Interwar Britain* (Princeton, NJ, 1994); Lucy Noakes, 'Demobilising the military woman: constructions of class and gender in Britain after the First World War', *Gender and History*, 19:1 (2007), 143–62.

8 Laura Beers, 'Is this man an anarchist? Industrial action and the battle for public opinion in interwar Britain', *Journal of Modern History*, 82:1 (2010), 30–60 at 37, 44–8.

9 Ross McKibbin, 'Class and conventional wisdom', in McKibbin, *Ideologies of Class*; Green, *Ideologies of Conservatism*, p. 133; James Smyth, 'Resisting Labour: Unionists, Liberals and moderates in Glasgow between the wars', *Historical Journal*, 46:2 (2003), 375–401 at 380.

10 *Popular View*, May 1922, pp. 8–9; *Straight Forward (Birmingham)*, September 1920, p. 4; *Birmingham Mail*, 16 April 1921, p. 4; Harold Smith, *Unpopular Opinions: A Diary of Political Protest* (London, 1922), pp. 13, 17.

11 *Home and Politics*, November 1922, p. 16.

12 *Home and Politics*, May 1921, p. 12; see also July 1921, p. 10; *Conservative Woman (Leeds)*, May 1921, p. 5; October 1921, p. 1.

13 Watson, *Fighting Different Wars*, pp. 264–5; Noakes, 'Demobilising the military woman'.

14 Jessica Meyer, *Men of War: Masculinity and the First World War in Britain* (Basingstoke, 2009), p. 161; for soldiers' attachment to domesticity during the war see Michael. Roper, 'Nostalgia as an emotional experience during the First World War', *Historical Journal*, 54 (2011), 421–51

15 *The Times*, 23 April 1920, p. 17; 27 April 1920, p. 12; 28 April 1920, p. 12; *Comrades' Journal*, May 1920, p. 5.

16 *Daily Herald*, 1 September 1921, p. 3.

17 Noreen Branson, *Poplarism, 1919–1925: George Lansbury and the Councillors' Revolt* (London, 1979), p. 63.

18 *Daily Mail*, 1 September 1921, p. 11; see also *The Times*, 1 September 1921, p. 10.

19 *Daily Mail*, 2 September 1921, p. 4.

20 *Daily Mail*, 3 September 1921, p. 4; see also 1 September 1921, p. 11; *The Times*, 1 September 1921, p. 10.

21 *Manchester Guardian*, 2 September 1921, p. 7.

22 *The Times*, 5 October 1921, p. 10.

23 *Daily Mail*, 3 September 1921, p. 6.

24 *The Times*, 5 October 1921, p. 10.

25 *Comrades' Journal*, March 1921, pp. 2–3.

26 *The Times*, 21 May 1923, p. 9.

27 *Popular View*, July 1921, p. 20.

28 Deborah Cohen, *The War Come Home: Disabled Veterans in Britain and Germany, 1914–1939* (Berkley, CA, 2001), pp. 21–2.

29 Ibid., pp. 5, 7, 29, 50.
30 *Popular View*, January 1922, p. 13.
31 Ibid., November 1921, p. 11.
32 Lawrence, 'Transformation of British public politics', 197–201; Labour candidates' attitudes to rowdy politics are criticised in *Home and Politics*, February 1924, p. 5; *Conservative Agent's Journal*, October 1923, p. 222.
33 Erskine-Bolst stood as an independent Coalition candidate, but subsequently joined the Conservative Party. LRO, Preston, Blackpool Conservative Association MSS, PLC5/14/1, C.C. Erskine-Bolst scrapbook, August 1922 election address and 'Another lie!' handbill.
34 *Hackney and Kingsland Gazette*, 14 August 1922, p. 3; 16 August 1922, p. 3
35 LRO, PLC5/14/1, handbill in C.C. Erskine-Bolst scrapbook.
36 *Hackney and Kingsland Gazette*, 16 August 1922, p. 3.
37 The slogan 'Vote for Erskine-Bolst and keep the extremist out' was also employed, *Hackney and Kingsland Gazette*, 18 August 1922, p. 4.
38 *Hackney and Kingsland Gazette*, 21 August 1922, p. 3.
39 Andrew Thorpe, *The British General Election of 1931* (Oxford, 1991), p. 227.
40 *Home and Politics*, February 1924, p. 5.
41 *Conservative Woman (Leeds)*, November 1924, pp. 1–2.
42 Jarvis, 'Politics of gender', pp. 174–6, 178, 180–4.
43 Ibid., pp. 180–1.
44 Robert Rhodes James, *Memoirs of a Conservative. J.C.C. Davidson's Memoirs and Papers, 1910–37* (London, 1969), pp. 266–8.
45 Lawrence, *Electing Our Masters*, p. 127.
46 *Conservative Agent's Journal*, February 1925, pp. 40–1; March 1926, pp. 37–8.
47 For a discussion of this subject see David Thackeray, 'Building a peaceable party: Masculine identities in British Conservative politics, c. 1903–24', *Historical Research* (2012), http://onlinelibrary.wiley.com/doi/10.1111/j.1468-2281.2012.00600.x/pdf.
48 Jarvis, 'Politics of gender', pp. 176–7, 183; *Conservative Clubs Gazette*, November 1919, p. 77; June 1920, p. 67; August 1920, p. 92; October 1920, p. 115; BCUA MSS, Ladywood Division Unionist Association MSS, Executive Committee meeting, 23 January 1924; National Library of Scotland, Edinburgh, Dumbartonshire Conservative Association MSS, Acc.12264, Executive Committee minutes, 16 December 1922.
49 Terence Young, *Becontree and Dagenham: A Report Made for the Pilgrim Trust* (London, 1934), p. 192.
50 Young, *Becontree and Dagenham*, pp. 222–3.
51 Phillips and Tavener, *Women's Work in the Labour Party*, p. 11.
52 Labour Party MSS, microfiche, pamphlets card 92, Philip Snowden, 'The housewife's budget', 1924/84; see also 'I am voting Labour', 1924/31; 'Food prices down', 1924/2; 'Why all workers by hand or brain should join the Labour Party', 1924/49.
53 Labour Party MSS, microfiche, pamphlets card 92, 'To working women: Remember! A well spent rate is the truest economy', 1924/92; see also 'Why all workers by hand or brain should join the Labour Party' 1924/49; card 72, 'Do you know how important the County Council election will be for your children' 1922/8; card 79, 'Mrs. Job's talks. Why women should vote Labour' 1922/44; *Labour Woman*, 1 June 1921, p. 94; 1 March 1922, p. 41.

54 Henry James Houston and Lionel Valdar, *Modern Electioneering Practice* (London, 1922), p. 20.

55 *Home and Politics*, August 1921, p. 21; see also June 1921, p. 19; August 1921, p. 12; September 1921, p. iii; June 1923, p. 8; September 1923, p. 13.

56 Jarvis, 'Mrs. Maggs and Betty', 132.

57 *Conservative Agent's Journal*, May 1926, p. 3.

58 Houston and Valdar, *Modern Electioneering Practice*, p. 643.

59 *Home and Politics*, October 1923, p. 7.

60 *Conservative Woman (Leeds)*, June 1921, p. 7; March 1922, p. 9.

61 Ibid., May 1921, p. 11; September 1921, pp. 10–11.

62 *Conservative Woman (Leeds)*, March 1921, pp. 6–8; April 1921, p. 3.

63 *Yorkshire Post*, 17 October 1924, pp. 6, 11.

64 Ibid., 14 July 1923, p. 10; 20 July 1923, p. 10; 27 July 1923, p. 9.

65 For Anne Chamberlain see biographical appendix.

66 Hilda Chamberlain was chairman of the Hampshire Federation of Women's Institutes. *Home and Politics*, October 1923, pp. 3–4.

67 Neville Chamberlain to Hilda Chamberlain, 26 September 1920, in Self (ed.), *Neville Chamberlain Diary Letters*, vol. 1, p. 388.

68 *Conservative Agent's Journal*, April 1922, p. 10; Phillips and Tavener, *Women's Work in the Labour Party*, p. 12; Eleanor Davis, 'Cottage meetings', *Home and Politics*, July 1923, p. 5; *Lloyd George Liberal Magazine*, November 1920, pp. 80–1.

69 *Home and Politics*, March 1921, p. 2; *Straight Forward (Birmingham)*, January 1921, p. 4.

70 *Straight Forward*, February 1921, p. 2; April 1921, p. 6; December 1921, p. 3.

71 Worcestershire Conservative Association Minutes, 22 February 1908; Lloyd MSS, GLLD16/62, *Stafford Chronicle*, 27 July 1912, cutting; BCUA MSS, Ladywood Division Unionist Association minutes, agent's report 1923–24.

72 CPA, ARE9/11/1, South Eastern Area, Women's Parliamentary Committee minutes, 31 July 1920.

73 Houston and Valdar, *Modern Electioneering Practice*, p. 144.

74 Alice Williams MSS, 7AHW/H/1, Alice Williams memorandum, 21 January 1919 discussed the democratic ideals of the WIs.

75 *Conservative Agent's Journal*, April 1922, pp. 10–11.

76 For the Fuschia Clubs see NUCA, *Handbook on Constituency Organisation*, p. 115; *Home and Politics*, March 1927, p. 14; a similar organisation existed in Wharfedale, Yorkshire, *Conservative Woman (Leeds)*, March 1921, p. 9.

77 *Labour Organiser*, January 1922, p. 14.

78 Gillian Scott, *Feminism and the Politics of the Working Woman: The Women's Co-operative Guild, 1880s to the Second World War* (London, 1998), pp. 3–4.

79 *Home and Politics*, March 1921, p. 2; October 1923, pp. 3–4.

80 Ibid., November 1923, p. 5; see also January 1924, p. 9.

81 For the work of 'Ebury workers' in the Edwardian period see *Berrow's Worcester Journal*, 3 May 1913, pp. 3, 7; Thompson, *Imperial Britain*, pp. 56–7.

82 For example, of the twelve women members of the Chelmsford Unionist Association executive committee, nine were the wives, sisters or daughters of sitting male members. Nigel Keohane, 'The Unionist Party and the First World War' (PhD dissertation, University of London, 2005), pp. 242–3.

83 Figures who subsequently joined the Lloyd George Liberals formed the core membership of the pro-conscription Liberal War Committee, Matthew Johnson,

'The Liberal War Committee and the Liberal advocacy of conscription in Britain, 1914–1916', *Historical Journal*, 51 (2008), 399–420.

84 See Martin Swartz, *The Union of Democratic Control in British Politics during the First World War* (Oxford, 1971).

85 For the publication's financial problems see *Women's Liberal Magazine*, December 1920, p. 153.

86 For rare examples of advice on organisation in *Federation News* before 1924 see Harold Storey, 'What is a study circle?', March 1923, p. 19; 'Practical hints on election work', December 1923, p. 81.

87 'Discussion of election methods', *Liberal Agent*, October 1920, p. 7.

88 For the use of specialist literature by Liberal organisers see *Liberal Agent*, July 1921, p. 19.

89 *Liberal Women's News*, June 1925, p. 2; October 1927, p. 120.

90 Maguire, *Conservative Women*, p. 80; Martin Pugh, *Women and the Women's Movement in Britain, 1914–1999* (Basingstoke, 2nd edition, 2000), p. 131.

91 Walker, 'Party political women', p. 169; Pugh, *Women and the Women's Movement*, p. 140.

92 See for example Wolverhampton Conservative and Unionist Association MSS, D/SO/27/23, NUCA, *Women of Today and Tomorrow* (1928).

93 For a discussion of the changing fortunes of the national dailies in the 1930s see McKibbin, *Classes and Cultures*, p. 506.

94 CPA, CCO170/5/47, A.R. Linforth to Joseph Ball, 13 February 1929.

9

The multiple identities of anti-socialism

In 1925 Frank Gray, the former Liberal MP for Oxford, recounted his experiences of recent election campaigns. For Gray, the most salient feature of the post-1918 electorate was its lack of settled political allegiances: 'the non-political section of the community is much larger [than before the war], and is indeed placed by some experts at as much as fifty percent… [who] take no active part at an election and are politically unpledged'.[1] Given these circumstances Gray argued that the budding politician needed to appeal to the various sectors of local society if he wished to succeed.[2]

Few politicians were likely to have shared Gray's zeal for attending countless club concerts, flower shows and football matches. Nonetheless, recent work has highlighted that the idea of employing what Sidney Webb referred to as 'stratified electioneering' – effectively breaking voters down into a variety of interest groups that could be targeted individually – became an important concern for all the major parties between the wars.[3] Much of this work has focused on the dissemination of national campaigns, and we now know much about the media strategies developed by party press and publicity departments in London.

All the same, the local campaign was arguably more important in the 1920s than it had been before the war. Political literature became more expensive to produce and auxiliary organisations could no longer run campaigns in support of a candidate without contributing to their election expenditure. In 1909 the Tariff Reform League alone had produced over fifty-three million copies of its literature, the Conservative Party did not manage to publish in such quantities in any post-war election year until 1929.[4] Moreover, it should also be remembered that this was a period when the local press thrived, particularly in large towns where evening papers flourished, free from competition with the national dailies.[5]

After 1918 local politics became a pressing concern for Conservatives as, although a Labour parliamentary majority appeared unlikely, achieving control of municipal councils provided it with a key means of expanding its support base through the provision of efficient public services, thereby laying the foundations for future success in national contests.[6] Local authorities accounted for 40 per cent of welfare spending between the wars, significantly expanding their role in the provision of public housing and maternal and infant welfare services.[7] In response to Labour advances in local politics, it became common for Conservative constituency associations to produce localised versions of national party publications such as *Popular View* and *Man in the Street* during the 1920s. This enabled supporters to keep up to date with party activities in their neighbourhoods, learn about the work being undertaken by local councils and thereby canvass effectively in the annual municipal elections.[8]

In an influential essay Ross McKibbin has accorded class a central role in explaining the Conservatives' electoral success between the wars. McKibbin outlines how the party portrayed itself as the defender of 'the public' against the sectional interests of organised labour. As part of this strategy, Conservative propaganda nurtured hostile 'conventional wisdoms' critical of organised labour, enabling them to win the votes of most of the middle class and much of the working class, particularly women. The anti-waste agitation of the early 1920s is seen as playing an important role in rallying support for the deflationary policies pursued by successive governments after 1920. In McKibbin's reading, the Conservative Party's calls for an end to government waste enabled it to expand its membership significantly, with these increases being concentrated overwhelmingly in middle-class constituencies.[9]

Whilst this approach highlights one of the key reasons for the Conservatives' success in appealing to the mass electorate after 1918, we should not neglect the plurality of party identities which existed across the country between the wars.[10] The circulation of the national popular press surged in the early 1920s, with the *Daily Mail*, a key supporter of the anti-waste agitation, claiming 1.5 million readers.[11]

Many activists in southern England were undoubtedly keen to support the reactionary anti-socialism promoted by such papers, but a reliance on this type of rhetoric could be seen as an electoral liability elsewhere. Northcliffe and Rothermere's papers were unreliable allies for the Conservative Party.[12] The anti-waste groups, who called for drastic retrenchment and an end to government extravagance, were often seen by Conservatives as being excessively negative in their politics and overly focused on defending the narrow interests of the middle classes. Given this, the intervention of press-supported Anti-Waste League (AWL) candidates against Conservatives during by-elections angered many party activists.

Conservatives in cities like Leeds and Birmingham promoted a more consensual form of anti-socialist politics, focused on their local efforts towards the amelioration of social conditions and the integration of working-class activists into the party. The rise of this more progressive style of activism, which focused on material interests, can be explained by Labour's attempts to counteract sensationalist anti-socialist propaganda. In cities where Labour plausibly promoted moderate reforms in local government Conservatives proved more reluctant to tar their opponents with Bolshevik or extreme socialist associations. Ultimately, it was the

Conservative Party's ability to develop a variety of anti-socialist identities in the localities, building on their Edwardian experiments with targeted electioneering, that was key to its successful negotiation of the challenge of class politics after the war.

The politics of anti-waste was far from static, as this was a cause that various political actors sought to represent. Undoubtedly though, the middle classes formed the backbone of this movement. Formed in May 1919, the Middle Classes Union (MCU) was the first significant organisation which operated chiefly to campaign against government 'extravagance'. The union highlighted the plight of the black-coated worker, thereby providing a challenge to trade union claims to represent hard-pressed working families. A key part of the initial attraction of the agitation for Conservatives was its assertion that the government's concessions to organised labour imperilled the state's finances and led to the imposition of unfair burdens on the middle classes. The Conservative MP, Sir Harry Brittain, championed the anti-waste cause as he felt that the Lloyd George government: 'falls easily into the habit of remembering only, [and] dealing only with the *vocal* working-classes...Labour is flattered, balloons on success and eventually achieves an arrogance which finds at last a too complaisant Government hard pressed to make further and still further concessions'.[13]

Despite its initial claims to act as a moderating centrist force in British politics, the anti-waste agitation grew increasingly reactionary under the influence of the conservative press lords. Lord Rothermere, the proprietor of the *Daily Mirror* and *Sunday Pictorial*, was particularly vocal in his calls for a stringent programme of economy. In his opinion, government spending needed to be cut back to late-Victorian levels and the country would benefit from a 'gradual deflation of the currency', which could be achieved by reducing expenditure by 33–50 per cent.[14] Local MCU leaders went further, often resorting to a belligerent rhetoric to express their frustrations with organised labour's growing assertiveness. At a meeting in Kingston-on-Thames, Mr C.W. Burge implored his audience to stop industrial militants steamrollering over middle-class interests: 'even here in England there were wild-eyed and wild-haired men who spoke as through...the men who were in the middle class...the men who gave solidarity to our national enterprises – were a mere useless excrescence which should be ruthlessly cut from the fabric of our society'.[15] Addressing the first annual general meeting of the Scottish MCU, its chairman, Sir William MacEwan went further, even claiming that only those who paid income tax should be entitled to the vote, and called for reduced government spending on education and housing.[16]

The increasingly vitriolic tone of MCU language reflected growing tensions between labour and capital. In May 1920 London dockers refused to load a ship bound with arms for Poland, then at war with Soviet Russia. Councils of action were subsequently formed, which formulated plans for a General Strike and protested at the government's supposed support for the arming of anti-Soviet forces. This episode outraged Conservatives, who felt that organised labour was prepared to bully government by using unconstitutional actions in the name of preventing a war with Russia that Britain did not intend to fight.[17] Tensions also grew as a result of the fraught position within the mining industry. Consumer groups were angered by government increases in the price of coal over summer 1920 and antagonised further by trade union calls for wage increases, and the calling of a miners' strike during that autumn.[18] Trade union membership surged during 1920, peaking at over eight million.[19] Given the tense climate in industrial relations and the growing assertiveness of the unions, the MCU grew rapidly as a counter-force, claiming over a hundred thousand subscribing members by November 1920.[20]

The strength of the MCU was overwhelmingly concentrated in southern England. This region accounted for 115 of the 148 branches listed in the union's journal, the *New Voice*, in April 1920.[21] Around this time, the anti-waste agitation had a particularly potent appeal in London and affluent towns in south-east England like Henley-on-Thames. In these areas Conservative associations reported that their traditional supporters were growing apathetic and becoming increasingly reluctant to associate themselves with the Lloyd George Coalition due to its apparent failure to cut wasteful expenditure and high taxes.[22] In Reading the MCU had supported twelve candidates in cooperation with the local chamber of commerce at the 1920 elections, championing the idea of businessmen's government. Eleven of these candidates were returned, usually in straight fights against Labour. Following this success the local branch of the MCU thrived, rising in strength from 210 to 1,300 members in the year after October 1920.[23] The organisation also prospered in Brighton in Sussex. Of the ten wards where there were contests in 1921, the MCU fought seven. Labour and MCU supporters both won four victories and independents filled the other two seats.[24] The MCU's campaign was notable for its strident calls for economy, and a Labour candidate in neighbouring Hove believed that the MCU should be rechristened 'Mean, Cruel and Unkind [for] that is their policy'.[25] The creation of the AWL by Esmond Harmsworth, the son of the *Daily Mail's* proprietor, in January 1921 can be seen as another sign of the growing strength of support for anti-coalitionist and deflationary politics. Nonetheless, like the MCU, the AWL's strength was concentrated in traditionally safe Conservative seats in south-east England; this region accounted for all of the by-election victories it achieved in 1921.[26]

It should come as no surprise that the anti-waste agitation thrived in London and its environs. The Conservative-linked Municipal Reform

Party had held London County Council since 1907 on a platform of low expenditure. During the early 1920s, the increasingly assertive presence of Labour on the London County Council gave the city's anti-socialist forces a new lease of life. Labour had held only one seat on the LCC before the war, but increased its representation to fifteen in March 1919. Over the course of the next year, the Labour-led decision to award high pay rises for municipal employees in Poplar raised the ire of many Conservatives, who felt that the council leader, George Lansbury, was pursuing reckless spending based on class interests.[27] In August 1920 the MCU journal stated bluntly: 'It is a fact that no-one can deny that the Labour machine is largely controlled by men of extreme views who, like "Lord Lansbury of Moscow", have been hypnotised by Lenin and are working with him to bring about the world-revolution'.[28]

A strident anti-socialist politics, focused on attacking the supposed iniquities of 'Poplar finance', thrived in the capital and came to dominate the campaign of the Municipal Reform Party during the LCC elections in March 1922. The Municipal Reformers' manifesto appealed to electors in blunt terms. Voters were implored to consider:

Whether the forces which make for revolution and overthrow of the established social order are to be given power to use the machinery of London government, not with a single eye to the efficient discharge of municipal duties, but rather as an instrument for promoting Socialist schemes and Communist policy. The sinister and deliberate acts of revolt...are the outcome of the policy and work of the London Labour Party and its Communist allies.[29]

Clearly this language had a great resonance for many electors. Voters deserted the Progressives as Municipal Reformers presented themselves as the bulwark of anti-socialism in the capital.

Table 9.1 *Composition of the London County Council (seats)*

Party	Before March 1922	After March 1922
Municipal Reform	68	82
Progressive	40	26
Labour	15	16

Local Conservative leaders in rural southern England often employed sensationalist anti-socialist discourses, much like their colleagues in the metropole. Here it was the Liberal Party rather than Labour which was most likely to form the main obstacle to Conservative dominance. Consequently, the dangers of letting Labour take power by voting Liberal were often highlighted. Percy Hurd, who became prospective Conservative candidate for Devizes, Wiltshire, in February 1924, spent much of his energies in tainting the Liberals by association with the minority Labour government which they had let into power. Hurd presented Poplarism as unabashed Communism, and suggested that Labour had little understanding about the interests of agricultural workers and ex-servicemen.[30] The Conservatives took the seat at the 1924 election, benefiting from a 25 per cent swing against the Liberals. In Tory Sussex party leaders went further in their attempts to highlight the threat of socialism, paying a women who had been 'in the hands of the Bolsheviks' to give lectures to its branches. These appear to have been highly successful; indeed, the association's leaders claimed that it was difficult to cope with the high demand for the lecturer's services.[31]

Presenting Labour as fiscally reckless and unable to govern responsibly in the public interest provided one of the core foundations of the Conservative Party's strategy during the early 1920s. As we saw in the previous chapter, Conservatives argued that the actions of Poplar's councillors demonstrated that the Labour Party was a threat to constitutional government. Nonetheless, accounts of anti-waste politics have tended to present it as monolithic, neglecting the contested nature of who represented the cause and the varied forms that anti-socialism, more broadly, took across the regions. Outside its heartland of south-east England, mainstream Conservative support for the class-based, *revanchist* discourse propounded by groups like the MCU and AWL was more partial and contingent than has been usually been supposed.[32]

As early as spring 1921, party leaders were expressing their frustrations with the reactionary rhetoric promoted by groups like the MCU. Lord Salisbury, a prominent anti-coalitionist, felt that the MCU had struggled to live up to its original ideal of acting as a centre ground between labour and capital: 'I rather dislike a Class Union. I have always protested against the Labour Party on that ground, and if the Middle Classes Union becomes powerful, it will greatly accentuate the evil of the Labour Party'.[33] Lord Salisbury's fears that the MCU ran the risk of dividing politics along class lines to the detriment of Conservatism were shared by his brother, Robert Cecil. For Cecil the MCU's key fault was a 'purely negative' approach which was 'against all change unless it can be shown to be of direct advantage to their class interests'. In Cecil's thinking, such a 'passive conservatism' could not offer an answer to the challenges that Conservatives faced in reconciling themselves to the realities of democratic politics.[34] Salisbury and Cecil subsequently created their own anti-waste organisation, the People's Union for Economy, in response to their fears that the politics of anti-waste was being presented in unduly narrow terms.

It has been argued that the Conservative Party's growth in membership during the 1920s was overwhelmingly concentrated in middle-class constituencies and owed much to its ability to promote class stereotypes hostile to the culture of the organised working class.[35] But it is far from clear that there was a ready-made anti-socialist 'public' for national leaders to mould at this time. It must be conceded that several of the largest party associations during the 1920s were situated in affluent constituencies. Of the thirteen regional divisions of the Women's Unionist Organisation, the South-Eastern Counties Division (Kent, Surrey and Sussex) had the largest membership, claiming sixty-two thousand supporters in 1923.[36] Yet in such areas the women's Conservative organisation was not so much expanding in the immediate post-war years as re-establishing its Edwardian strength. Amongst the largest WUO branches in the early 1920s were Newbury, Berkshire (5,300 members) and Horsham, Sussex, where over one-fifth of the female electorate were members of the WUO; both constituencies already had thriving women's organisations before 1914.[37] Aside from the south-east counties, by 1923 the WUO had also developed substantial memberships in areas with a strong tradition of working-class Unionism such as Lancashire and Cheshire (sixty thousand supporters) and the West Midlands (forty thousand).[38]

The need to widen the Conservatives' appeal was compounded by the difficulties which the party faced in gaining active middle-class support because of the variety of community organisations which competed for activists' time. In a 1923 article for the *Conservative Agent's Journal*, E.J. Forster, agent for Newbury, noted that: 'It was not very long ago that an Agent could rely both in urban and rural districts on not only the loyal support but hearty co-operation of that portion of the community, which for want of a better word is termed the middle-class'. Yet in the present 'too many agents would, I fear, reply that the active middle-class support, especially amongst men, is by no means proportionate to their responsibilities...such associations as the Farmers Union, the Chambers of Trade and Commerce up and down the country, [and] the Middle Classes Union' were competing for their attention. Forster concluded, 'a further result has been a withdrawal, partial or complete, from all active participation in political work, either educational or organising, and so the Conservative cause in particular suffers'.[39] These difficulties in gaining the active support of 'known' Conservatives may have partly resulted from the decline of pre-war 'non-party' traditions in local politics caused by hostile Labour Party interventions against sitting councillors.[40] The formation of Liberal–Conservative coalitions in local government was portrayed as a means to remove politics from municipal affairs and return to traditions of businessmen's government.[41]

Whilst growing uncertainties about their middle-class support base encouraged Conservatives to develop a more consensual politics with a wide appeal, the main reason why the party could not rely on a purely negative anti-socialism was that Labour was making significant strides to refute claims that it was attached to 'Bolshevik' methods and wasteful expenditure.[42] Anti-waste organisations were relatively weak outside southern England as their virulent anti-socialist discourses did not necessarily chime with the identity of local Labour movements. Recent local studies of Labour's progress in areas such as South Wales and Lancashire have demonstrated that the party spent much of its energies on expanding its presence in municipal government and promoting bread-and-butter reforms, such as improving maternal welfare services, expanding public housing provision and providing cheap municipal transport services.[43]

This was also the case in much of West Yorkshire. Since the Edwardian period, Leeds Labour had focused on using municipal government as a means to promote social reform, challenging the Liberals' ability to represent progressive opinion. Before 1914 they had been able to win municipal victories in industrial inner-city wards such as East and West Hunslet, which had previously been Liberal strongholds.[44] Leeds Labour pursued the same strategy after the war. The Labour-sponsored *Weekly Citizen* presented a moderate face and focused on gaining support from the middle classes, claiming that they had much to gain from the party's efforts to avoid extravagant spending, reduce council rates and cut the cost of trams.[45] Labour claimed that only it could produce efficient public services and reduce the waste which had been created by the Lloyd George government.[46] At the heart of the *Weekly Citizen*'s strategy was an attempt to avoid politics dividing on class lines: 'The middle classes, whatever they may consider themselves are in the main workers', whose interests, the paper claimed, would be best served by joining their respective trade unions.[47] The *Weekly Citizen* noted that many lower middle-class tenants sought to benefit under Labour schemes to build houses for rents of under £20 per annum.[48]

Conservative Central Office's 'Tranquillity' strategy during the 1922 general election compounded the existing problems which West Yorkshire Conservatives faced in presenting themselves as a progressive alternative to Labour. Bonar Law's election address, written by Leo Amery, claimed that a Conservative administration would create 'a sense of stability and of immunity from acute political controversy', in contrast to Lloyd George's reckless foreign policies and inflationary government, which had supposedly exacerbated the socialist menace.[49] In practice, this meant that Conservative Central Office in London promoted an essentially negative anti-socialism, focused on highlighting the turmoil which would ensue were a Labour government to be elected. A series of leaflets gruesomely outlined the horrors that socialism had inflicted on Russia, instructing Britons to avoid a similar fate by voting Conservative. One pamphlet showed graphic illustrations of emaciated families living a wretched existence under Soviet tyranny, with the slogan: 'This is what socialism means in Russia, keep it out of Britain by voting for the Conservative and Unionist candidate'.[50] Another claimed that Labour would abandon India to potential capture by Russian Bolsheviks. Ending on a sinister note, the voter was told that some Labour leaders supported 'bloody revolution'. Electors were instructed to support the Conservatives and 'vote to keep your right to vote'.[51]

In Wakefield, West Yorkshire, the Labour candidate, Albert Bellamy, sought to present the Conservative leadership as out of touch with the problems of his community. Campaigning at the 1922 election, he told an audience: 'When Mr. Bonar Law promises you tranquillity that means in effect that none of the measures for social reform are going to be carried out because they cost money…We are not going to have peace and tranquillity in this land whilst we have a single man, woman or child that needs food or proper clothing'.[52] The Labour campaign clearly ruffled the Conservative candidate, Geoffrey Ellis, who took pains to counter claims that Bonar Law would oversee a reactionary administration, imperilling the pensions

Figure 9.1: 'Bonar Law and Sound Government. Vote Unionist', Conservative Party leaflet, 1922 general election

system.[53] In the end, the Conservative majority in Wakefield was reduced from 3,246 to a mere 618.

West Yorkshire Conservatives sought to counter Labour claims that their policies were inimical to working-class interests by presenting a progressive image in local politics. In March 1922 the *Yorkshire Post* stressed the need 'to deprecate any policy tended to produce a party founded only on an anti-Labour basis, which could have no other effect than to throw moderate working-class voters into the arms of extreme Labour'.[54] The Conservatives made significant breakthroughs in urban constituencies by promoting social reforms in municipal government. In 1914 Liberals had held four of Leeds' parliamentary seats, with Labour controlling the other. And yet by 1923 Labour and the Conservatives held an even share of the city's six seats, with the latter party victorious in the mixed industrial/business districts of Leeds Central as well as the northern suburbs.[55] Sir Charles Wilson, elected at the Leeds Central by-election in July 1923, was emblematic of the city's paternalistic and progressive strand of Conservatism. During the campaign he trumpeted his record in advancing unemployment relief, superannuated pensions and championing working families' interests as leader of the city council.[56] In Yorkshire towns like Bradford and Barnsley, Conservatives sought to present a progressive image by forming coalitions with the Liberal Party in municipal government. The success of anti-Labour coalitions in these towns during the 1920s built on their records in extending council housing and improving transport and welfare services.[57]

The identity of Conservative anti-socialism could differ significantly between adjoining regions. In largely rural Worcestershire, where the Liberal Party posed the main challenge to Conservative hegemony, activists commonly made scaremongering claims about the socialist threat, much as their colleagues did in southern England. At the annual meeting of the county's WUO in 1921, speakers made lurid claims that Labour's extremist wing was growing in authority and would unleash the forces of Bolshevism on Britain if given power. One woman speaker claimed that Labour 'was not a Labour party at all, it [is] a revolutionary party'. A local party grandee, Lord Deerhurst took this theme further, imploring his audience to work whole-heartedly for the Conservative cause, insisting that at the next general election: 'They would have a clear issue before them in Worcester; it would be the Union Jack or the Red Flag...If this country fell and the Labour party triumphed it would mean the breaking up of civilisation'.[58]

Such an approach lacked plausibility in the industrial districts of nearby Birmingham. Although Conservative control of the city council was never seriously threatened between the wars, Labour's significant advances in Birmingham's industrial heartlands caused deep concern during the early 1920s. A sub-committee of the Birmingham Conservative Association noted that thirteen wards had contested in the city at both the 1920 and 1921 elections. Whereas the Conservative poll in these wards had risen by 3 per cent between the contests, the Labour poll increased by 72 per cent. These troubling results led to the creation of a Unionist Propaganda Committee, in an attempt to counter Labour's advances.[59]

Much as in Leeds, Labour's advances in Birmingham relied on Labour councillors' attention to bread-and-butter reforms such as improving municipal amenities, cutting the cost of trams and gas, and improving housing stock. Birmingham Labour activists focused on offering concrete policies to improve the welfare of the local community and engaged in local charities and relief funds.[60] Percy Shurmer, who became councillor for the deprived city-centre ward of St Martin's in 1921, provides a good example of Birmingham's moderate brand of Labour politics. In a municipal election leaflet Shurmer encouraged the people of Deritend to put their trust in him: 'Stand by the man who has stood by you, who prevented many evictions! Has made landlords repair property! Had your yard lamp lit!…vote for Shurmer. His next work: gas and taps in all houses.'[61]

Men like Shurmer could hardly be tarred with the Poplar brush, and consequently Birmingham Conservatives sought to nurture a progressive, neighbourhood-centred politics to counter the rise of Labour in the city. During 1921 party literature in Birmingham criticised the anti-waste movement's calls for a drastic retrenchment in government expenditure.[62] In his *Notes for Unionist Workers and Speakers*, produced for that year's municipal elections, Leo Amery, the Conservative MP for Sparkbrook, instructed his supporters avoid the *revanchist* tone of the MCU and AWL whilst canvassing: 'Begin by pointing out that you don't denounce working men's wives for extravagance because they can't feed their families for the same money as they could before the War…How many anti-waste speakers could make their own home budget pass the tests they impose on the National budget?'[63] Speakers were implored to point out the useful work that the Coalition government was already doing in the direction of realistic retrenchment through the activities of the Geddes committee: 'It is useless to ask for impossibilities, or to think that we can scrap the Army or the Navy or throw all our real national and imperial responsibilities overboard'.[64] Nonetheless, calls for moderation in economy sat uneasily with scaremongering attacks on the supposed extremism of Labour candidates in the Birmingham Conservative magazine, *Straight Forward*.[65]

All the same, after their poor showing at the 1921 municipal elections, Birmingham Unionists sought to reassert their progressive credentials, cutting down references to Labour extremism, championing rent restrictions and promoting a major house-building programme.[66] John Smedley-Crooke exemplified Conservative attempts to match Birmingham Labour's community appeal.[67] By no means a conventionally gifted orator and hamstrung by a poorly funded local association, he managed to hold the deprived constituency of Deritend, Birmingham, from 1922 to 1929 and from 1931 to 1945.[68] Smedley-Crooke's service as an MP was distinguished by his paternalistic care for his constituents, particularly ex-servicemen.[69] Before becoming an MP he had played a prominent role in the working of the Unity Relief Fund, organised by ex-servicemen's organisations to aid the many members who had been made unemployed as a result of the post-war economic slump. By May 1921 the fund had raised over £100,000 and the Birmingham committee was providing four thousand meals a day to out-of-work ex-servicemen.[70] Smedley-Crooke subsequently involved himself heavily in the work of the British Legion in the city. Birmingham Conservative leaders commonly engaged in the work of local charitable funds, often organised in cooperation with the *Birmingham Mail*, which supported the party.[71]

Conservative MPs in the industrial constituencies of Birmingham experimented with surgeries during the 1920s, further expanding their appeal to community. Smedley-Crooke ran 'at home' sessions where constituents could consult him about their problems. A local councillor noted that these surgeries were valuable, as 'many of these people are so illiterate that they do not know how to take advantage of the facilities which have been provided'.[72] Similarly, Neville Chamberlain regularly went 'slumming', as he put it, visiting constituents' homes to discuss local affairs.[73] Furthermore, Conservative MPs tapped into the city's Nonconformist social culture by speaking at the Digbeth Institute, a church and community centre with which Smedley-Crooke was closely associated. The institute provided concerts, adult education classes and a club room for the surrounding slum areas of Deritend.[74] Smedley-Crooke replicated the neighbourhood-centred politics of the local Labour movement exemplified by Percy Shurmer, and even produced ten thousand copies of a leaflet telling constituents his life story, reinforcing the personal nature of his appeal.[75]

Despite their attempts to reach out to working class voters, Conservative constituency associations often remained dominated by narrow oligarchies, much as they had done before the war. In part, this was a matter of finance. Constituency associations continued to rely heavily on the financial support of the parliamentary candidate and a small band of businessmen and local worthies. Only a handful of working-class Conservative councillors were elected in Birmingham and Sheffield between the wars.[76] Much of the debate about the need to retain 'known' Conservatives, whose energies appear to have been increasingly diverted into wider non-party civic organisations, resulted from concerns about the financial resources of the local party. In the Erdington constituency of Birmingham, Arthur Steel-Maitland spent around £450 to £500 a year on supporting the constituency association. Local businesses also made substantial contributions to Conservative activities in Erdington. GEC, the Metropolitan Carriage Company and Wolseley contributed donations amounting to £400 in 1929.[77] With such financial assistance came status within the running of constituency associations. In nearby Deritend twenty-five businessmen were responsible for the constituency's polling districts.[78]

Despite the growing influence of professionalisation through the work of agents, effective power remained concentrated in middle-class hands in cities such as Birmingham. Steel-Maitland decided that his wife should become chairman of the Washwood Heath Women's Unionist Association rather than a local activist as the latter was 'sufficiently near to the others in social standing that they might be jealous of her'.[79] If anything, elite patronage may well have been an advantage in what was still a highly paternalistic and deferential society. Henry Houston, who had overseen several successful campaigns by anti-waste candidates during the early 1920s in southern England, observed that 'happy is the agent who has on his staff a woman who holds the keys to the humble homes of the division. She must be of good breeding, for the working woman still loves "a lady".'[80]

The problems experienced in Birmingham were representative of a wider picture. Whilst the Conservative Party had developed a variety of discursive appeals which sought to connect with a largely working-class electorate, it often proved unwilling or unable to democratise the activities of constituency associations. During the 1920s correspondents in the *Conservative Agent's Journal* complained that many constituency associations relied on their member or candidate for funding, thereby undermining their independence.[81] In 1929 one contributor voiced his concern that few men of moderate means were able to stand for the party, noting that 'a [Conservative] candidate whose election expenses are paid has rarely a chance of fighting a division which can be won'.[82] By the 1930s only between a third and a quarter of constituency associations were self-supporting, and they tended to be safe Conservative seats concentrated in south-east England.[83]

There were a variety of anti-socialist identities which the Conservative Party presented across the nation during the early 1920s. Although the class-based politics of groups such as the AWL appealed to many, especially in south-east England, its calls for severe retrenchment were greeted with scepticism by activists in other regions, who felt that they needed a progressive appeal to challenge that of their rivals. Negative anti-socialist rhetoric ebbed and flowed in appeal throughout the inter-war period, gaining in resonance in periods when labour militancy appeared at its most threatening, such as during the 1924 election and around the time of the general strike in 1926.

In the West Midlands and northern industrial districts Conservative activists began to develop an alternative politics, centred on neighbourhood interests and offering moderate social reform balanced with steady government. Such appeals built on the populist cultures developed by the pre-1918 party. Unionists had presented themselves as guardians of social justice before the war: advocating measures to help tenant farmers buy property, supporting a review of National Insurance to help casual workers and presenting tariff reform as a programme which would benefit both producers' and consumers' welfare.

There were clear limits to the Conservatives' reconciliation to democratic politics, and the creation of demotic appeals focused on a largely working-class public did not lead to a substantial change in the composition of party leadership structures. The appeal of Conservative figures such as Annie Chamberlain and John Smedley-Crooke was rooted in their promotion of a paternalistic form of social leadership. But it is likely that the party would have faced even greater setbacks and difficulties in winning the support of the post-war electorate in cities like Birmingham and Leeds had it not been for its sustained attempts to engage with working-class communities and develop a progressive appeal after 1918. Aside from shoring up the party's position in urban Britain during the 1920s, Conservative activists' spade-work at this time may well have provided the basis for their substantial breakthroughs in urban constituencies at the 1931 election, following the discrediting of the outgoing Labour government's economic record.

Notes

1 Frank Gray, *Confessions of a Candidate* (London, 1925), p. 19; see also *Conservative Agent's Journal*, March 1923, p. 58.
2 Gray, *Confessions of a Candidate*, pp. 34, 91.
3 Lawrence, *Electing Our Masters*, pp. 119–20; Jarvis, 'Class politics in the 1920s', 64, 80–2; Beers, *Your Britain*, chs 2, 8–9.
4 Lawrence, *Electing Our Masters*, p. 110; Scally, *Origins of the Lloyd George Coalition*, p. 95; Beers, *Your Britain*, p. 18.
5 The *Investigated Press Circulations* for 1932 found that 66–82 per cent of households in Birmingham, Bristol, Leeds, Liverpool, Manchester, Newcastle and Plymouth took a local paper regularly. For a more detailed discussion of local press readership see McKibbin, *Classes and Cultures*, pp. 505–6.
6 *Home and Politics*, October 1921, p. 10; for the importance of municipal politics to the identity of local Labour parties see Mike Savage, 'Urban politics and the rise of the Labour Party, 1919–39', in Lynn Jamieson and Helen Corr (eds), *State, Private Life and Political Change* (Basingstoke, 1990), pp. 204–23 at pp. 209–11; Duncan Tanner, 'Gender, civic culture and politics in South Wales: explaining Labour's municipal policy, 1918–39', in Matthew Worley (ed.), *Labour's Grassroots: Essays on the Activities and Experiences of Local Labour Parties and Members, 1918–1945* (Aldershot, 2005), pp. 170–93.
7 Daunton, *Trusting Leviathan*, p. 300.
8 Amongst the most successful of these ventures were in Chippenham in Wiltshire and Banbury in Oxfordshire, where localised editions of *Popular View* achieved

circulations of 5,000 and 11,500 respectively. *Conservative Agent's Journal*, April 1925, pp. 84–5; *Popular View in North Oxfordshire*, April 1926, p. 15.

9   McKibbin, 'Class and Conventional Wisdom', pp. 267–9, 273, 285, 292–3.

10   For the varied cultures of local Conservatism between the wars see Geraint Thomas, 'Conservatives and the culture of "national" government between the wars' (PhD dissertation, University of Cambridge, 2010); James K. Dearling, 'The language of Conservatism in Lancashire between the wars: a study of Ashton-under-Lyme, Chorley, Clitheroe, Royton and South Salford' (PhD dissertation, University of Manchester, 2002); Bates, 'Conservative Party in the constituencies'.

11   Colin Seymour-Ure, 'The press and the party system', in Gillian Peele and Chris Cook (eds), *The Politics of Reappraisal, 1918–1939* (London, 1975), pp. 232–57 at p. 237.

12   For Northcliffe and Rothermere see biographical appendix.

13   Sir Harry Brittain, 'Middle classes mobilise!', *Review of Reviews*, 59, May 1919, pp. 316–17.

14   *Sunday Pictorial*, 17 August 1919 and 7 December 1919, cited in Cowling, *Impact of Labour*, p. 50.

15   *New Voice*, 15 May 1920, p. 15.

16   *Glasgow Herald*, 23 October 1919 cited in Smyth, 'Resisting Labour', p. 380; for the reactionary nature of MCU rhetoric see also Leo Maxse's speech to a Brighton meeting in *Southern Weekly News (Brighton)*, 30 April 1921, p. 7.

17   *The Times*, 14 August 1920, pp. 6, 11; 16 August 1920, p. 11.

18   Kenneth Morgan, *Consensus and Disunity: The Lloyd George Coalition Government, 1918–1922* (Oxford, 1979), pp. 62–71, 137.

19   H.A. Clegg, *A History of British Trade Unions since 1889. Vol. 2: 1911–33* (Oxford, 1985), p. 570.

20   *New Voice*, November 1920, p. 3.

21   James Peters, 'Anti-socialism in British politics, c. 1900–22' (D. Phil dissertation, University of Oxford, 1992), p. 312.

22   City of Westminster Archives, London, Westminster Conservative Association MSS, CON487, H.A. Collins report, 21 April 1920; Bonar Law MSS, BL99/3/24, George Younger to Andrew Bonar Law, 19 March 1920.

23   *Berkshire Chronicle (Reading)*, 28 October 1921, p. 10; *Reading Standard*, 29 October 1921, p. 5.

24   *Southern Weekly News (Brighton)*, 5 November 1921, p. 7, Braybon comfortably won the Queen's Park ward as an independent, although he also stated that he was a member of the MCU.

25   Ibid.

26   Harmsworth was MP for the Isle of Thanet, Kent. T.A. Polson was elected as an independent MP for Dover in January 1921, and joined the AWL when it was formed shortly afterwards. The AWL achieved subsequent by-election victories in Hertford and St George's, Westminster, and supported a series of independent Conservative candidates in the south-east during the 1922 general election.

27   John Shepherd, *George Lansbury: At the Heart of Old Labour* (Oxford, 2002), pp. 189, 194.

28   *New Voice*, 16 August 1920, p. 9.

29   *Ratepayer*, January 1922, p. 105; for the role that attacks on 'Poplar' finance played in the campaign see also *The Times*, 16 February 1922, p. 7, 27 February 1922,

p. 7; *Daily Mail*, 20 February 1922, p. 14, 24 February 1922, p. 6; *Morning Post*, 22 February 1922, p. 5; *Woolwich Herald*, 17 February 1922, p. 2.

30 Wiltshire and Swindon History Centre, Chippenham, Devizes Conservative Association MSS, 2305/48, *Wiltshire, Berkshire and Hampshire County Paper*, 22 February 1924, *Wiltshire Gazette*, 28 February 1924, 6 March 1924, cuttings in Percy Hurd scrapbook; see also *Popular View in North Oxfordshire*, May 1924, p. 3, June 1924, p. 3.

31 West Sussex Record Office, Chichester, Chichester Women's Unionist Association MSS, Add.12090, Executive Committee minutes, 21 October 1920.

32 For interpretations of the anti-waste cause which have portrayed it as broadly representative of the Conservative grassroots in general see McKibbin, 'Class and conventional wisdom', p. 268; Green, *Ideologies of Conservatism*, pp. 122–5.

33 Cecil MSS, fols 85–6, Lord Salisbury to Robert Cecil, 6 May 1921.

34 Cecil MSS, fols 92–7, Robert Cecil to Lord Salisbury, 18 May 1921.

35 McKibbin, 'Class and conventional wisdom', p. 267; Jarvis, 'British Conservatism and class politics in the 1920s', pp. 63, 73–5, 80; McCrillis, *British Conservative Party in the Age of Universal Suffrage*, pp. 47, 76–8, 95.

36 *Home and Politics*, June 1923, p. 8.

37 *Conservative Agent's Journal*, January 1921, p. 13; *Home and Politics*, February 1922, p. 14.

38 *Home and Politics*, June 1923, p. 8.

39 E.J. Forster, 'The middle classes and Conservative organisation', *Conservative Agent's Journal*, October 1923, p. 199; for Birmingham leaders' complaints about the apathy of 'known' middle-class Conservatives see BCUA MSS, Executive Committee minutes, 18 October 1923, 7 January 1924, 14 November 1924.

40 For the idea that the 'party ticket' was holding men back from standing for municipal office see *Manchester Guardian*, 26 October 1921, p. 3.

41 Dearling, 'Language of Conservatism in Lancashire', pp. 110–12.

42 The literature on Labour's responses to anti-socialism in inter-war Britain has largely focused on politics at a national level, to date. See Beers, *Your Britain*; Lawrence, 'Labour and the politics of class'.

43 For the moderate strategies of Labour in Lancashire politics see *Northern Daily Telegraph (Blackburn)*, 29 October 1919, p. 3; Dearling, 'Language of Conservatism in Lancashire', p. 175; Savage, *Labour Movement in Preston*, pp. 36–63, 134–87 ; for Wales see Duncan Tanner, 'The pattern of Labour politics, 1918–1939', in Duncan Tanner, Chris Williams and Deian Hopkin (eds), *The Labour Party in Wales, 1900–2000* (Cardiff, 2000), pp.113–39 at pp.117–24; Elizabeth Andrews, Labour's woman organiser in Wales, focused much of her attention on campaigning for improved municipal amenities. See her articles for the *Colliery Workers' Magazine* republished in Andrews, *A Woman's Work is Never Done*, pp. 71, 76–9; After the 1922 LCC elections Herbert Morrison sought to rebuild the support base of the London Labour Party, arguing that it could only take control of municipal government in the capital by winning middle-class support through moderate reforms. See *Labour Organiser*, October 1923, pp. 16–19; *London Labour Chronicle*, August 1922, p. 1; February 1923, pp. 1, 8; May 1923, pp. 1–2.

44 Raymond Dalton, 'Labour and the municipality: Labour politics in Leeds, 1900–1914' (PhD dissertation, University of Huddersfield, 2000), pp. 97–8, 154–6; Tanner, *Political Change and the Labour Party*, pp. 259–60.

45 *Leeds Weekly Citizen*, 14 October 1921, p. 2; 21 October 1921, p. 2; 19 May 1922, p. 2.

46 Ibid., 18 February 1921, p. 3.

47 *Leeds Weekly Citizen*, 28 January 1921, p. 3.

48 Ibid., 19 May 1922, p. 2.

49 Amery MSS, AMEL4/10, Leo Amery to Andrew Bonar Law, 22 October 1922.

50 CPA, microfiche 0.396.220, pamphlet 1922/74, 'Bonar Law and Sound Government. Vote Unionist' (1922); for other contemporaneous examples of claims that Labour's programme made it unelectable see *Popular View*, November 1922, p. 20; *Marylebone Mercury*, 28 October 1922, p. 4; *Southern Weekly News (Brighton)*, 4 November 1922, p. 9, 11 November 1922, p. 9.

51 CPA, microfiche 0.396.211, pamphlet 1921/16, 'A "Labour" government? What it would do and how it would do it' (1921).

52 *Wakefield Express*, 11 November 1922, p. 12.

53 *Yorkshire Post*, 9 November 1922, p. 11; *Wakefield Express*, 11 November 1922, p. 13.

54 *Yorkshire Post*, 4 March 1922, p. 8.

55 The Conservatives were aided by the professional and business vote accounting for up to 20 per cent of the Leeds Central electorate, but winning over industrial workers was seen as a determining factor in contests within this constituency, see *The Times*, 26 July 1923, p. 12.

56 *Yorkshire Post*, 14 July 1923, p. 10; 20 July 1923, p. 10; 27 July 1923, p. 9.

57 Sam Davies and Bob Morley, *County Borough Elections in England and Wales, 1919–1938: A Comparative Analysis* (Aldershot, 3 vols, 1999–2006), vol. 1, pp. 11–16 and vol. 2, p. 24; The Conservatives' appeal in Bradford also built on their attacks on the 'prodigal spending' of the Labour administration in the town, which had won a majority in the council elections of 1919. See for example, *Yorkshire Post*, 1 November 1921, p. 5; *Bradford Daily Argus*, 1 November 1922, p. 8.

58 *Berrow's Worcester Journal*, 21 May 1921, p. 3.

59 The Conservative poll in these thirteen wards increased from 33,992 votes to 35,077, Labour's poll grew from 20,837 to 35,899 between 1920 and 1921. BCUA MSS, Executive Committee minutes, 21 November 1921.

60 Birmingham University Library, Neville Chamberlain MSS, NC5/10/23, Patrick Hannon to Neville Chamberlain, 1 November 1924.

61 Cited in John Boughton, 'Working class politics in Birmingham and Sheffield, 1918–1931' (PhD dissertation, University of Warwick, 1985), p. 121.

62 *Straight Forward (Birmingham)*, June 1921, p. 6; for Neville Chamberlain's belief that anti-waste had a limited electoral appeal in the West Midlands see Neville Chamberlain to Hilda Chamberlain, 15 January 1921, 16 July 1921 in Self (ed.), *Neville Chamberlain Diary Letters*, vol. 2, pp. 37, 72.

63 Amery MSS, AMEL4/9, *Notes for Unionist Workers and Speakers [Sparkbrook]*, n.d. [1921].

64 Ibid.

65 See for example *Straight Forward (Birmingham)*, September 1920, p. 4; August 1921, p. 7; October 1921, p. 4; see also *Birmingham Mail*, 16 April 1921, p. 4.

66 *Straight Forward (Birmingham)*, October 1922, p. 2; Neville Chamberlain, MP for Ladywood, had told his sister in March 1922 that 'to go to the country purely on economy and anti-Socialism seems bad tactics to me', Neville Chamberlain to Hilda Chamberlain, 26 March 1922, in Self (ed.,) *Neville Chamberlain Diary Letters*, vol. 2, p. 104.

67 For Smedley-Crooke see biographical appendix.
68 Hannon MSS, HNN138/2, Patrick Hannon, 'Notes for memoirs', n.d. [c. 1959]; for the difficulties of gaining subscriptions in this deprived constituency see BCUA MSS, Management Committee minutes, 12 March 1926.
69 Amongst other events, Smedley-Crooke organised large-scale children's Christmas parties and outings. See BCUA MSS, John Smedley Crooke report to meeting of management committee, 12 March 1926.
70 *The Times*, 21 May 1921, p. 8; *Comrades Journal*, March 1921, pp. 2–3; April 1921, p. 12.
71 Boughton, 'Working class politics in Birmingham and Sheffield', pp. 418–19.
72 BCUA MSS, Councillor Thomas Bishop supplementary verbal report to meeting of management committee, 12 March 1926.
73 Neville Chamberlain to Ida Chamberlain, 7 January 1922, in Self (ed.), *Neville Chamberlain Diary Letters*, vol. 2, pp. 89–90.
74 For the work of the institute see Birmingham Central Library, Digbeth Institute MSS, CC2.
75 BCUA MSS, Chief Agent's report, meeting of management committee, 14 January 1927.
76 Boughton, 'Working class politics in Birmingham and Sheffield', pp. 159, 415.
77 Ibid., p. 159 .
78 BCUA MSS, Executive Committee minutes, 14 October 1927.
79 Arthur Steel-Maitland to Gradwell [his election agent], 3 February 1922, Steel-Maitland MSS, GD193/95/3, cited in Boughton, 'Working class politics in Birmingham and Sheffield', p. 415.
80 Houston and Valdar, *Modern Electioneering Practice*, p. 148.
81 *Conservative Agent's Journal*, August 1920, p. 15; March 1924, p. 45.
82 *Conservative Agent's Journal*, August 1929, p. 128; Ramsden provides numerous examples of prominent Conservative MPs who acted as the main source of funds for their constituency associations, see his *Age of Balfour and Baldwin*, pp. 245–7.
83 Ramsden, *Age of Balfour and Baldwin*, p. 248.

10

Baldwin's party?

In June 1923 *Home and Politics* published an article based on a recent speech given by Stanley Baldwin at a Conservative women's meeting. Seeking to explain the potentially rather arid issue of why the sugar duty had not been reduced, Baldwin observed that: 'every woman is a Chancellor of the Exchequer in her own right as housewife. I am, as Chancellor of the Exchequer, the housewife of the nation. Women can realise my task if they imagine themselves living in a house which is mortgaged to the hilt. I have many clients for my favours.'[1] Within a fortnight Baldwin had replaced the chronically ill Andrew Bonar Law as Conservative Party leader and prime minister. Whereas Bonar Law had received little attention in popular party magazines such as *Popular View* and *Home and Politics*, Baldwin and his wife appeared regularly in such publications, often employing the populist style which had been a feature of the appeal to women as the 'domestic chancellors of the exchequer'.[2]

Party literature portrayed Baldwin as the personification of constructive Conservative leadership, placing the cause of nation above party or class interest.[3] When the 1923 election resulted in no parliamentary majority for any one party, *Popular View* depicted Asquith, the Liberal Party leader, as having to choose to back either Ramsay MacDonald, supported by a rabble carrying the banner of the 'Socialistische Arbeiter Internationale', or a pipe-smoking Baldwin, who represented the interests of the home and family.[4]

Thereafter, Baldwin became an increasingly iconic figure, perhaps more so than any political leader since Gladstone, featuring prominently in Conservative Party posters and pioneering the use of newsreel and radio to address an audience of millions.[5]

It should come as no surprise, therefore, to learn that Stanley Baldwin's leadership is generally portrayed as being integral to the Conservative Party's success between the wars, unifying the disparate factions within the party and creating a Conservative middle ground. Baldwin promoted an anti-socialist politics which identified the party with constitutionalism, moderate social reform and the national interest.[6] For Philip Williamson, Baldwin's accession to the party leadership in 1923 was a vital turning point, enabling the Conservatives to distance themselves from the reactionary image which had been created by the anti-waste agitation.[7] In this reading, the party's resounding election victory in 1924, and subsequent dominance of British politics, owed much to Baldwin's moderate and progressive

Figure 10.1: Front cover of *Popular View*, January 1924

approach, which appealed to much of the working class and many erstwhile Liberal voters.[8]

The discourse of 'Baldwinite Conservatism' offered a brand of constructive anti-socialism which had a significantly wider appeal than the Edwardian tariff reform campaign or the press-led anti-waste agitation of the early 1920s. Nonetheless, the symbiotic relationship between the party's national leadership and grassroots organisations has been underestimated. True, Williamson rightly stresses the role that grassroots activists played in promoting the discourse of 'Baldwinite Conservatism'.[9] But their creative agency should also be emphasised. Before Baldwin became party leader in 1923, organisations like Annie Chamberlain's Unionist Women's Institutes were already promoting a brand of Conservative activism which attempted to inculcate values of good citizenship, to break down traditional class barriers and to promote a positive appeal. Baldwin's rhetoric was effectively mediated and disseminated through conversations with groups like the Women's Unionist Organisation.

★

During the 1922 election Bonar Law's 'Tranquillity' strategy focused on associating Labour with reckless schemes of tax appropriation and public spending, based on class interests.[10] But whilst Bonar Law was returned with a parliamentary majority, the most salient feature of the contest was the dramatic rise in Labour's share of the popular vote and representation at Westminster. By contrast, the Conservative vote remained relatively static.

Table 10.1 *General election results, 1918 and 1922*

	1918	1922
Conservative MPs	358	345
Share of vote (%)	36	38.2
Labour MPs	63	142
Share of vote (%)	22.2	29.5
Liberal MPs	161	116
Share of vote (%)	25.6	29.1

Figures from David Butler and Gareth Butler, *British Political Facts, 1900–1994* (Basingstoke, 7th edition, 1994), pp. 214–15.

Given the problems which the Conservatives had faced at the 1922 election, Baldwin's decision to come out in support of tariff reform a few months after becoming party leader in 1923 seems a less surprising decision than has sometimes been implied.[11]

Tariff reform had played a key role in rejuvenating Unionism as a popular movement in the 1900s, it was subsequently an obvious policy to adopt for a leader who wished to reorientate the Conservative Party by offering it a positive programme. At this time, Leo Amery, a long-standing supporter of tariff reform, felt that a 'positive policy' was needed to stall Labour's growth otherwise the Conservatives risked becoming 'a mere vested interests anti-Socialist little Englander party'.[12] In his lectures at the party's Philip Stott College in autumn 1923, which were subsequently published as *Imperial and National Economics*, Amery voiced his fear that Conservatism risked falling into 'a mere negative opposition to Socialism, identifying ourselves more and more in the process with class interests and laisser-faire theory'.[13] For Amery, Baldwin's decision to go to the country on the issue of tariff reform was a godsend.

The party's advocacy of tariff reform at the December 1923 election greatly aided Conservatives in the old heartlands of tariff reform, resulting in a clean sweep for the party in Birmingham. The protectionist cause also made inroads in some regions of chronic unemployment. In Stockton, County Durham, the young Conservative candidate, Harold Macmillan, felt that tariff reform provided a boon to his campaign as protectionist claims that British industry was being undercut by foreign 'dumpers' resonated with his many out-of-work constituents.[14] But in 1923 tariff reform was ultimately unable to offer Conservatives a programmatic politics which could unite the party across the country. Baldwin's campaign failed to overcome existing hostility to protection in the heartlands of free trade. This was most notably the case in Lancashire, where the Conservatives suffered numerous losses and managed to win only a single seat in Manchester and Salford. Several candidates stood as Conservative free traders in the county, defying the national leadership and reopening the wounds of the Edwardian period. Liberals were able to achieve a slew of victories by using the old 'your bread will cost you more' cries, which were widely seen as having a particularly emotive appeal for the new women voters.[15] Ultimately both tranquillity and tariff reform proved unattractive to much of the Conservative Party. Leaders' attempts to develop a national appeal had only served to exacerbate regional tensions.

And yet, the Conservatives made a significant recovery over the following year under Baldwin's leadership, after protection had been dropped from the party programme. In fact, the October 1924 election was comfortably the most successful that the Conservatives fought between the Armistice and the economic nadir which followed the Wall Street Crash. This triumph relied on the ineffectuality and divisions of the Liberal opposition and the Conservative Party's ability to shape a wide-ranging anti-socialist politics compatible with a variety of local Conservatisms.

Table 10.2 *Conservative Party performance at general elections, 1918–29*

Election	Conservative seats	Share of vote (%)
December 1918	358	36
November 1922	345	38.2
December 1923	258	38.1
October 1924	419	48.3
May 1929	260	38.2

Figures from Butler and Butler, *British Political Facts, 1900–1994*, pp. 214–15.

During the 1924 campaign the Conservatives and Liberals took pains to allege that the minority Labour government had pandered to Communist influences. The *Unionist Canvassers' Handbook* produced for the election began by addressing the 'Campbell case' which had brought down MacDonald's administration. It was alleged that Labour backbenchers had put pressure on the attorney-general to withdraw a prosecution against John Campbell, editor of the Communist *Workers Weekly*, who had published an article encouraging soldiers to engage in sedition and treason. The longest section of the handbook focused on Labour's Russian treaty, which provided the Soviet government with a loan and abandoned British subjects' claims to compensation of property which they had lost in the revolution.[16] It is this background which explains why the Zinoviev Letter stunt provoked widespread controversy. Three days before the election the *Daily Mail* had published a letter allegedly sent from Zinoviev, the leader of Comintern, to Arthur McManus, of the Communist Party of Great Britain, encouraging British Communists to intensify their agitation. The Zinoviev Letter, which was a forgery, acted as the denouement of the Conservatives' campaign to stress the links between Labour and Socialist extremism.

Tory activists in south-east England, where 'Poplarism' and anti-waste had recently provided the Conservatives with electoral trump cards, unsurprisingly made much of the apparent increase in the assertiveness of extreme socialist forces, as signalled by the Campbell case. In his election address, Major Astor, the Conservative candidate for Dover, claimed that Labour 'has placed Russian Bolshevists before our own Dominions'. Meanwhile, in South Islington T.F. Howard suggested that the Labour rowdyism which had apparently been a feature of the campaign was the harbinger of more sinister forces. Howard went as far as placing details of the worst cases of Labour supporters' electoral violence in the windows of his election headquarters, coupled with the claim that 'a British electorate will not countenance Russian methods of suppression'.[17]

The alleged iniquities perpetrated by the MacDonald government also enabled Conservatives in other regions to sidestep the moderate identity of local Labour movements and attack socialism in more belligerent terms than usual. In Birmingham Amery focused on the supposed extremist influence behind the Labour administration: 'They will never stand up to Communist or Bolshevik pressure...A Socialist Government is a Government under Bolshevik influence'. The Russian loan was dismissed as a reckless gamble with taxpayers' money: 'Was greater folly ever conceived of outside of an asylum?'[18] In nearby Walsall, Conservatives suggested that the Zinoviev Letter demonstrated that Labour was backed by foreigners and lacking in patriotism.[19]

But Conservatives did not rely solely on anti-socialist scaremongering; under Baldwin's leadership they also took care to stress their plans for progressive social reforms. In 1924 the party was able to blend positive and negative anti-socialisms and national and local appeals more successfully than at any election during that decade. In particular, Conservatives championed the 1923 Housing Act introduced by Neville Chamberlain, and their support for continued rent restrictions. This appeal was promoted with vigour in Birmingham, where the Conservatives' success at recent municipal elections was seen as being largely reliant on their commitment to house building.[20] Chamberlain encouraged voters to support Conservative house-building plans because they facilitated owner-occupation and placed less pressure on local authorities for funding than the Labour Housing Act introduced by John Wheatley in 1924. It was claimed that the cost to the taxpayer of houses built under the Conservatives' 1923 Act would be £75 cash value, as opposed to £160 under the Wheatley scheme.[21] The Conservatives' Rent Restrictions Act was also promoted as a measure to protect tenants from unscrupulous landlords who would otherwise be free to charge any rent they wished.[22] Chamberlain's housing scheme authorised the building of 160,000 houses in a year and was presented nationally as the centrepiece in the Conservatives' commitment to progressive social reform. Aside from housing, the Conservatives also promised a commission on food prices, committed themselves to widows' pensions and a rise in old age pensions.

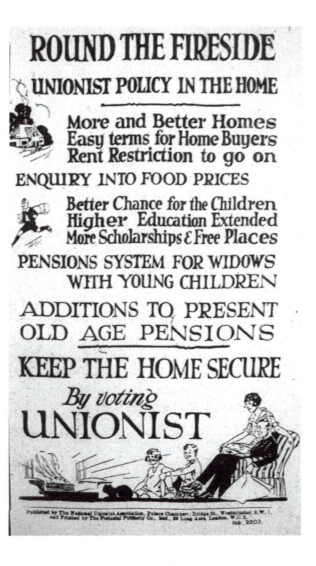

Figure 10.2: 'Round the fireside', Conservative Party leaflet, 1924 general election

★

In 1924 the Conservatives were greatly aided by the ineffectual campaigning of their Liberal rivals, who were subsequently reduced to a rump of forty MPs. Conservatives presented the Liberals as an obstacle to progressive government during the election.[23] Whilst Baldwin's support for tariff reform at the 1923 election had lost the Conservatives their majority, it did at least demonstrate that the party was keen to find a radical solution to the ongoing unemployment problem. Labour, whilst committed to free trade, was convinced that relying on the mantra of the cheap white loaf, famously celebrated by Edwardian Liberals, would no longer be adequate. Labour organisations had shaped a new politics of the consumer during the First World War, focused on developing state food controls to make nutritious food accessible to all.[24] In addition, in 1923 its candidates tended to focus as much on the wider issues of unemployment and housing as on the defence of free trade.[25]

Although the recently reunited Liberal Party won 158 seats at the 1923 election, theirs was a Pyrrhic victory. Tensions continued to exist between the Asquith and Lloyd George wings of the party, which meant that the Liberals lacked an effective and coherent strategy. In particular, the parliamentary party had a muddled relationship with the minority Labour government, formed in January 1924, which depended on Liberal support. Liberals voted three ways in the 'Poplar' debate on poor law relief and on the Labour proposal to discontinue support for the Singapore naval base. Morale was further damaged by the failure of the Liberals' proposed Electoral Reform Bill, which would have secured a measure of proportional representation, aiding the electoral position of the party.[26] From spring 1924 onwards Lloyd George urged his colleagues to oppose a number of government bills, and became a particularly keen critic of Labour unemployment policies. However, his line was opposed by Asquith and the bulk of the parliamentary party.[27] These continued tensions hampered organisational efficiency; Lloyd George refused to provide the Liberal Party with major funding until late on during the 1924 election campaign, which meant it was only able to field 343 candidates in this contest.[28]

Hamstrung by these continuing divisions, the Liberal Party lacked an effective programme at the 1924 election which could compete with the proposals offered by Labour and the Conservatives. Rather than adapt their appeals to the new post-war employment conditions, as their opponents had, Liberals tended to trot out familiar pre-war slogans. For instance, in Sparkbrook, Birmingham, the Liberal candidate, Finnemore, produced a leaflet with echoes of the 1906 election, proclaiming: 'Women voters! Your hands hold the key of the cupboard. Will you welcome food taxers? Will you let them loot your larder?'[29] By the early 1920s, the Liberal Party had lost much of the reforming impetus which had fuelled Edwardian New

Liberalism. Admittedly, the party's 1924 election manifesto offered some progressive reforms, such as slum clearance and reform of the leasehold system to aid owner-occupation.[30] Nonetheless, in areas where the party had continuous success in the immediate post-war years, such as rural Wales, south-west England and parts of East Anglia, Liberalism relied on Gladstonian issues like the defence of Nonconformity, orthodox free trade, temperance and security for tenant farmers.[31]

The flaws in the Liberals' reliance on traditional cries are demonstrated by the parties' comparative performance at the 1923 and 1924 elections in Norfolk. In 1923 the Liberal *Eastern Daily Press* had stressed that tariff reform would be inimical to agricultural workers' interests as it would mean farmers paying higher prices for their machinery, without getting any protection for their produce.[32] But the Liberals, in advocating free trade, could not offer a solution to unemployment levels, which remained stubbornly over one million and increasingly appeared to be systemic rather than a cyclical phenomenon in line with pre-war trends.

Table 10.3 *Parliamentary seats won at Norfolk elections, 1922–24*

Year	Conservative	Liberal	Labour
1922	4	3	1
1923	1	3	4
1924	6	1	1

The claim of the Norwich Liberal candidate, Copeman, that free trade had raised Britain 'to the highest pitch of prosperity in trade and commerce' must have had a hollow ring for many a voter suffering from the effects of the economic slump.[33] The Liberals' rivals in Norfolk offered constructive policies which went beyond the free trade and tariff reform debate. Labour focused on strengthening its support amongst agricultural trade unionists by calling for a restoration of the Corn Production Act of 1920, which continued the guaranteed price regime for food producers introduced during the war. Noel Buxton, a former Liberal MP appointed minister of agriculture in 1924, led Norfolk Labour demands for a 30s. minimum wage for agricultural workers and a rural house-building programme.[34]

Norfolk Conservatives developed a progressive politics, which had similarities with the anti-socialist politics nurtured by urban Tories in areas like Leeds and Birmingham. It must be conceded that there was a negative element to the Conservatives' agricultural policy in 1924. Tories protested at Labour's plans to introduce a central board for agricultural workers' wages, claiming that it neglected local conditions and might increase rural unemployment.[35] All the same, Norfolk Conservatives also focused on reforms such as the Chamberlain Housing Act, rent restrictions and the Workmen's Compensation Act.[36] By contrast, the Norfolk Liberal campaign essentially relied on electors' fear of Labour's capital levy and the Conservatives' advocacy of tariff reform.[37]

Although the Liberals won three Norfolk seats in 1923, the party's narrow focus on protecting the current fiscal order became problematic when their rivals dropped the controversial issues of tariff reform and the capital levy at the next year's election. As elsewhere, the Conservatives made dramatic breakthroughs in the county at the 1924 election by coupling a progressive programme with attacks on the Liberals' decision to vote in a socialist administration.[38] In Norwich, Fairfax portrayed the Conservatives as the true friends of the consumer: 'In spite of Mr. Snowden's free breakfast table, the ordinary housekeeping bill did not appear to be going down'. He supported Baldwin's call for a commission to investigate high food prices. Fairfax also attacked Snowden's reluctance to give £20 million to fund widows' pensions whilst lending £40 million to the 'bankrupt Bolsheviks'.[39]

The Liberals were left in a double bind in 1924, attacking the socialist policies of the Labour government which they had let in, whilst trying to portray Baldwin's party as reactionaries. Just as in Norfolk, the Liberal Party in south-west England made several breakthroughs in 1923, aided by fear of higher prices under tariff reform at a time of agricultural depression, before experiencing a series of setbacks the following year due to its failure to develop a distinct identity and a positive programme.[40] Even when Lloyd George adopted radical public works schemes to deal with unemployment at the 1929 election, activists in traditional Liberal heartlands like Devon and Cornwall tended to focus on the old creed of free trade and retrenchment.[41]

Ultimately, the Liberals' malaise resulted from its failure to build on the legacy of New Liberalism, which had enabled the party to flourish during the 1900s, and their retreat back into trusted Victorian slogans. In consequence, they struggled to find adequate solutions to the problems of post-1918 society.[42] In the mid-1920s the Conservatives, who had built on the traditions of Liberal Unionism through the work of the Edwardian popular leagues, and Labour, which had been able to recruit many Liberals after 1914, arguably appeared the most credible successors to the progressive administration which Asquith had overseen.[43]

The Liberals' problems did not simply relate to the difficulties they faced in developing new policies which could appeal to the wider, post-war electorate, they also struggled to adapt to the changing cultural environment of politics. This meant that the Conservatives rapidly became the dominant anti-socialist force in British politics. The Liberal Party's decline as a viable challenger to the Conservatives' status as the leading anti-socialist party was hastened most noticeably by its growing difficulties in harnessing the Nonconformist vote. In 1929 the *Church Times* claimed that 'until the war, probably eighty percent of Nonconformists voted Liberal, and the Liberal *debacle* of 1924 is to be directly traced to the secession of the Nonconformists, for a variety of reasons, to Labour and the Conservatives'.[44] Barry Doyle's study of Norwich elites has suggested that after 1918 younger generations identified less than their elders did with the chapel-based social culture which had sustained the Liberal Party in the town.[45] The First World War created new opportunities for socialising which went beyond denominational lines, and it may be supposed that the concurrent rise of secular, non-party organisations further challenged the position of Nonconformity in associational life. The Women's Institutes were one such organisation which sought to erode traditional divides between church and chapelgoers, often becoming the main social centre for women in villages.[46]

Nonconformity had been vital to the success of the pre-war Liberal Party. Opposition to the Unionists' 1902 Education Act and the campaigns for Welsh disestablishment and Irish home rule galvanised radical Nonconformity in Edwardian Britain. Around two hundred churchmen sat on the Liberal benches in the 1906 parliament.[47] Nonetheless, many of the issues which had rallied the Nonconformist conscience carried little weight in politics after the First World War. Irish home rule and Welsh disestablishment were enacted in 1921, and religious issues ceased to have their former influence on policies towards schooling following the 1918 Education Act. Furthermore, the Labour Party could assert that it represented the Nonconformist interest, with forty-five free churchmen sitting on their benches following the 1924 general election.[48] The Conservative Party, under Baldwin's leadership, also staked a claim to represent Nonconformity, with key figures in his cabinets such as William Joynson-Hicks and the Chamberlains enjoying good relations with the free churches.[49] Baldwin's personal appeal to Nonconformists was further strengthened during the 1930s when he emphasised the Christian roots of Britain's identity, which were diametrically opposed to the values promoted by totalitarian dictators on the continent.[50]

Non-party associations grew to play an increasingly prominent role in Britain's associational life during the First World War when a number of voluntary organisations supplemented the state's efforts to mobilise manpower and resources, playing a vital role, for example, in fundraising, army recruitment and the administering of pensions claims.[51] After the war a number of recently formed voluntary organisations such as the WIs and British Legion continued to play an important role in British civic life. It is clear that the Conservatives were markedly more effective in developing an appeal to these non-party interests than their Liberal rivals. Since the First World War Conservatives such as Mary Maxse and the Duchess of Atholl had valued non-party movements because they appeared to offer a means to break down the traditional social barriers which had inhibited the party's growth in industrial areas before 1914. As we have seen, Conservative activists developed strong bonds with non-party cultures during the early 1920s. Annie Chamberlain's social clubs imitated the organisation of the WIs, and Conservatives celebrated the creation of the British Legion which, they claimed, had removed party politics from the question of ex-servicemen's welfare.[52] Conservative constituency associations appear to have made great use of speakers and literature from non-party organisations, as these services were often available at a nominal cost. A National Union of Conservative Associations handbook produced in 1925 noted that propaganda literature 'is offered free by non-party organisations to such an extent that the [Conservative] Central Office is frequently expected to forgo its charges' for pamphlets, leaflets and other publications'.[53]

All the same, Ross McKibbin's claim that Conservatives informally colonised non-party associational life and turned these organisations into 'secondary agents of Toryism' is problematic.[54] Each of the main political parties, not least the Conservatives, expressed some wariness regarding the activities of non-party movements.[55] Even into the 1930s Conservatives expressed fears that rival parties would come to dominate decision-making in the local bodies of organisations like the WIs unless their supporters made an effort to attend meetings.[56] After the First World War, all parties understood that their meetings needed a strong social and ostensibly apolitical element if they were to attract large numbers of new voters, especially women. The Conservatives may ultimately have been most successful in developing a 'non-political' appeal but they were certainly not acting in isolation. Nor was there anything particularly novel about the appeal of such cultures in inter-war Britain. The rapid growth of the Primrose League and Women's Liberal Federation in the late-Victorian period owed much to their function as social centres, and this was especially true in rural areas, where these organisations' annual dance or summer fete was often the main social event of the year.[57]

Non-party organisations did not provide a cloak for Conservatives to infiltrate associational life, although in practice the party drew on many members with experience in such movements. Conservatives saw party and non-party associations as filling separate, albeit complementary spheres in Britain's associational culture. It remained common for party leaders to hold office in non-party organisations throughout the inter-war years and beyond.[58] When a resolution was submitted for discussion at the WIs conference in 1921, proposing that party officials should not be able to hold posts within the WIs, it caused outrage amongst Conservative women, who subsequently played a prominent role in defeating the motion.[59] After 1923, Stanley Baldwin cultivated an appeal which transcended party politics, with his regular addresses to non-party civic organisations and his claims to put country before party. But this should not be seen as an innovation in Conservative leadership: rather, Baldwin was building on his supporters' existing attempts to cultivate close relations with non-party movements.

What seems puzzling is that the Liberal Party also sought to develop a similar non-political culture but with nothing like the success of their Conservative rivals. Admittedly, some of Liberal women's clubs, which resembled Annie Chamberlain's Unionist Women's Institutes, appear to have achieved impressive growth. In Penzance, isolated in south Cornwall, membership grew from 50 to 540 in four years. Weekly meetings usually began with a thirty-minute concert, there would be a sing-song or a dance, with a ten- to fifteen-minute talk on politics and obligatory cup of tea sandwiched in between. The High Wycombe Liberal Women's Club hit upon a similar winning formula, combining an informal discussion on current affairs with a sewing club and yet more afternoon tea.[60] But these were scattered achievements.

It may have been the case that, whereas Conservatives saw non-party associations as complementing their own work to develop political education and responsible citizenship, non-party activism may have proved a more attractive route for erstwhile Liberals than participation in its beleaguered party organisation. Certainly, the *Liberal Agent* suggested that recruiting new blood was a problem. One correspondent voiced his frustrations in early 1921: 'Do not our women's organizations in the main, still comprise a few enthusiastic women – not exactly young – but loyal and true workers, remnants of the pre-war era'.[61] This state of affairs should not come as much of a surprise given that Liberalism was a divided force. The League of Nations Union (LNU) was one non-party organisation which drew support from large numbers of Liberal activists, and erstwhile Liberals. This body tapped into the party's traditional Nonconformist support base, particularly in Wales, where strong links were forged with the free churches. LNU meetings in some regions began with prayer or took place on church premises.[62] Overall, free church congregations made up more than three-quarters of the LNU's corporate membership.[63] We may surmise that working within such an organisation, which had three hundred thousand members at its peak, offered a more appealing prospect than devoting one's service to the Liberal Party organisation.

Hopes of a Liberal revival were further hampered by changes in local political cultures, which in turn aided Baldwin's attempts to promote a 'constitutional' discourse which could unite the majority of the electorate against socialism. Most notably, the independent Liberal press declined between the wars, with the consolidation of rival Liberal and Conservative newspapers in many towns.[64] Likewise, Conservative–Liberal pacts became a common feature in inter-war local elections, usually with the Conservatives eventually emerging as the dominant partner. This was much to the frustration of a correspondent in the *Liberal Women's News*, who feared that the growth of municipal alliances was demoralising the party.[65] During the 1920s in many towns the Liberal Party gradually weakened as a distinct and independent force, enabling the Conservatives to present themselves as the only party that could provide a realistic alternative to a Labour government. Although Baldwin played an important role in aiding the Liberals' decline, he was also aided by the activities of grassroots activists who established new forms of organisation and developed links to wider associational cultures, thereby expanding the appeal of Conservative politics.

Baldwin's leadership was a product of the cultural transformation of popular Unionism which had begun in the Edwardian period. As a backbencher representing Bewdley, Worcestershire, before the war, he had been a member of the Tariff Reform League and held close relations with the Women's Unionist and Tariff Reform Association. A thriving women's organisation existed in Baldwin's Worcestershire constituency and played a vital role in distributing literature, registration work, campaigning in outlying villages and fundraising.[66] Many of Baldwin's preoccupations: nurturing non-party interests, combining anti-socialism with moderate social reform and developing a pluralistic programme which could appeal to a variety of new voters, and women in particular, built on the existing concerns of party activists. Yet at the same time the early years of Baldwin's leadership heralded a new era of Conservative politics, in which the authority of central office was strengthened and party appeals became more uniform.

When tariff reformers had sought to reform the culture of popular Unionism during the Edwardian period they were largely acting in defiance of Conservative Central Office, whose leadership they regarded as ineffectual. The 1911 Unionist reorganisation placed several of Joseph Chamberlain's supporters in prominent positions within the Conservative Party hierarchy. But auxiliary leagues acting outside the formal party structure continued to play a vital role in shaping the popular identity of Unionist politics, much to the frustration of some Conservative agents, who felt that they weakened the authority and finances of constituency party associations.[67] This changed after 1918 when auxiliary leagues were no longer able to spend unlimited sums at elections without contributing to the expenses of the candidate they supported.

Significantly, it was not until 1925 that the Empire Industries Association was formed to replace the defunct TRL. Yet Henry Page Croft, who led the new movement, set himself against forming a national branch network along the lines of the Edwardian tariff leagues. Both he and the former chairman of the TRL, Viscount Duncannon, thought this would be an inefficient and expensive form of organisation.[68] Page Croft instead focused on creating an effective press and publicity department.[69] In doing so, he was influenced by the growing professionalisation of political campaigning, which was increasingly being inspired by commercial marketing. In 1922 Houston and Valdar's election manual stressed that the political agent should act as a 'publicity expert': 'One such expert, with half a dozen assistants who know their job can win elections against a battalion of "earnest workers". Winning elections is really a matter of salesmanship, little different from marketing any branded article.'[70]

Conservative Central Office expanded its influence over the dissemination of the party's programme during the 1920s through the development of its lobby press service, which provided a steady stream of articles and notes that papers were free to localise. In June 1927 Conservative Central Office estimated that newspapers printed 353 leading articles, 535 notes and 35 special articles based on materials provided by the press service.[71] This practice of providing material from central office which could be adapted for local use was a feature of the party's magazines, which appeared in a profusion of local editions. [72] Yet this did not necessarily lead to any straightforward 'nationalisation' of Conservative campaigning. Whilst the Conservative Party hired the Benson's agency to coordinate a national poster campaign in 1929, local parties were still able to select the posters they wished to display.[73] By the mid-1920s central office's influence was beginning to be felt in some surprising areas. During the Edwardian period local activists had done much to shape the popular culture of tariff reform, creating political plays and holding pageants. Yet after the war head office in London was taking a lead in developing this feature of party propaganda. A series of 'Plays for Patriots' was developed to provide material for dramatic societies formed by local constituency associations. Central office also provided suggestions for pageants in connection with Empire Day celebrations and assisted in providing films for local meetings.[74]

Under the chairmanship of J.C.C. Davidson after 1926, the Conservative Party was restructured, with an increased emphasis on professionalisation. Cooperation between Conservative Central Office and the Women's Unionist Organisation increased markedly and a National Association of Conservative and Unionist Women's Organisers was set up in 1927.[75] Under Davidson's leadership, Conservative Central Office's efforts at promoting political education expanded too. An examination board for agents was set up and the activities of Stott College, which provided courses for Conservative workers, grew significantly. By 1927 it was training one thousand activists a year, and was eventually replaced in 1929 by a new, larger college at Ashridge.[76]

We should not exaggerate the centralisation of authority within the Conservative Party during the latter half of the 1920s. It was not until the 1930s that newsreel and radio, which Baldwin was the first major politician to master, came to play a decisive role in elections. In 1929 only a quarter of households held radio licences.[77] Furthermore, whilst Baldwin's leadership may have helped reconcile the different strands of Conservative anti-socialism which existed in the country in 1924, he struggled to present the party as a force for progressive government at the next election in 1929, frustrating many grassroots activists.[78] Nor were the regional divisions which had afflicted the Conservatives during the early 1920s, and beforehand, entirely overcome by the 1924 victory. Beaverbrook's Empire Crusade, a campaign for imperial preference which rocked the party in the early 1930s, relied on much the same south-east England populist base as the anti-waste agitation had done a decade earlier.[79] It was arguably only during the years of National Government after 1931 that the party was able to reconcile the competing interests of local and national Conservatisms.[80]

By the mid-1920s the Conservatives had established an ascendant position within British politics and seriously undermined the Liberals as a realistic party of government. This achievement had looked far from certain in 1918 when popular enthusiasm for party politics was at its nadir and the Conservatives were uncertain whether they could appeal to the new working-class voters whom they had struggled to enthuse in the Edwardian period. The Conservatives' success after the war could not be taken for granted and was reliant on actively constructing new appeals and reshaping the party's culture to meet the challenges of a new mass electorate. And yet 1918 was not a *tabula rasa*; rather the Conservatives built on the reforms that they had made since the 1900s. Activists' experiences of working in the Edwardian popular conservative leagues and wartime voluntary organisations meant that on the ground Conservative cultures were adaptable, able to develop localised appeals and to interact with wider associational cultures. Furthermore, the party's embrace of more sophisticated methods of targeted electioneering meant that it became less reliant on programmatic politics. By the mid-1920s the Conservatives were able to offer a variety of localised and gendered appeals, often responding to innovations in electioneering made by Labour. By contrast, the Liberals failed to modernise to the same degree and increasingly relied on their traditional core support in rural, Nonconformist Britain.

Notes

1 *Home and Politics*, June 1923, p. 3.
2 See for example *Home and Politics*, January 1922, p. 3; August 1923, p. 3; *Home and Empire*, March 1930, p. 3; May 1930, p. 3; December 1930, p. 3; August 1931, p. 5; December 1931, p. 3.
3 *Home and Politics*, December 1923, p. 8; January 1924, p. 4.

4 *Popular View*, January 1924, p. 1.
5 CPA, 'Safety First! Stanley Baldwin the man you can trust', 1929-09; 'Trust Baldwin. He will steer you to safety', 1929-32; 'I hear they want more Baldwin', 1929-33; 'The man for peace and security', 1935-09; 'Baldwin and prosperity for me', 1935-10; 'Stand by the National Government', 1935-25; for Baldwin's mastery of modern mass media see Nicholas, 'Construction of a national identity'; T.J. Hollins, 'The Conservative Party and film propaganda between the wars', *English Historical Review*, 96 (1981), pp. 359–69; John Ramsden, 'Baldwin and film', in Nicholas Pronay and D.W. Spring (eds), *Propaganda, Politics and Film, 1918–45* (London, 1982), pp. 126–43.
6 Williamson, *Stanley Baldwin*, pp. 32–3 , 150–1, 342–3; David Jarvis, 'Stanley Baldwin and the ideology of the Conservative response to socialism, 1918–1931' (PhD dissertation, University of Lancaster, 1991), p. 479; McKibbin, *Parties and People*, pp. 62–3; Bill Schwarz, 'The language of constitutionalism: Baldwinite Conservatism', in *Formations of Nation and People* (London, 1984), pp. 1–18.
7 Williamson, *Stanley Baldwin*, p. 206.
8 Ibid., p. 33.
9 Ibid., p. 153.
10 For examples of anti-socialist scaremongering during the election campaign see *Popular View*, November 1922, p. 20; *Marylebone Mercury*, 28 October 1922, p. 4; *Southern Weekly News (Brighton)*, 4 November 1922, p. 9; 11 November 1922, p. 9.
11 For the micro-politics of Baldwin's adoption of tariff reform in 1923 see Robert C. Self, 'Conservative reunion and the general election of 1923: A reassessment', *Twentieth Century British History*, 3:3 (1992), 249–73; Nick Smart, 'Debate. Baldwin's blunder? The general election of 1923', *Twentieth Century British History*, 7:1 (1996), 110–39 and the reply, Robert C. Self, 'Baldwin's blunder. A rejoinder to Smart on 1923', *Twentieth Century British History*, 7:1 (1996), 140–55.
12 Amery MSS, AMEL7/17, Leo Amery diary, 20 February 1923, 16 November 1923.
13 CPA, microfiche 0.396.225, L.S. Amery, *National and Imperial Economics* (1923/6); for Amery's aims for these lectures see Amery MSS, AMEL7/17, Leo Amery diary, 22 September 1923.
14 Harold Macmillian, *Winds of Change, 1914–1939* (London, 1966), p. 146.
15 Randolph S. Churchill, *Lord Derby: 'King of Lancashire'* (London, 1959), pp. 525–41; *Manchester Guardian*, 20 November 1923, p. 12; 7 December 1923, p. 8; *Blackpool Gazette*, 8 December 1923, p. 8.
16 CPA, microfiche 0.396.249, *Unionist Canvassers Handbook* (1924).
17 *The Times*, 27 October 1924, p. 7; for further Conservative claims that Labour was putting Russia's interests before Britain's see, for example, the election addresses of Ernest Taylor (Finsbury) and Charles Du Cann (Rotherhithe), Bristol University, National Liberal Club MSS, DM668, British election addresses, 1924, vol. 1.
18 Amery MSS, AMEL4/12, 'Vote for Amery!' Leo Amery election pamphlet (1924); Oliver Locker Lampson, the Conservative candidate in Handsworth, Birmingham, described the Russian loan as giving money to murderers. National Liberal Club MSS, DM668, British election addresses , 1924, vol. 1.
19 Dean, *Town and Westminster*, pp. 100–1.
20 *Birmingham Post*, 2 November 1922, p. 5; for the Unionist housing policy in Birmingham see *Straight Forward (Birmingham)*, October 1922, p. 2.

21 CPA, microfiche 0.396.249, Neville Chamberlain, *The Housing Question*, 1924/34; microfiche, 0.396.276, 'Two housing acts', 1924/237.

22 For Chamberlain's defence of rent restrictions see *The Times*, 29 October 1924, p. 7.

23 *Home and Politics*, December 1923, p. 8.

24 Trentmann, *Free Trade Nation*, pp. 193–213; see also Frank Trentmann, 'Bread, milk and democracy in modern Britain: consumption and citizenship in twentieth-century Britain', in Martin J. Daunton and Matthew Hilton (eds), *The Politics of Consumption: Material Culture and Citizenship in Britain and America* (Oxford, 2001), pp. 129–63.

25 Trentmann, *Free Trade Nation*, p. 223; Keith W.D. Rolf, 'Tories, tariffs and elections: The West Midlands in English politics, 1918–1935' (PhD dissertation, University of Cambridge, 1974), p. 202.

26 Paul Adelman, *The Decline of the Liberal Party, 1910–1931* (Harlow, 2nd edition, 1995), p. 47.

27 Ibid., p. 50.

28 Chris Wrigley, *Lloyd George* (Oxford, 1992), p. 127.

29 Amery MSS, AMEL4/11, Finnemore election handbill (1923).

30 For the manifesto see *Liberal Magazine*, November 1924, pp. 648–52.

31 Kenneth Morgan, 'The new Liberalism and the challenge of Labour: the Welsh experience, 1885–1929', *Welsh History Review*, 6 (1973), 288–312 at 290; Michael Dawson, 'Liberalism in Devon and Cornwall, 1910–1931: "the old time religion"', *Historical Journal*, 38:2 (1995), 425–37 at 425; Garry Tregidga, *The Liberal Party in South West Britain since 1918: Political Decline, Dormancy and Rebirth* (Exeter, 2000), pp. 46, 55; Doyle, 'Urban Liberalism and the "lost generation"', 617.

32 *Eastern Daily Press (Norwich)*, 8 November 1923, p. 4.

33 Ibid., 22 November 1923, p. 3.

34 *Eastern Daily Press (Norwich)*, 21 November 1923, p. 8; 27 November 1923, pp. 4, 8; for Norfolk Labour see Clare Griffiths, *Labour and the Countryside: The Politics of Rural Britain, 1918–1939* (Oxford, 2007), pp. 72, 326–7.

35 *Popular View in North Oxfordshire*, July 1924, p. 3; September 1924, p. 3.

36 *Eastern Daily Press (Norwich)*, 23 November 1923, p. 4.

37 Ibid., 6 December 1923, p. 4.

38 For this strategy at a national level see CPA, microfiche 0.396.274, 'Who put the Socialists in?' (1924/65).

39 *Eastern Daily Press (Norwich)*, 16 October 1924, p. 7.

40 Tregidga, *Liberal Party in South-West Britain*, pp. 34–7.

41 Dawson, 'Liberalism in Devon and Cornwall', 430.

42 The key examination of the influence of New Liberal ideas within the party's Edwardian culture is provided by Clarke, *Lancashire and the New Liberalism*, chs 7–15; For the post-war culture of Liberalism see in particular Michael Bentley, *The Liberal Mind, 1914–1929* (Cambridge, 1977); Michael Freeden, *Liberalism Divided: A Study in British Political Thought, 1914–1939* (Oxford, 1986).

43 Catherine Cline, *Recruits to Labour: The British Labour Party, 1914–1931* (Syracuse, NY, 1963).

44 *Church Times*, 24 May 1929 cited in Koss, *Nonconformity in British Politics*, p. 181.

45 Doyle, 'Urban Liberalism and the "lost generation"'.

46 For the WIs' initial successes in breaking down these social barriers see Alice Williams MSS, 7AHW/H/1, Alice Williams memorandum, 21 January 1919. Alice

Williams was the National Federation of Women's Institutes' secretary at this time.

47　Koss, *Nonconformity in British Politics*, p. 77.

48　Ibid., p. 174.

49　Ibid., p. 177.

50　See Philip Williamson, 'Christian Conservatives and the totalitarian challenge, 1933–40', *English Historical Review*, 115 (2000), 607–42.

51　Peter Grant, 'Voluntarism and the impact of the First World War', in Matthew Hilton and James McKay (eds), *The Ages of Voluntarism: How we Got to the Big Society* (Oxford, 2011), pp. 27–46.

52　See ch. 8.

53　National Union of Conservative Associations, *Handbook on Constituency Organisation* (London, 1925), p. 26; links between the Conservative Party and non-party organisations appear to have been consolidated further by the period of National Government after 1931, see Thomas, 'Conservatives and "national" government", pp. 145–9.

54　McKibbin, *Parties and People*, p. 94.

55　For examples of wariness towards non-party organisations expressed by activists from across the political spectrum see McCarthy, 'Parties, voluntary associations and democratic politics in interwar Britain', 901–7.

56　CPA, CCO170/2/1/1, National Society of Women's Organisers' minutes, 30 September 1936.

57　Lynch, *Liberal Party in Rural England*, pp. 51, 85; Robb, *Primrose League, 1883–1906*.

58　Hinton, *Women, Social Leadership, and the Second World War*, p. 56; for Conservative attempts to encourage close relations with local charitable and voluntary organisations see *Home and Empire*, January 1932, p. 12.

59　*Home and Politics*, June 1921, p. iii; *Conservative Agent's Journal*, March 1921, pp. 3, 9; NFWI MSS, 5FWI/A/2/3/01, report of Women's Institutes general meeting, 3 May 1921, pp. 431–57.

60　*Liberal Women's News*, May 1927, p. 75; June 1927, p. 95.

61　*Liberal Agent*, January 1921, p. 13.

62　Helen McCarthy, 'Democratizing British foreign policy: rethinking the Peace Ballot, 1934–1935', *Journal of British Studies*, 49:2 (2010), 358–87 at 374, 378, 381.

63　Helen McCarthy, *The British People and the League of Nations: Democracy, Citizenship and Internationalism, c. 1918–45* (Manchester, 2011), p. 54.

64　Lawrence, *Electing Our Masters*, p. 101; In 1910–11 there had been thirty-six major provincial daily papers which supported the Liberal Party in England, as opposed to thirty-three backing the Unionists. Blewett, *Peers, the Parties and the People*, p. 302.

65　Sam Davies and Bob Morley, 'Electoral turnout in county borough elections, 1919–1938', *Labour History Review*, 71:2 (2006), 167–86 at 169; 'Conservative and Liberal pacts by a young Liberal', *Liberal Women's News*, February 1927, p. 26.

66　*Berrow's Worcester Journal*, 3 May 1913, p. 3; 23 May 1914, pp. 2, 6.

67　For Conservative agents' frustrations with the multiplication of independent auxiliary leagues see *Conservative Agent's Journal*, April 1910, pp. 19–20; October 1910, p. 105; June 1911, pp. 14–15; July 1914, pp. 89–90.

68　Page Croft, *My Life of Strife*, p. 179; Amery MSS, AMEL7/18, Amery diary, 26 February 1924.

69　Page Croft, *My Life of Strife*, p. 179.

70 Houston and Valdar, *Modern Electioneering Practice*, p. 14.

71 Richard Cockett, 'The party, publicity, and the media', in Anthony Seldon and Stuart Ball (eds), *Conservative Century: The Conservative Party Since 1900* (Oxford, 1994), pp. 547–77 at pp. 551–2.

72 Ramsden has claimed that there were 144 local editions of Conservative Party publications by 1928, see his *Age of Balfour and Baldwin*, p. 233.

73 Lawrence, *Electing Our Masters*, p. 111.

74 *Conservative Agent's Journal*, February 1926, p. 42.

75 Rhodes James, *Memoirs of a Conservative*, pp. 226–8; Ramsden, *Age of Balfour and Baldwin*, p. 236 .

76 For the development of Ashridge College see Clarisse Berthézene, *Les Conservateurs Britanniques dans la Bataille des Idées, 1929–1954: Ashridge College, Premier Think Tank Conservateur* (Paris, 2011).

77 Lawrence, *Electing Our Masters*, pp. 97–100; Dearling, 'Conservatism in Lancashire between the wars', p. 16.

78 BCUA MSS, letters relating to the West Birmingham constituency, E.R. Canning to Austen Chamberlain, 21 June 1929; Thomas, 'Conservatives and "national" government', ch. 1.

79 Ball, *Baldwin and the Conservative Party*, ch. 3.

80 See Thomas, 'Conservatives and "national" government'.

Conclusion

British politics and society went through unprecedented upheavals during the opening decades of the twentieth century. Yet the question of how the Conservatives adapted to this changing environment on the ground has not received sufficient attention. The main studies of political history which transcend the First World War tend to focus on the familiar story of the decline of the Liberal Party and the rise of Labour.[1] Yet it is only by analysing how the Conservatives competed as a popular movement with their rivals on the Left that we can understand how the electoral map was transformed during the early twentieth century, the era when Britain became a true democracy.

The Conservative Party's revival during the early twentieth century was aided by changes in the structure of the state and the problems encountered by their rivals. Between 1906 and 1924 the role of the state advanced rapidly, through extended welfare provision and the introduction of wartime controls over industry and food supply. Whilst Unionist claims that tariff reform would be the best way to fund social reforms had repeatedly failed to find favour at Edwardian elections, the post-war settlement was well suited to the party's patriotic rhetoric. In particular, the Conservatives were able to successfully promote a deflationary economic regime which protected propertied interests whilst fighting off Labour claims for a significant expansion in the unemployment 'dole'.

Moreover, the decline of the Liberal Party organisation after 1914 proved uniquely advantageous to the Conservatives. Recent research has demonstrated that Labour made great strides during the course of the inter-war period in developing support bases outside its traditional heartlands. Its ability to create appeals aimed at rural workers, housewives and white-collar workers may well have played a crucial role in laying the foundations for its landslide election victory in 1945.[2] Labour had had to build gradually from a weak support base amongst these groups in many areas of the country after 1918. By contrast, the Unionist alliance had already taken significant steps to develop cross-community appeals during the Edwardian period.

Although the Conservatives' ascendancy in inter-war politics was aided and abetted by structural factors, the party's dramatic revival cannot be understood without acknowledging the crucial importance of its attempts to cultivate more progressive and demotic forms of politics after 1903. Unionist activists were not merely the passive beneficiaries of Liberal dissension and wartime social change; they had to actively reshape their culture to engage with a mass electorate, many of whom were assumed to lack long-held party loyalties. Joseph Chamberlain's tariff reform campaign played a seminal role in kick-starting these attempts to widen the appeal of Unionist politics.

As is well known, tariff reform proved a highly contentious policy, dividing Unionist activists and alienating many traditional supporters, particularly in the industrial north.[3] These rifts contrasted markedly with the success which conservative organisations, such as the Primrose League, had achieved during the late-Victorian period, developing a wide appeal across the classes, both sexes, and nationwide.[4] But to put too much emphasis on this is to miss the point. Earlier conservative associational cultures were not removed by the onset of the tariff reform campaign; rather, the development of the tariff leagues was a response to a growing sense that existing conservative organisations were failing to respond effectively to the advances made by the Liberal Party in the early 1900s.

Despite its wide-ranging concerns, tariff reform was clearly no panacea to cure the Unionists' ills; far from it. The Unionist alliance lost three successive general elections in Edwardian Britain whilst supporting tariff reform. Stanley Baldwin's ill-advised decision to base his 1923 campaign around the need for protective tariffs lost the Conservatives their parliamentary majority and reinforced the policy's reputation as a vote-loser. But although Chamberlain's followers were unable to convince the electorate to abandon free trade during the Edwardian period, they managed to create a new culture of Unionist activism better suited to dealing with the challenges of twentieth-century politics.

Unionist activists were already taking substantial steps to reduce their dependence on tariff reform and to develop a wide-ranging programme in the immediate years before the First World War. They developed cross-community appeals through their opposition to Irish home rule and National Insurance and their development of a land reform programme based on Jesse Collings's proposals. Rather than being merely passive beneficiaries of existing hostility to Liberal policies, they crafted campaigns to reflect the characteristics of different constituencies, thereby constructing, rather than simply reflecting, popular antipathy towards Liberal reforms. The Unionist Party sought to present itself as the guardian of social justice, defending social groups harassed by ill-advised Liberal policies.

Unionist politicians in Edwardian Britain built on the populist appeals of the 'cakes and ale' Toryism of the the 1870s and 1880s but were able to develop a more wide-ranging appeal to working-class men: they claimed that a protected economy would increase families' affluence, an overhaul of National Insurance legislation would aid the casual worker and that tenant farmers stood to benefit from smallholdings. The Edwardian period was also a crucial period in advancing women's positions within Unionist activism. By making housewives central to the fiscal debate, tariff reformers encouraged women to pursue a more assertive political role than they had been able to experience within the Primrose League before 1903. The rapid development of the Women's Unionist and Tariff Reform Association in the 1900s partly explains the party's success in appealing to women after 1918, since the Conservatives clearly enjoyed a substantial head-start over Labour in organising the female electorate. In some regions, the women's tariff association already constituted the dominant form of Unionist organisation during the Edwardian period. WUTRA claimed three hundred thousand members in 1914, although this figure should be treated with caution given the reluctance that political organisations had at this time towards striking non-subscribers off their membership lists.[5]

Nonetheless, we should be careful not to exaggerate the influence that these new cultures of activism had in shaping the Conservative Party's later success. The identity of Unionist politics differed significantly across the regions in Edwardian Britain. In some places, Tory politicians had already developed populist cultures in the late Victorian period which were little affected by the convulsions of the tariff reform campaign. This was notably the case in Liverpool, where Archibald Salvidge controlled the Working Men's Conservative Association from 1892 onwards. The city's populist Unionism relied heavily on Protestantism and anti-Irish sentiment.[6] Salvidge's patriarchal control of the Conservative organisation meant that the Tariff Reform League struggled to develop a foothold in Liverpool.[7] In addition, the organisation of popular Unionism appears to have stultified in regions where free trade remained strong such as the Lancashire cotton towns and west Yorkshire. In these regions the Primrose League remained a major force, but continued to be locked in Victorian modes of operation, providing an effective social organisation but remaining a less satisfactory electoral ally. It was not until the revival of the Irish home rule controversy in 1912 that the Unionists had an effective policy which rallied activists across the nation and enabled organisations such as WUTRA and the Primrose League to work together closely.

Even so, the First World War threw up a variety of new challenges which threatened to scupper the efforts which activists had made to widen the appeal of Unionist politics in the Edwardian period. Radical right organisations gained support from Conservatives frustrated by the stalemate on the Western Front and the apparent ineffectuality of the war leadership. Policies which had previously been at the core of Unionist politics before the war, such as tariff reform and opposition to Irish home rule, were reshaped, and, despite occasionally being propelled to the centre of political controversy after 1918, lost their earlier influence within the

Conservative programme. The most alarming wartime development of all for Conservatives was the dramatic rise of the Labour Party.

Trade union membership surged, peaking at over eight million in 1920. There had been a substantial working-class electorate before the war when the Unionist alliance had fallen to three consecutive election defeats and struggled to develop popular organisations which could appeal to organised labour. The vast expansion of the electorate following the Representation of the People Act in 1918 meant that from then on the vast majority of voters would be drawn from this social class.

Yet the experiences of the First World War played an important role in laying the foundations for the Conservative Party's post-war success. During the early years of the conflict there had been widespread sympathy amongst mainstream Conservatives towards the patriotic politics of radical right organisations such as the British Workers League. Yet, as Britain's war position grew increasingly precarious during 1917, the radical right's demagoguery came to be seen as a destabilising force which risked creating a stronger anti-war opposition. Unionist activists showed a remarkable unity in supporting the war effort and the party leadership; breakaway movements such as Henry Page Croft's National Party were never able to offer a serious alternative. The Unionist Party's patriotic unity stood in marked contrast to the factionalism and division which the Labour and Liberal parties experienced as a result of differing attitudes to the conduct of the war. Moreover, Unionist activists developed links with non-party movements through their participation in war work organisations, which played an important role in shaping the identity of the post-war party on the ground.

The Conservative Party's success after 1918 owed much to its ability to offer a broad range of policies and target multiple interest groups, building on the adaptable and demotic cultures of Unionist activism developed during the Edwardian period and war years. The identity of the party differed markedly across the regions during the 1920s. South-east England had been a hotbed of the wartime radical right, and reactionary forms of Conservatism thrived here during the early 1920s through the essentially negative anti-socialism promoted by the Anti-Waste League and Middle Classes Union, as well as local party associations. Their politics relied strongly on middle-class grievances and the 'Poplarism' controversy in London was used to suggest that Labour was not fit to govern responsibly in the public interest.

Nevertheless, relying solely on an essentially negative, class-based anti-socialist politics was a strategy fraught with danger for the Conservatives given the great strides which Labour organisations made to widen their authority amongst workers during the war and its aftermath. Labour was able to begin to move beyond its traditional, male working-class support base during the

1920s. In particular, the party's presentation of itself as the 'housewives' champion', embracing issues such as the creation of a consumers' council, appears to have played an important role in its 1929 election victory.

The moderate identities constructed by local Labour movements in many regions made the reactionary politics of organisations such as the Anti-Waste League appear less plausible outside its south-east England heartland. In regions such as Birmingham, Leeds and Norfolk Conservatives subsequently sought to promote a consensual politics which would broaden the social bases of their appeal across the community. During the early 1920s the party managed to develop significant popular organisations in industrial districts. The work of female activists like Annie Chamberlain, who built a Unionist working women's organisation based on the model of the Women's Institutes, was crucial to this achievement. Conservative activists focused much of their attention on local issues and championed the social reforms enacted by the party in municipal government during the 1920s.

At the same time, Conservative politicians developed links to charitable organisations involved in the welfare of deprived ex-servicemen's families and challenged the claims of their Labour opponents to speak for the interests of this section of society, thereby heading off calls for a radical overhaul of the unemployment insurance system. The development of these varied forms of Conservatism enabled the party to consolidate its position in many industrial seats in regions like Birmingham, and make several gains in areas which had previously been Liberal strongholds, like Leeds and Norfolk, despite the significant expansion of the working-class electorate. This is not to say that the organisation of Conservative politics became more democratic in the 1920s – the leadership of most constituency associations continued to be dominated by traditional elites who were expected to fund the party's day-to-day running.

After the First World War both Labour and the Conservatives were reluctant to allow politics to divide along lines of class and actively developed cross-community appeals. The Liberals struggled to win a large following amongst the new post-war electorate given that their rivals created broad support bases and sought to monopolise the centre ground in British politics. This was most apparent in local politics, where the Liberal Party lost its distinct independent identity in many towns, being relegated to a junior partner in anti-Labour municipal alliances. But perhaps the most striking feature of the Liberals' post-war malaise was their inability to develop a mass-supported women's organisation which could attract the new female voter after 1918. In comparison with its rivals, the Women's Liberal Federation appeared distinctly old-fashioned during the 1920s, and it struggled to attract a higher membership than it had enjoyed before the war.

The electoral recovery of the Conservative Party in early twentieth-century Britain was rooted in the efforts of local activists. For much of this period, and especially prior to the 1911 Unionist reorganisation, Conservative Central Office was seen as an incubus to modernisation. Activists intent on widening the appeal of Unionist politics directed much of their energies towards extra-parliamentary leagues formally independent of party control. In several respects Baldwin's ascent to the Conservative Party leadership in 1923 signalled a new era for the party. Baldwin was able to position the Conservatives as a centrist party of nation which safeguarded constitutionalism and democracy. Williamson is right to stress the importance of Baldwin's leadership to the party's enduring success: his moderate and consensual politics made him the main public persona of the National Government for much of the 1930s. At the same time, he was able to appeal to the right-wing of the party, most infamously by appointing the puritanical William Joynson-Hicks as home secretary in 1924.

Under Baldwin's leadership Conservative Central Office became more significant in directing the party's media strategy and operations than it had been previously. The fate of the Empire Crusade in 1930–31 demonstrated the difficulties of operating Conservative grassroots campaigns outside party channels during the Baldwin era. In some senses Beaverbrook's newspaper campaign in support of imperial preference resembled the strategies employed by radical right organisations during the First World War and anti-waste organisations in the early 1920s, focusing on winning by-elections and developing a grassroots movement on the back of a press campaign. Yet, while there was widespread sympathy amongst Conservatives towards Beaverbrook's call to introduce empire tariff preferences, many were angered by his methods.[8] Baldwin was highly effective in questioning the validity of the press lord's intervention in Conservative politics. Speaking on the eve of the St George's, Westminster, by-election in March 1931, he attacked Beaverbrook for seeking 'power without responsibility – the prerogative of the harlot throughout the ages'.[9] With the tightening of laws on election expenditure after 1918 it became increasingly difficult to run independent pressure group campaigns, which had been a major feature of Edwardian elections. As such, Baldwin was able to present Beaverbrook's campaign as the machinations of an over-mighty press lord intent on expanding his own influence in politics.

Stanley Baldwin was certainly a key figure in shaping the Conservative Party's identity after 1923, but his influence should not be exaggerated. The local party meeting remained central to electioneering between the wars.[10] Moreover, local parties mediated the appeals produced by central office in London and continued to give Conservatism a diverse identity across the regions during the National Government years in the 1930s.[11]

Activists did much to shore up Baldwin's leadership during its difficult early years and they also shaped the public presentation of Baldwinite Conservatism by focusing on aspects of party policy which corresponded with their own interests. Baldwin's inclusive and consensual brand of politics was itself both a product of the popular Conservative revival which had begun in the 1900s and its culmination.

Notes

1. Duncan Tanner, 'Class voting and radical politics: the Liberal and Labour parties, 1910–31', in Jon Lawrence and Miles Taylor (eds.), *Party, State and Society: Electoral Behaviour in Britain since 1820* (Aldershot, 1997), pp. 106–30; Peter Clarke, *Liberals and Social Democrats* (Cambridge, 1978); Wilson, *Downfall of the Liberal Party*; McKibbin, *Evolution of the Labour Party, 1910–1924*; Trentmann acknowledges the growing appeal of the Conservative rhetoric of the patriotic consumer in the 1920s, but is mainly concerned with the shift from Liberal to Social Democratic consumer discourses after the Great War. See his *Free Trade Nation*, ch. 4; for an important exception to the historiography see Ramsden, *Balfour and Baldwin*.

2. Griffiths, *Labour and the Countryside*; Lawrence, 'Labour and the politics of class'; Beers, *Your Britain*.

3. For detailed analyses of the divisions which tariff reform caused at constituency level see Witherell, 'Political cannibalism'; Sykes, 'Confederacy and the purge of the Unionist free traders'.

4. Peter Marsh, *The Discipline of Popular Government: Lord Salisbury's Domestic Statecraft, 1881–1902* (Hassocks, 1978), pp. 204–5; Roberts, '"Villa Toryism" and popular Conservatism in Leeds', pp. 222–4; Coetzee, 'Villa Toryism', p. 44.

5. In 1943 it was noted that the Junior Imperial League had a pre-war 'propaganda figure' for membership of 250,000 and an actual active membership of around 100,000. Correspondence with area agents, June–August 1943, CPA, CCO506/4/7.

6. Salvidge, *Salvidge of Liverpool*, pp. 62–4.

7. Ibid., p. 85.

8. For the hostile reaction to the Empire Crusade amongst Conservative leaders see Leo Amery, 'The crisis in the Unionist Party', *Nineteenth Century and After*, April 1930, p. 447.

9. A.J.P. Taylor, *Beaverbrook* (London, 1972), p. 305; see also *Home and Empire*, March 1930, pp. 3–4.

10. Lawrence, *Electing Our Masters*, pp. 103–8.

11. See Thomas, 'Conservatives and "national" government'.

Biographical appendix

Amery, Leopold (1873–1955). Unsuccessful candidate for East Wolverhampton, 1906, 1908, January 1910; Bow and Bromley, December 1910; Unionist MP for Sparkbrook, Birmingham, 1911–18; South Birmingham 1918–45. War service in Europe, 1914–16; deputy secretary to the War Cabinet, 1917–19; parliamentary under-secretary at Colonial Office (under Viscount Milner) 1919–21; parliamentary secretary for the Admiralty, 1921–22; first lord of the Admiralty 1922–24; colonial secretary 1924–29. Supporter of National Service League; founder of British Covenant campaign; chairman of Tariff Reform League management committee; stopped active work with the TRL after autumn 1917.

Atholl, Duchess of (Katharine Stewart-Murray, 1874–1960). Marchioness of Tullibardine between 1899 and 1917; husband was Unionist MP for West Perthshire, January 1910–17, inherited dukedom in 1917. President of Perthshire Women's Unionist Association, 1908–18; supporter of National League for Opposing Women's Suffrage; war work in Egypt; Unionist MP for Kinross and West Perthshire, 1923–38; first woman to serve in a Conservative government as parliamentary secretary to the Board of Education, 1924–29.

Bottomley, Horatio (1860–1933). Liberal MP for Hackney South, London 1906–10; retained seat as an independent in December 1910; expelled from parliament when found bankrupt in 1912; independent MP for Hackney South, 1919–22. Founded *John Bull* newspaper in 1906; prominent recruitment speaker during the First World War; played active role in the by-election campaigns of several independent candidates during 1916–18; supported anti-waste candidates during 1919–21; found guilty of fraud in 1922, expelled from parliament and spent five years in gaol.

Bridgeman, Caroline (née Parker, 1873–1961). Wife of William Bridgeman, who served as Unionist MP for Oswestry, Shropshire, 1906–29, home secretary, 1922–24, first lord of the Admiralty, 1924–29. Founded Oswestry Women's Unionist Association in 1904; vice-chairman of Women's Unionist and Tariff Reform Association; member of British Women's Covenant committee; involved in work of Women's Land Army during the First World War; chairman of Women's Unionist Organisation, 1918–25 and National Union of Conservative Associations, 1926–27; retired from political life simultaneously with her husband in 1929.

Chamberlain, Anne (1883–1967). Wife of Neville Chamberlain. President of Ladies Committee of the Birmingham Navy League from 1915; founded Unionist Women's Institute movement in 1919; president of Ladywood, Birmingham Women's Unionist Association and West Midlands Women's Unionist Organisation from 1918.

Derby, Lord (Edward Stanley, seventeenth Earl of Derby, 1865–1948). Known as Lord Stanley until he succeeded to the peerage in 1908. Conservative MP for West Houghton, Lancashire, 1892–1906; president of Liverpool Workingmen's Conservative Association (Archibald Salvidge served as the association's chairman); opponent of tariff reform, played important role in precipitating crisis which led to Bonar Law memorial of 1913; director-general of recruiting, 1915–16; secretary of state for war, 1916–18; British ambassador to France, 1918–20.

Fisher, Victor (1870–1954). Member of the Fabian Society and Social Democratic Federation (later British Socialist Party) during the Edwardian period; co-founded Socialist National Defence Committee in 1915; this formed the basis of the British Workers League, which Fisher served as honorary secretary, 1916–18. Edited *British Citizen and Empire Worker*, 1916–18; ended active work for BWL around the time of the 1918 general election. Unsuccessful contests in Stourbridge, Worcestershire, National Democratic Party (BWL), 1918; West Ham, London, Conservative, 1923.

Goulding, Edward (1862–1936, appointed Baron Wargrave, 1922). Unionist MP for Devizes, Wiltshire, 1895–1906; City of Worcester, 1908–22. Chaired Tariff Reform League organisation committee, 1905–13; chairman of Rolls Royce from 1921.

Hannon, Patrick (1871–1963). Unsuccessful contests, East Bristol, January and December 1910; Unionist MP for Moseley, Birmingham, 1921–50. Acted as a vice-president of the Tariff Reform League, 1910–14; Navy League general secretary, 1911–18; director of British Commonwealth Union, 1918–23.

Lyttelton, Edith (née Balfour, 1865–1948). Wife of Alfred Lyttelton. Honorary secretary of the Victoria League; supporter of Liberal Women's Unionist Association and Women's Unionist and Tariff Reform Association; served on executive of National Union of Women Workers; involved in Help the Ulster Women campaign; founder of War Refugees Committee in 1914; appointed deputy director of women's branch of the Ministry of Agriculture in 1917; British substitute delegate to the League of Nations Union, 1923, 1926–28, 1931.

Maxse, Mary (née Wyndham, 1870–1944). Chairman of Women's Tariff League, 1905–6 and Women's Unionist and Tariff Reform Association, 1906–18. Wartime work for agricultural and pensions committee and the Women's Institutes.

Northcliffe, Viscount (Alfred Harmsworth, 1865–1922). Unsuccessful candidate for Portsmouth, 1895; brother of Viscount Rothermere. Began publication of the *Daily Mail* in 1896 and the *Daily Mirror* in 1903; purchased *The Times* in 1908. Supported independent candidates during 1916 by-elections; director of propaganda, 1917–18. Northcliffe's papers supported the Anti-Waste League's campaigns in the early 1920s.

Page Croft, Henry (1881–1947). Unsuccessful contest, Lincoln, 1910; Conservative MP for Christchurch, Hampshire, 1910–18; Bournemouth, Hampshire, 1918–45 (1918–22 as National Party member); Tariff Reform League organising committee vice-chairman, 1913–16, chairman 1916–17. War service in France, 1914–16; founded National Party in 1917, severing relations with Conservative Party and TRL; returned to the Conservative Party in 1921; chairman of Empire Industries Association.

Pemberton-Billing, Noel (1881–1948). Unsuccessful contest, Mile End, London, January 1916 and four by-elections during 1941; independent MP for Hertford, March 1916–21. Formed Vigilante Party in 1917, ran candidates at wartime by-elections in Clapham and East Finsbury, London. Keen critic of government air policy during the First World War; unsuccessfully sued by Maud Allen for libel. Made lurid allegations about the sexual 'perversions' of public figures in court during summer 1918; forcibly removed from House of Commons in July 1918 for disregarding the authority of the chair.

Rothermere, Viscount (Harold Harmsworth, 1868–1940). Brother of Viscount Northcliffe. Worked with Northcliffe to establish *Daily Mail* and *Daily Mirror*; acquired *Sunday Pictorial* in 1915; founded Anti-Waste League in 1921.

Smedley-Crooke, James (1861–1951). MP for Deritend, Birmingham, 1924–29, 1931–45; honorary treasurer of Midland Division of Comrades of the Great War; involved in Birmingham British Legion and Digbeth Institute.

Willoughby de Broke, Lord (Richard Greville Verney, 1869–1923). MP for Rugby, 1895–1900; president of Imperial Maritime League; founded League for the Support of Ulster in 1912.

Bibliography

Unpublished

Personal Papers

Amery, Leo (Churchill College, Cambridge)
Atholl, Duchess of (Blair Castle, Perthshire)
Balfour, Arthur (British Library, London)
Bonar Law, Andrew (Parliamentary Archives, London)
Bridgeman, Caroline (Shropshire Archives, Shrewsbury)
Bridgeman, William (Shropshire Archives, Shrewsbury)
Cecil, Robert (British Library, London)
Churchill, Winston (Churchill College, Cambridge)
Hannon, Patrick (Parliamentary Archives, London)
Lloyd, George (Churchill College, Cambridge)
Lloyd George, David (Parliamentary Archives, London)
Long, Walter (British Library, London)
Maxse family (West Sussex Record Office, Chichester)
McKenna, Reginald (Churchill College, Cambridge)
Morrison-Bell, Arthur (Parliamentary Archives, London)
Morrison-Bell, Ernest (Devon Record Office, Exeter)
Mosley, Oswald (Birmingham University Library)
Page Croft, Henry (Churchill College, Cambridge)
Sandars, J.S. (Bodleian Library, Oxford)
Steel-Maitland, Arthur (National Archives of Scotland, Edinburgh)
Stephen, Jessie (Ruskin College, Oxford)
Townsend, St Clair (Women's Library, London)
Upcher of Sheringham (Norfolk Record Office, Norwich)
Wargrave, Baron (Parliamentary Archives, London)
Williams, Alice (Women's Library, London)
Willoughby de Broke, Lord (Parliamentary Archives, London)

Other manuscript sources

Birmingham Conservative and Unionist Association (Birmingham Central Library)
Blackpool Conservative Association (Lancashire Record Office, Preston)
Chichester Women's Unionist Association (West Sussex Record Office, Chichester)
Conservative Party MSS (Bodleian Library, Oxford)
Darwen Conservative Association (Lancashire Record Office, Preston)
Devizes Conservative Association (Wiltshire and Swindon History Centre, Chippenham)
Digbeth Institute (Birmingham Central Library)

Dumbartonshire Conservative Association (National Library of Scotland, Edinburgh)

Fawcett Society (Women's Library, London)

Garstang Primrose League habitation (Lancashire Record Office, Preston)

Labour Party (microfiche, People's History Museum, Manchester)

London Municipal Society (Guildhall Library, London)

Municipal Reform Party posters (London Metropolitan Archives)

National Federation of Women's Institutes MSS (Women's Library, London)

National Liberal Club (Bristol University)

National Party (Bodleian Library, Oxford)

National War Aims Committee, T102 (National Archives, London)

Petworth House Archive (West Sussex Record Office, Chichester)

Primrose League Grand Council (Bodleian Library, Oxford)

Scottish Conservative and Unionist Association (National Library of Scotland, Edinburgh)

South Oxfordshire Conservative Association MSS (Oxfordshire Record Office, Oxford)

Tariff Commission (London School of Economics)

Walsall Local History Centre Special Collections, 1910 elections material

War Reserve Collection (Cambridge University Library)

West Perthshire Unionist Association (Perth and Kinross Council Archive, Perth)

West Worcestershire Conservative Association (Worcestershire Record Office, Worcester)

Westminster Conservative Association (City of Westminster Archives, London)

Wolverhampton Conservative and Unionist Association (Wolverhampton Archives)

Women at Work Collection (Imperial War Museum, London, Microfilm)

Women's Suffrage Autograph Collection (Women's Library, London, Microfilm)

Published primary sources

Newspapers

Berkshire Chronicle (Reading)

Berrow's Worcester Journal

Birmingham Daily Mail (Birmingham Mail after 1918)

Birmingham Post

Blackpool Gazette

Bradford Daily Argus

Cheshire Daily Echo

Colne and Nelson Times

Consett and Stanley Chronicle

County Express for Worcestershire and Staffordshire (Stourbridge)

Daily Chronicle

Daily Express

Daily Herald

Daily Mail

Daily News and Leader

Darwen Gazette

D.P.'s Daily Paper

East London Observer

Eastern Daily Press (Ipswich and Norwich editions)

Evening Star (Ipswich)
Finsbury Weekly News
Fulham Chronicle
Hackney and Kingsland Gazette
Hampshire Advertiser (Southampton)
Hebden Bridge and Calder Vale Gazette
Henley and South Oxfordshire Standard
Hyde Reporter
Islington News and Hornsey Gazette
Leeds Weekly Citizen
Leicester Mercury
London Labour Chronicle
Manchester Guardian
Manchester Weekly Times
Marylebone Mercury
Midland Evening News (Wolverhampton)
Midland Mail (Market Harborough)
Morning Post
Newmarket Journal
North Wales Guardian
Northampton Herald
Northern Daily Telegraph (Blackburn)
Reading Standard
Shoreditch Observer
Southern Weekly News (Brighton)
Scotsman
Swansea and Glamorgan Herald
The Times
Todmorden and District News
Wakefield Express
Walthamstow, Leyton and Chingford Guardian
West London Observer
Wimbledon Herald
Woolwich Herald
Yorkshire Observer (Bradford)
Yorkshire Post

Journals and periodicals

Parliamentary Debates

Bioscope
British Citizen and Empire Worker
Comrades' Journal
Conservative Agent's Journal
Conservative and Unionist
Conservative Clubs Gazette
Conservative Woman (Leeds)
Covenanter

Federation News
Free Trader
Home and Empire
Home and Politics
Imperialist
John Bull
Labour Leader
Labour Organiser
Labour Woman
Lady's Realm
Liberal Agent
Liberal Magazine
Liberal Women's News
Lloyd George Liberal Magazine
Monthly Notes (Imperial Tariff Committee)
Monthly Notes (Tariff Reform League)
New Crusader (Women's Peace Crusade)
New Voice (Middle Classes Union)
Nineteenth Century and After
Notes for Speakers (Tariff Reform League)
Our Flag
Outlook
Popular View
Popular View in North Oxfordshire
Primrose League Gazette
Ratepayer
Review of Reviews
Straight Forward (Birmingham)
Tariff Reformer and Empire Monthly
Women's Liberal Magazine
Workers' Dreadnought

Diaries and memoirs

Amery, Leo, *My Political Life* (London, 3 vols, 1953–55)
Andrews, Elizabeth, *A Woman's Work Is Never Done*, ed. Ursula Masson (Dinas Powys, 2006, originally published 1957)
Macmillan, Harold, *Winds of Change, 1914–1939* (London, 1966)
Page Croft, Henry, *My Life of Strife* (London, 1948)
Ramsden, John (ed.), *Real Old Tory Politics: Political Diaries of Sir Robert Sanders, First Lord Bayford, 1910–35* (London, 1984)
Rhodes James, Robert , *Memoirs of a Conservative. J.C.C. Davidson's Memoirs and Papers, 1910–37* (London, 1969)
Self, Robert (ed.), *Neville Chamberlain Diary Letters* (Aldershot, 4 vols, 2000–5)
Williamson, Philip (ed.), *The Modernisation of Conservative Politics: The Diaries and Letters of William Bridgeman, 1904–1935* (London, 1988)
Winterton, Earl, *Orders of the Day* (London, 1953)

Contemporary publications

Arbuthnot, G.A. (ed.), *The Primrose League Election Guide* (London, 1914)

Bagge, Lillian Mary (ed.), *The Unionist Workers Handbook* (London, 1912)

Blackburn, Helen (ed.), *A Handbook for Women Engaged in Social and Political Work* (London, 2nd edition, 1895)

Bohun Lynch, J.G., *The Complete Amateur Boxer* (London, 1913)

Bridges, John A., *Reminiscences of a Country Politician* (London, 1906)

Cambray, P.G. *The Game of Politics: A Study of the Principles of British Political Strategy* (London, 1932)

Chance, Sir William, *Industrial Unrest: The Reports of the Commissioners (July 1917) Collated and Epitomised* (London, 1917)

Collings, Jesse, *The Colonization of Rural Britain: a Complete Scheme for the Regeneration of British Rural Life* (London, 2 vols, 1914)

Free Trade Union, *Photographic Reproductions of our Brilliantly Coloured Picture and Word Posters* (London, n.d., c.1905)

Gore, John (ed.), *Mary Maxse, 1870–1944: A Record Compiled by her Family and Friends* (London, 1946)

Gosling, Harry, *Peace: How to Get it and Keep it* (London, n.d. [c. 1917–18])

Gray, Frank, *Confessions of a Candidate* (London, 1925)

Hall, B.T., *Our Fifty Years: The Story of the Working Men's Club and Institute Union* (London, 1912)

Hamilton, M.A. (Iconoclast), *Margaret Bondfield* (London, 1924)

Henderson, Arthur, *Aims of Labour* (London, 1918)

Houston, Henry James and Valdar, Lionel, *Modern Electioneering Practice* (London, 1922)

Imperial Tariff Committee, *General Election 1910: A Handbook for Unionist Canvassers* (Birmingham, 1909)

Lawrence Lowell, A., *The Government of England* (New York, 2 vols, 2nd edition, 1912)

Lee, John A., *Todmorden and the Great War, 1914–1918* (Todmorden, 1922)

Long, Walter, *Memories* (London, 1923)

Masterman, C.F.G., *The Condition of England* (London, 1909)

Maxse, Mary, *Tariff Reform and Cheap Living* (London, 1910)

McLaren, Barbara, *Women of the War* (New York, 1918)

Mid-Worcestershire Tariff Reform Association, *The Carpet Trade and the Fiscal Question* (Kidderminster, 1904)

Moreton, Amy H., *Freedom in Happy England: A Tariff Reform Play* (Nuneaton, 1911)

National Union of Conservative Associations, *Handbook on Constituency Organisation* (London, 1925)

Oliver, F.S., *Ordeal by Battle* (London, 1915)

Peel, Mrs C.S. [Dorothy], *A Year in Public Life* (London, 1919)

Phillips, Marion and Tavener, Grace, *Women's Work in the Labour Party: Notes for Speakers' and Workers' Classes* (London, 1923)

Reynolds, Stephen, Woolley, Bob and Woolley, Tom, *Seems So! A Working Class View of Politics* (London, 1911)

Richards, H.C., *The Candidates' and Agents' Guide in Contested Elections* (London, 4th edition, 1904)

Seymour Lloyd, J., *Elections and How to Fight Them* (London, revised edition, 1909)

Smith, Harold, *Unpopular Opinions: A Diary of Political Protest* (London, 1922)

Soutter, Francis William, *Fights for Freedom: The Story of My Life* (London, 1925)

Tariff Reform League, *Annual Report* (London, 1913)

Young, Terence, *Becontree and Dagenham: a Report Made for the Pilgrim Trust* (London, 1934)

Published secondary works

Adelman, Paul, *The Decline of the Liberal Party, 1910–1931* (Harlow, 2nd edition, 1995)

Aubel, Felix, 'The Conservatives in Wales, 1880–1935', in Martin Francis and Ina Zweiniger-Bargielowska (eds), *The Conservatives and British Society, 1880–1990* (Cardiff, 1996), pp. 96–110

Auspos, Patricia, 'Radicalism, pressure groups, and party politics: From the National Education League to the National Liberal Federation', *Journal of British Studies*, 20:1 (1980), 184–204

Ball, Stuart, *Baldwin and the Conservative Party: The Crisis of 1929–1931* (New Haven, CT, 1988)

—— 'Local Conservatism and the evolution of the party organization', in Stuart Ball and Anthony Seldon (eds), *Conservative Century: The Conservative Party since 1900* (Oxford, 1994), pp. 261–314

—— 'National politics and local history: the regional and local archives of the Conservative Party, 1867–1945', *Archives*, 22 (1996), 27–59

—— and Seldon, Anthony (eds), *Conservative Century: The Conservative Party since 1900* (Oxford, 1994)

Beaumont, Caitriona, 'Moral dilemmas and women's rights: the attitude of the Mothers' Union and Catholic Women's League to divorce, birth control and abortion in England, 1928–1939', *Women's History Review*, 16:4 (2007), 463–85

Beckett, I.F.W., *The Army and the Curragh Incident, 1914* (London, 1986)

Beers, Laura, 'Counter-Toryism: Labour's response to anti-socialist propaganda, 1918–1939', in Matthew Worley (ed.), *The Foundations of the Labour Party: Identities, Cultures and Perspectives, 1900–39* (Aldershot, 2009), pp. 231–54

—— 'Is this man an anarchist? Industrial action and the battle for public opinion in interwar Britain', *Journal of Modern History*, 82:1 (2010), 30–60

—— *Your Britain: Media and the Making of the Labour Party* (Cambridge, MA, 2010)

Bentley, Michael, *The Liberal Mind, 1914–1929* (Cambridge, 1977)

—— (ed.), *Public and Private Doctrine: Essays in British History Presented to Maurice Cowling* (Cambridge, 1993)

Berthézene, Clarisse, *Les Conservateurs Britanniques dans la Bataille des Idées, 1929–1954: Ashridge College, Premier Think Tank Conservateur* (Paris, 2011)

Biagini, Eugenio F., *British Democracy and Irish Nationalism, 1876–1906* (Cambridge, 2007)

Bibbings, Lois, 'Images of manliness: the portrayal of soldiers and conscientious objectors in the Great War', *Social and Legal Studies*, 12:3 (2003), 335–58

Bingham, Adrian, '"Stop the flapper vote folly": Lord Rothermere, the *Daily Mail*, and the equalization of the franchise, 1927–28', *Twentieth Century British History*, 13:1 (2002), 17–37

Black, Lawrence, 'The lost world of Young Conservatism', *Historical Journal*, 51 (2008), 991–1024

Blewett, Neal, *The Peers, the Parties and the People: The General Elections of 1910* (London, 1972)

Bourke, Joanna, *Dismembering the Male: Men's Bodies, Britain and the Great War* (London, 1996)

Branson, Noreen, *Poplarism, 1919–1925: George Lansbury and the Councillors' Revolt* (London, 1979)

Breitenbach, Esther, and Gordon, Eleanor (eds), *Out of Bounds: Women in Scottish Society, 1800–1945* (Edinburgh, 1992)

Bush, Julia, *Behind the Lines: East End Labour, 1914–1919* (London, 1984),

—— *Women Against the Vote: Female Anti-suffragism in Britain* (Oxford, 2008)

Butler, David and Butler, Gareth, *British Political Facts, 1900–1994* (Basingstoke, 7th edition, 1994)

Cannadine, David, 'The context, performance and meaning of ritual: the British monarchy and the "invention of tradition", c. 1820–1977', in Eric Hobsbawm and Terence Ranger (eds), *The Invention of Tradition* (Cambridge, 1983), pp. 263–307

Cawood, Ian, 'Joseph Chamberlain, the Conservative Party and the Leamington Spa candidature dispute of 1895', *Historical Research*, 79 (2006), 554–77

Churchill, Randolph S., *Lord Derby: 'King of Lancashire'* (London, 1959)

Clarke, P.F., *Lancashire and the New Liberalism* (Cambridge, 1971)

—— 'The electoral position of the Liberal and Labour parties, 1910–1914', *English Historical Review*, 90 (1975), 828–36

—— *Liberals and Social Democrats* (Cambridge, 1978)

Clegg, H.A., *A History of British Trade Unions since 1889. Vol. 2: 1911–33* (Oxford, 1985)

Cline, Catherine, *Recruits to Labour: The British Labour Party, 1914–1931* (Syracuse, NY, 1963)

Cockett, Richard, 'The party, publicity, and the media', in Anthony Seldon and Stuart Ball (eds), *Conservative Century: The Conservative Party since 1900* (Oxford, 1994), pp. 547–77

Coetzee, Frans, *For Party or Country: Nationalism and the Dilemmas of Popular Conservatism in Edwardian England* (Oxford, 1990)

—— 'Villa Toryism reconsidered: Conservatism and suburban sensibilities in late-Victorian Croydon', in E.H.H. Green (ed.), *An Age of Transition: British Politics, 1880–1914* (Edinburgh, 1997), pp. 29–47

—— and Coetzee, Marilyn Shevin, 'Rethinking the Radical Right in Germany and Britain before 1914', *Journal of Contemporary History*, 21:4 (1986), 515–37

Cohen, Deborah, *The War Come Home: Disabled Veterans in Britain and Germany, 1914–1939* (Berkley, CA, 2001)

Conley, Mary A., *From Jack Tar to Union Jack: Representing Naval Manhood in the British Empire, 1870–1918* (Manchester, 2009)

Connell, R.W., *Masculinities* (Cambridge, 1995)

—— and Messerschmidt, J.W., 'Hegemonic masculinity: rethinking the concept', *Gender and Society*, 19:6 (2005), 829–59

Cornford, James, 'The transformation of Conservatism in the late nineteenth century', *Victorian Studies*, 7:1 (1963), 35–66

Cowling, Maurice, *The Impact of Labour, 1920–1924: The Beginning of Modern British Politics* (Cambridge, 1971)

Craig, David M., '"High politics" and the "New Political History"', *Historical Journal*, 53 (2010), 453–75

Craig, F.W.S. (ed.), *British Parliamentary Election Results, 1885–1918* (Chichester, 1974)

Daunton, Martin, *Trusting Leviathan: The Politics of Taxation in Britain, 1799–1914* (Cambridge, 2001)

—— and Hilton, Matthew (eds), *The Politics of Consumption: Material Culture and Citizenship in Britain and America* (Oxford, 2001)

Davies, R.R. and Jenkins, Geraint H. (eds), *From Medieval to Modern Wales* (Cardiff, 2004)

Davies, Sam and Morley, Bob, *County Borough Elections in England and Wales, 1919–1938: A Comparative Analysis* (Aldershot, 3 vols, 1999–2006)

—— 'Electoral turnout in county borough elections, 1919–1938', *Labour History Review*, 71:2 (2006), 167–86

Davis, John, 'The enfranchisement of the urban poor in late-Victorian Britain', in Peter Ghosh and Lawrence Goldman (eds), *Politics and Culture in Victorian Britain: Essays in Memory of Colin Matthew* (Oxford, 2006), pp. 95–117

Dawson, Graham, *Soldier Heroes: British Adventure, Empire, and the Imagining of Masculinities* (London, 1994)

Dawson, Michael, 'Liberalism in Devon and Cornwall, 1910–1931: "The old time religion"', *Historical Journal*, 38:2 (1995), 425–37

Dean, Kenneth J., *Town and Westminster: A Political History of Walsall from 1906–1945* (Walsall, 1972)

Douglas, Roy, 'The background to the "Coupon" Election arrangements', *English Historical Review*, 86 (1971), 318–36

—— 'The National Democratic Party and the British Workers' League', *Historical Journal*, 15:3 (1972), 533–52

Doyle, Barry M., 'Urban Liberalism and the "lost generation": politics and middle-class culture in Norwich, 1900–1935', *Historical Journal*, 38:3 (1995), 617–34

Dutton, David, *'His Majesty's Loyal Opposition': The Unionist Party in Opposition, 1905–1915* (Liverpool, 1992)

Edwards, Andrew and Griffith, Wil, 'Welsh national identity and governance, 1918–1945', in Duncan Tanner, Chris Williams, W.P. Griffiths and Andrew Edwards (eds), *Debating Nationhood and Governance in Britain, 1885–1939: Perspectives from the Four Nations* (Manchester, 2006), pp. 118–45

Evans, Neil, '"A nation in a nutshell": the Swansea disestablishment demonstration of 1912 and the political culture of Edwardian Wales', in R.R. Davies and Geraint H. Jenkins (eds), *From Medieval to Modern Wales* (Cardiff, 2004), pp. 214–29

Evans, Stephen, 'The Conservatives and the redefinition of Unionism, 1912–21', *Twentieth Century British History*, 9:1 (1998), 1–27

Feldman, David and Stedman Jones, Gareth (eds), *Metropolis London* (London, 1989)

—— and Lawrence, Jon (eds), *Structures and Transformations in Modern British History: Papers for Gareth Stedman Jones* (Cambridge, 2011)

Fergusson, James, *The Curragh Incident* (London, 1964)

Finlay, Richard, 'Scottish Conservatism and Unionism since 1918', in Martin Francis and Ina Zweiniger-Bargielowska (eds), *The Conservatives and British Society, 1880–1990* (Cardiff, 1996), pp. 111–26

Fitzpatrick, David, *Politics and Irish Life, 1913–1921: Provincial Experience of War and Revolution* (Cork, 1977)

Francis, Martin and Zweiniger-Bargielowska, Ina (eds), *The Conservatives and British Society, 1880–1990* (Cardiff, 1996)

Freeden, Michael, *Liberalism Divided: A Study in British Political Thought, 1914–1939* (Oxford, 1986)

Ghosh, Peter and Goldman, Lawrence (eds), *Politics and Culture in Victorian Britain: Essays in Memory of Colin Matthew* (Oxford, 2006)

Gollin, Alfred, *Balfour's Burden: Arthur Balfour and Imperial Preference* (London, 1965)

Grant, Peter, 'Voluntarism and the impact of the First World War', in Matthew Hilton and James McKay (eds), *The Ages of Voluntarism: How we Got to the Big Society* (Oxford, 2011), pp. 27–46

Graves, Pamela M., *Labour Women: Women in British Working-class Politics, 1918–1939* (Cambridge, 1994)

Grayzel, Susan R., '"The outward and visible sign of her patriotism": women, uniforms and National Service during the First World War', *Twentieth Century British History*, 8 (1997), 145–64

—— 'Nostalgia, gender and the countryside: placing the "Land Girl" in First World War Britain', *Rural History*, 10:2 (1999), 155–70

Green, E.H.H., 'Radical Conservatism: the electoral genesis of tariff reform', *Historical Journal*, 28:3 (1985), 667–92

—— 'The strange death of Tory England', *Twentieth Century British History*, 2:1 (1991), 67–88

—— *The Crisis of Conservatism: The Politics, Economics and Ideology of the British Conservative Party, 1880–1914* (London, 1995)

—— *Ideologies of Conservatism* (Oxford, 2002)

—— (ed.), *An Age of Transition: British Politics, 1880–1914* (Edinburgh, 1997)

Gregory, Adrian, '"You might as well recruit Germans": British public opinion and the decision to conscript the Irish in 1918', in Adrian Gregory and Senia Pašeta (eds), *Ireland and the Great War: 'A War to Unite us All?'* (Manchester, 2002), pp. 113–32

—— *The Last Great War: British Society and the First World War* (Cambridge, 2008)

Griffiths, Clare, *Labour and the Countryside: The Politics of Rural Britain, 1918–1939* (Oxford, 2007)

Gullace, Nicoletta, *'The Blood of our Sons': Men, Women and the Renegotiation of British Citizenship during the Great War* (Basingstoke, 2002)

Harrison, Brian, 'For church, queen and family: the Girls' Friendly Society, 1874–1920', *Past and Present*, 61:1 (1973), 107–38

Haste, Cate, *Keep the Home Fires Burning: Propaganda in the First World War* (London, 1977)

Hendley, Matthew, '"Help us to secure a strong, healthy, prosperous and peaceful Britain": the social arguments of the campaign for compulsory military service in Britain, 1899–1914', *Canadian Journal of History*, 30 (1995), 262–88

Hilton, Matthew and McKay, James (eds), *The Ages of Voluntarism: How we Got to the Big Society* (Oxford, 2011)

Hinton, James, *Women, Social Leadership, and the Second World War: Continuities of Class* (Oxford, 2002)

Hoare, Philip, *Wilde's Last Stand: Decadence, Conspiracy and the First World War* (London, 1997)

Hobsbawm, Eric and Ranger, Terence (eds), *The Invention of Tradition* (Cambridge, 1983)

Hollins, T.J., 'The Conservative Party and film propaganda between the wars', *English Historical Review*, 96 (1981), pp. 359–69

Hollis, Patricia, *Ladies Elect: Women in English Local Government, 1865–1914* (Oxford, 1987)

Horne, John, 'Remobilizing for "total war": France and Britain, 1917–18', in John Horne (ed.), *State, Society and Mobilization in Europe during the First World War* (Cambridge, 1997), pp. 195–211

Howarth, Janet, 'The Liberal revival in Northamptonshire, 1880–1895: a case study in late nineteenth century elections', *Historical Journal*, 12:1 (1969), 78–118

Howe, Anthony, *Free Trade and Liberal England, 1846–1946* (Oxford, 1997)

Jackson, Daniel M., *Popular Opposition to Irish Home Rule in Edwardian Britain* (Liverpool, 2009)

Jamieson, Lynn and Corr, Helen (eds), *State, Private Life and Political Change* (Basingstoke, 1990)

Jarvis, David, 'Mrs. Maggs and Betty: the Conservative appeal to women voters in the 1920s', *Twentieth Century British History*, 5:2 (1994), 129–52

—— 'British Conservatism and class politics in the 1920s', *English Historical Review*, 111 (1996), 59–84

——'The Conservative Party and the politics of gender, 1900–1939', in Martin Francis and Ina Zweiniger-Bargielowska (eds), *The Conservatives and British Society, 1880–1990* (Cardiff, 1996), pp. 172–93

——'The shaping of Conservative electoral hegemony, 1918–39', in Jon Lawrence and Miles Taylor (eds), *Party, State and Society: Electoral Behaviour in Britain since 1820* (Aldershot, 1997), pp. 131–52

Jeffrey, Tom, 'The suburban nation: politics and class in Lewisham', in David Feldman and Gareth Stedman Jones (eds), *Metropolis London* (London, 1989), pp. 189–216

Johnson, Matthew, 'The Liberal War Committee and the Liberal advocacy of conscription in Britain, 1914–1916', *Historical Journal*, 51 (2008), 399–420

Jones, G.W., *Borough Politics: A Study of the Wolverhampton Town Council, 1888–1964* (London, 1969)

Kennedy, Paul and Nicholls, Anthony (eds), *Nationalist and Racialist Movements in Britain and Germany before 1914* (London, 1981)

Kennedy, Thomas C., 'Troubled Tories: dissent and confusion concerning the party's Ulster policy, 1910–1914', *Journal of British Studies*, 46:4 (2007), 570–93

Keohane, Nigel, *The Party of Patriotism: The Conservative Party and the First World War* (Farnham, 2010)

Kingsley Kent, Susan, *Making Peace: The Reconstruction of Gender in Interwar Britain* (Princeton, NJ, 1994)

Koss, Stephen, *Nonconformity in Modern British Politics* (London, 1975)

Kushner, Tony and Lunn, Kenneth (eds), *The Politics of Marginality: Race, the Radical Right and Minorities in Twentieth Century Britain* (London, 1990)

Laurence, Sue, 'Moderates, municipal reformers, and the issue of tariff reform, 1894–1934', in Andrew Saint (ed.), *Politics and the People of London: the London County Council, 1889–1965* (London, 1989), pp. 93–102

Lawrence, Jon, 'Class and gender in the making of urban Toryism, 1880–1914', *English Historical Review*, 108 (1993), 629–52

—— *Speaking for the People: Party, Language and Popular Politics in England, 1867–1914* (Cambridge, 1998)

—— 'Contesting the male polity: the suffragettes and the politics of disruption in Edwardian Britain', in Amanda Vicery (ed.), *Women, Privilege and Power: British Politics, 1750 to the Present* (Stanford, CA, 2001), pp. 201–26

—— 'Review of Sam Davies and Bob Morley ed., *County borough election results in England and Wales, 1919–1938: a comparative analysis* (Aldershot, 2 vols, 1999–2000)', *English Historical Review*, 118 (2003), 462–4

—— 'Forging a peaceable kingdom: war, violence and the fear of brutalization in post-First World War Britain', *Journal of Modern History*, 75:3 (2003), 557–89

—— 'The transformation of British public politics after the First World War', *Past and Present*, 190 (2006), 185–216

—— 'Public space/political space', in Jay Winter and Jean Louis-Robert (eds), *Capital Cities at War: Paris, London, Berlin, 1914–1919. Vol. 2: A Cultural History* (Cambridge, 2007), pp. 280–312

—— *Electing Our Masters: The Hustings in British Politics from Hogarth to Blair* (Oxford, 2009)

—— 'Labour and the politics of class, 1900–1940', in David Feldman and Jon Lawrence (eds), *Structures and Transformations in Modern British History: Papers for Gareth Stedman Jones* (Cambridge, 2011), pp. 237–60

—— and Taylor, Miles (eds), *Party, State and Society: Electoral Behaviour in Britain since 1820* (Aldershot, 1997)

Levine, Philippa, '"Walking the streets in a way no decent women should": women police in World War One', *Journal of Modern History*, 66 (1994), 34–78

Light, Alison, *Forever England: Femininity, Literature and Conservatism between the Wars* (London, 1991)

Lynch, Patricia, *The Liberal Party in Rural England, 1885–1910: Radicalism and Community* (Oxford, 2003)

Machin, G.I.T., *Politics and the Churches in Great Britain, 1869 to 1921* (Oxford, 1987)

Maguire, G.E., *Conservative Women: A History of Women and the Conservative Party, 1884–1997* (Basingstoke, 2000)

Marsh, Peter, *The Discipline of Popular Government: Lord Salisbury's Domestic Statecraft, 1881–1902* (Hassocks, 1978)

McCarthy, Helen 'Parties, voluntary associations and democratic politics in interwar Britain', *Historical Journal*, 50:4 (2007), 891–912

—— 'Democratizing British foreign policy: rethinking the Peace Ballot, 1934–1935', *Journal of British Studies*, 49:2 (2010), 358–87

—— *The British People and the League of Nations: Democracy, Citizenship and Internationalism, c. 1918–45* (Manchester, 2011)

McCrillis, Neal, *The British Conservative Party in the Age of Universal Suffrage: Popular Conservatism, 1918–1929* (Columbus, OH, 1998)

McEwen, John M., 'The press and the fall of Asquith', *Historical Journal*, 21:4 (1978), 863–83

McKibbin, Ross, *The Evolution of the Labour Party, 1910–1924* (Oxford, 1974)

—— *Ideologies of Class: Social Relations in Britain, 1880–1950* (Oxford, 1990)

—— *Classes and Cultures: England, 1918–1951* (Oxford, 1998)

—— *Parties and People: England, 1914–1951* (Oxford, 2010)

Meyer, Jessica, *Men of War: Masculinity and the First World War in Britain* (Basingstoke, 2009)

Millman, Brock, *Managing Domestic Dissent in First World War Britain* (London, 2000)

Monger, David, *Patriotism and Propaganda in First World War Britain: The National War Aims Committee and Civilian Morale* (Liverpool, 2012)

—— 'Transcending the nation: domestic propaganda and supranational patriotism in Britain, 1917–1918', in Tony Paddock (ed.), *Propaganda and the First World War* (forthcoming)

Moore, James R., 'Liberalism and the politics of suburbia: electoral dynamics in late-nineteenth century South Manchester', *Urban History*, 2 (2003), 225–50

—— *The Transformation of Urban Liberalism: Party Politics and Urban Governance in Late-Nineteenth Century England* (Aldershot, 2006)

Morgan, Kenneth, 'The New Liberalism and the challenge of Labour: the Welsh experience, 1885–1929', *Welsh History Review*, 6 (1973), 288–312

—— *Consensus and Disunity: The Lloyd George Coalition Government, 1918–1922* (Oxford, 1979)

—— *Rebirth of a Nation: Wales, 1880–1980* (Oxford, 1980)

Nicholas, Sian, 'The construction of a national identity: Stanley Baldwin, "Englishness" and the mass media in inter-war Britain', in Martin Francis and Ina Zweiniger-Bargielowska (eds), *The Conservatives and British Society, 1880–1990* (Cardiff, 1996), pp. 127–46

Noakes, Lucy, 'Demobilising the military woman: constructions of class and gender in Britain after the First World War', *Gender and History*, 19:1 (2007), 143–62

O'Day, Alan (ed.), *The Edwardian Age: Conflict and Stability, 1900–1914* (London, 1979)

O'Gorman, Frank, 'Campaign rituals and ceremonies: the social meaning of elections in England, 1780–1860', *Past and Present*, 135 (1992), 79–115

Offer, Avner, *Property and Politics, 1870–1914: Landownership, Law, Ideology and Urban Development in England* (Cambridge, 1981)

Packer, Ian, *Lloyd George, Liberalism and the Land: The Land Issue and Party Politics in England, 1906–1914* (Woodbridge, 2001)

Paddock, Tony (ed.), *Propaganda and the First World War* (forthcoming)

Panayi, Panikos, 'The British Empire Union in the First World War', in Tony Kushner and Kenneth Lunn (eds), *The Politics of Marginality: Race, the Radical Right and Minorities in Twentieth Century Britain* (London, 1990), pp. 113–28

—— *The Enemy in our Midst: Germans in Britain during the First World War* (Oxford, 1991)

Peele, Gillian and Cook, Chris (eds), *The Politics of Reappraisal, 1918–1939* (London, 1975)

Pelling, Henry, *Social Geography of British Elections, 1885–1910* (London, 1967)

Pennybacker, Susan D., *A Vision for London, 1889–1914: Labour, Everyday Life and the LCC Experiment* (London, 1995)

Phillips, Gregory D., 'Lord Willoughby de Broke: Radicalism and Conservatism', in J.A. Thompson and Arthur Meija (eds), *Edwardian Conservatism: Five Studies in Adaptation* (London, 1988), pp. 77–104

Pinto-Duschinsky, Michael, *British Political Finance, 1830–1980* (Washington, DC, 1981)

Pronay, Nicholas and Spring, D.W. (eds), *Propaganda, Politics and Film, 1918–45* (London, 1982)

Pugh, Martin, *Electoral Reform in War and Peace, 1906–18* (London, 1978)

—— *The Tories and the People* (Oxford, 1985)

—— *Women and the Women's Movement in Britain, 1914–1999* (Basingstoke 2nd edition, 2000)

Ramsden, John, *The Age of Balfour and Baldwin, 1902–1940* (London, 1978)

—— 'Baldwin and film', in Nicholas Pronay and D.W. Spring (eds), *Propaganda, Politics and Film, 1918–45* (London, 1982), pp. 126–43

Readman, Paul, 'The 1895 election and political change in late Victorian Britain', *Historical Journal*, 42:2 (1999), 467–93

—— 'The Conservative Party, patriotism, and British politics: the case of the general election of 1900', *Journal of British Studies*, 40:1 (2001), 107–45

—— *Land and Nation in England: Patriotism, National Identity, and the Politics of the Land, 1880–1914* (Woodbridge, 2008)

Rempel, Richard, *Unionists Divided: Arthur Balfour, Joseph Chamberlain and the Unionist Free Traders* (Newton Abbot, 1972)

Rendall, Jane (ed.), *Equal or Different: Women's Politics, 1880–1914* (Oxford, 1987)

Ridley, Jane, 'The Unionist Social Reform Committee, 1911–1914: wets before the deluge', *Historical Journal*, 30 (1987), 391–413

Rix, Kathryn, '"Go out into the highways and hedges": the diary of Michael Sykes, Conservative political lecturer, 1895 and 1907–8', *Parliamentary History*, 20:2 (2001), 209–31

—— '"The elimination of corrupt practices in British elections"? Reassessing the impact of the 1883 Corrupt Practices Act', *English Historical Review*, 123 (2008), 65–97

Robb, Janet Henderson, *The Primrose League, 1883–1906* (New York, 1942)

Roberts, Matthew, '"Villa Toryism" and popular Conservatism in Leeds, 1885–1902', *Historical Journal*, 94:1 (2006), 217–46

—— 'Constructing a Tory world-view: popular politics and the Conservative press in late-Victorian Leeds', *Historical Research*, 79 (2006), 115–43

Roper, Michael, 'Nostalgia as an emotional experience during the First World War', *Historical Journal*, 54 (2011), 421–51

Rüger, Jan, 'Nation, empire and navy: identity politics in the United Kingdom, 1887–1914', *Past and Present*, 185 (2004), 159–88

—— *The Great Naval Game: Britain and Germany in the Age of Empire* (Cambridge, 2007)

Russell, A.K., *Liberal Landslide: The General Election of 1906* (Newton Abbot, 1973)

Saint, Andrew (ed.), *Politics and the People of London: The London County Council, 1889–1965* (London, 1989)

Salvidge, Stanley, *Salvidge of Liverpool: Behind the Political Scene, 1890–1928* (London, 1934)

Savage, Mike, *The Dynamics of Working-class Politics: The Labour Movement in Preston* (Cambridge, 1987)

—— 'Urban politics and the rise of the Labour Party, 1919–39', in Lynn Jamieson and Helen Corr (eds), *State, Private Life and Political Change* (Basingstoke, 1990), pp. 204–23

—— and Miles, Andrew, *The Remaking of the British Working Class, 1840–1940* (London, 1994)

Scally, R.J., *The Origins of the Lloyd George Coalition: The Politics of Social-Imperialism, 1900–1918* (Princeton, NJ, 1975)

Schwarz, Bill, 'The language of constitutionalism: Baldwinite Conservatism', in *Formations of Nation and People* (London, 1984), pp. 1–18

Scott, Gillian, *Feminism and the Politics of the Working Woman: The Women's Co-operative Guild, 1880s to the Second World War* (London, 1998)

Searle, G.R., 'Critics of Edwardian society: the case of the radical right', in Alan O'Day (ed.), *The Edwardian Age: Conflict and Stability, 1900–1914* (London, 1979), pp. 79–96

Self, Robert C., 'Conservative reunion and the general election of 1923: a reassessment', *Twentieth Century British History*, 3:3 (1992), 249–73

—— 'Baldwin's blunder: a rejoinder to Smart on 1923', *Twentieth Century British History*, 7:1 (1996), 140–55

Seymour-Ure, Colin, 'The press and the party system', in Gillian Peele and Chris Cook (eds), *The Politics of Reappraisal, 1918–1939* (London, 1975), pp. 232–57

Shepherd, John, *George Lansbury: At the Heart of Old Labour* (Oxford, 2002)

Smart, Nick, 'Debate. Baldwin's blunder? The general election of 1923', *Twentieth Century British History*, 7:1 (1996), 110–39

Smith, Jeremy, *The Tories and Ireland, 1910–1914: Conservative Party Politics and the Home Rule Crisis* (Dublin, 2000)

Smyth, James, 'Rents, peace, votes: working-class women and political activity in the

First World War', in Esther Breitenbach and Eleanor Gordon (eds), *Out of Bounds: Women in Scottish Society, 1800–1945* (Edinburgh, 1992), pp. 174–96

—— 'Resisting Labour: Unionists, Liberals and moderates in Glasgow between the wars', *Historical Journal*, 46:2 (2003), 375–401

Stubbs, John, 'Lord Milner and patriotic Labour, 1914–1918', *English Historical Review*, 87 (1972), 717–54

—— 'The impact of the Great War on the Conservative Party', in Gillian Peele and Chris Cook (eds), *The Politics of Reappraisal, 1918–1939* (London, 1975), pp. 14–38

Summers, Anne, 'Militarism in Britain before the Great War', *History Workshop Journal*, 2 (1976), 104–23

—— 'The character of Edwardian nationalism: three popular leagues', in Paul Kennedy and Anthony Nicholls (eds), *Nationalist and Racialist Movements in Britain and Germany before 1914* (London, 1981), pp. 68–87

Swartz, Martin, *The Union of Democratic Control in British Politics during the First World War* (Oxford, 1971)

Sykes, Alan, 'The Confederacy and the purge of the Unionist free traders, 1906–1910', *Historical Journal*, 18:2 (1975), 349–66

—— *Tariff Reform in British Politics, 1903–1913* (Oxford, 1979)

—— 'The radical right and the crisis of Conservatism before the First World War', *Historical Journal*, 26:3 (1983), 661–76

—— 'Radical Conservatism and the working-classes in Edwardian England: the case of the Workers Defence Union', *English Historical Review*, 113 (1998), 1180–1209

Sykes, Sir Percy, *Sir Mortimer Durand* (London, 1926)

Tanner, Duncan, *Political Change and the Labour Party, 1900–1918* (Cambridge, 1990)

—— 'Class voting and radical politics: the Liberal and Labour parties, 1910–31', in Jon Lawrence and Miles Taylor (eds), *Party, State and Society: Electoral Behaviour in Britain since 1820* (Aldershot, 1997), pp. 106–30

—— 'The pattern of Labour politics, 1918–1939', in Duncan Tanner, Chris Williams and Deian Hopkin (eds), *The Labour Party in Wales, 1900–2000* (Cardiff, 2000), pp. 113–39

—— 'Gender, civic culture and politics in South Wales: explaining Labour's municipal policy, 1918–39', in Matthew Worley (ed.), *Labour's Grassroots: Essays on the Activities and Experiences of Local Labour Parties and Members, 1918–1945* (Aldershot, 2005), pp. 170–93

—— Williams, Chris and Hopkin, Deian (eds), *The Labour Party in Wales, 1900–2000* (Cardiff, 2000)

——, ——, Griffiths, W.P. and Edwards, Andrew (eds), *Debating Nationhood and Governance in Britain, 1885–1939: Perspectives from the Four Nations* (Manchester, 2006)

Taylor, A.J.P., *Beaverbrook* (London, 1972)

Thackeray, David, 'Rethinking the Edwardian crisis of Conservatism', *Historical Journal*, 54 (2011), 191–213

—— 'Building a peaceable party: masculine identities in British Conservative politics, c. 1903–24', *Historical Research* (2012), http://onlinelibrary.wiley.com/doi/10.1111/j.1468-2281.2012.00600.x/pdf

Thompson, Andrew S., *Imperial Britain: The Empire in British Politics, c. 1880–1932* (Harlow, 2000)

Thompson, J.A. and Meija, Arthur (eds), *Edwardian Conservatism: Five Studies in Adaptation* (London, 1988)

Thompson, James '"Pictorial lies"? Posters and politics in Britain, c. 1880–1914', *Past and Present*, 197 (2007), 177–210

Thorpe, Andrew, *The British General Election of 1931* (Oxford, 1991)

Tregidga, Garry, *The Liberal Party in South West Britain since 1918: Political Decline, Dormancy and Rebirth* (Exeter, 2000)

Trentmann, Frank, 'Bread, milk and democracy in modern Britain: consumption and citizenship in twentieth-century Britain', in Martin J. Daunton and Matthew Hilton (eds), *The Politics of Consumption: Material Culture and Citizenship in Britain and America* (Oxford, 2001), pp. 129–63

—— *Free Trade Nation: Commerce, Consumption, and Civil Society in Modern Britain* (Oxford, 2008)

Turner, John A., 'The British Commonwealth Union and the General Election of 1918', *English Historical Review*, 93 (1978), pp. 528–59

—— *British Politics and the Great War: Coalition and Conflict, 1915–1918* (New Haven, CT, 1992)

Urquhart, Diane (ed.), *Minutes of the Ulster Women's Unionist Council and Executive Committee* (Dublin, 2001)

Vernon, James, *Politics and the People: A Study in English Political Culture, c.1815–1867* (Cambridge, 1993)

Walker, Linda, 'Party political women: a comparative study of Liberal women and the Primrose League, 1890–1914', in Jane Rendall (ed.), *Equal or Different: Women's Politics, 1880–1914* (Oxford, 1987), pp. 165–91

Ward, Paul, *Red Flag and Union Jack: Englishness, Patriotism and the British Left, 1881–1924* (Woodbridge, 1998)

Ward, Stephen R., 'Intelligence surveillance of British ex-servicemen, 1918–1920', *Historical Journal*, 16:1 (1973), 179–88

Watson, Janet S.K., *Fighting Different Wars: Experience, Memory and the First World War in Britain* (Cambridge, 2004)

Williamson, Philip, 'The doctrinal politics of Stanley Baldwin', in Michael Bentley (ed.), *Public and Private Doctrine: Essays in British History Presented to Maurice Cowling* (Cambridge, 1993), pp. 181–208

—— *Stanley Baldwin: Conservative Leadership and National Values* (Cambridge, 1999)

—— 'Christian Conservatives and the totalitarian challenge, 1933–40', *English Historical Review*, 115 (2000), 607–42

—— 'The Conservative Party, 1900–1939: from crisis to ascendancy', in Chris Wrigley (ed.), *A Companion to Early Twentieth-Century Britain* (Oxford, 2003), pp. 3–22

Wilson, Trevor, *The Downfall of the Liberal Party, 1914–1935* (London, 1966)

Windscheffel, Alex, *Popular Conservatism in Imperial London, 1868–1906* (Woodbridge, 2007)

Winter, Jay and Robert, Jean Louis-Robert (eds), *Capital Cities at War: Paris, London, Berlin, 1914–1919. Vol. 2: A Cultural History* (Cambridge, 2007)

Witherell, Larry L., 'Political cannibalism among Edwardian Conservatives: Henry Page Croft, the confederacy and the campaign for East Hertfordshire, 1906–10', *Twentieth Century British History*, 8:1 (1997), 1–26

Wootton, Graham, *The Politics of Influence: British Ex-servicemen, Cabinet Decisions and Cultural Change (1917–57)* (Cambridge, MA, 1963)

Worley, Matthew (ed.), *Labour's Grassroots: Essays on the Activities and Experiences of Local Labour Parties and Members, 1918–1945* (Aldershot, 2005)

——— *The Foundations of the Labour Party: Identities, Cultures and Perspectives, 1900–39* (Aldershot, 2009)

Wrigley, Chris, *David Lloyd George and the British Labour Movement* (Hassocks, 1976)

——— *Lloyd George and the Challenge of Labour: The Post-war Coalition, 1918–1922* (London, 1990)

——— *Lloyd George* (Oxford, 1992)

——— (ed.), *A Companion to Early Twentieth-Century Britain* (Oxford, 2003)

Zweiniger-Bargielowska, Ina, 'Rationing, austerity and Conservative Party recovery after 1945', *Historical Journal*, 37:1 (1994), 174–97

Unpublished secondary sources

Barbary, Victoria, '"From platform to the polling booth"': political leadership and popular politics in Bolton and Bury, 1868–1906' (PhD dissertation, University of Cambridge, 2007)

Bates, J.W.B., 'The Conservative Party in the constituencies, 1918–39' (DPhil dissertation, University of Oxford, 1994)

Blanch, M.D., 'Nation, Empire and the Birmingham working-class, 1899–1914' (PhD dissertation, University of Birmingham, 1975)

Boughton, John, 'Working class politics in Birmingham and Sheffield, 1918–1931' (PhD dissertation, University of Warwick, 1985)

Carr, Richard, 'The phoenix generation at Westminster: Great War veterans turned Tory MPs, democratic political culture, and the path of British Conservatism from the Armistice to the Welfare State' (PhD dissertation, University of East Anglia, Norwich, 2010)

Cawood, Ian, 'The lost party: Liberal Unionism, 1886–1895' (PhD dissertation, University of Leicester, 2009)

Cooper, Tim, 'The politics of radicalism in suburban Walthamstow, 1870–1914' (PhD dissertation, University of Cambridge, 2004)

Dalton, Raymond, 'Labour and the municipality: Labour politics in Leeds, 1900–1914' (PhD dissertation, University of Huddersfield, 2000)

Dawson, A.M., 'Politics in Devon and Cornwall, 1900–1931' (PhD dissertation, University of London, 1991)

Dearling, James K., 'The language of Conservatism in Lancashire between the wars: a study of Ashton-under-Lyme, Chorley, Clitheroe, Royton and South Salford' (PhD dissertation, University of Manchester, 2002)

Good, Kit, 'England goes to war, 1914–15' (PhD dissertation, University of Liverpool, 2002)

Hancock, John W., 'The anatomy of the British Liberal Party, 1908–1918: a study of its character and disintegration' (PhD dissertation, University of Cambridge, 1992)

Jarvis, David, 'Stanley Baldwin and the ideology of the Conservative response to socialism, 1918–1931' (PhD dissertation, University of Lancaster, 1991)

Jesman, Christine, 'Conservative women, the Primrose League and public activity in Surrey and Sussex, c. 1880–1902' (DPhil dissertation, University of Sussex, 2008)

Jones, Grace A., 'National and local issues in politics: a study of East Sussex and Lancashire spinning towns, 1906–10' (PhD dissertation, University of Sussex, 1965)

Keohane, Nigel, 'The Unionist Party and the First World War' (PhD dissertation, University of London, 2005)

McIsaac, Pamela, '"To suffer and to serve": British military dependents, patriotism and gender in the Great War' (PhD dissertation, MacMaster University, 1997)

Monger, David, 'The National War Aims Committee and British patriotism during the First World War' (PhD dissertation, University of London, 2009)

Mylechreest, Denise, 'A singular Liberal: Richard Robert Fairbairn and Worcester politics, 1899–1941' (MPhil dissertation, University of Coventry, 2007)

Peters, James, 'Anti-socialism in British politics, c. 1900–22' (DPhil dissertation, University of Oxford, 1992)

Porter, Dilwyn, 'The Unionist tariff reformers, 1903–1914' (PhD dissertation, University of Manchester, 1976)

Rix, Kathryn, 'The party agent and English electoral culture, 1880–1906' (PhD dissertation, University of Cambridge, 2001)

Roberts, Matthew, 'W.L. Jackson, Leeds Conservatism and the world of villa Toryism, c. 1867–1900' (PhD dissertation, University of York, 2003)

Rolf, Keith W.D., 'Tories, tariffs and elections: the West Midlands in English politics, 1918–1935' (PhD dissertation, University of Cambridge, 1974)

Rüger, Jan, 'The celebration of the fleet in Britain and Germany, 1897–1914' (PhD dissertation, University of Cambridge, 2003)

Swaddle, K.M.O., 'Coping with a mass electorate: a study in the evolution of constituency electioneering in Britain, with special emphasis on the periods which followed the Reform Acts of 1884 and 1918' (DPhil dissertation, University of Oxford, 1990)

Thomas, Geraint, 'Constitutional reform and constitutional language in the Conservative Party, c. 1911–1929' (unpublished MS, 2008)

—— 'Conservatives and the culture of "national" government between the wars' (PhD dissertation, University of Cambridge, 2010)

Toye, Richard, '"Perfectly parliamentary"? The Labour Party and the House of Commons after 1918' (unpublished MS)

Vervaecke, Philippe, 'Dieu, la Couronne et l'Empire la Primrose League, 1883–2000: culture et pratiques politiques d'un movement Conservateur' (PhD dissertation, University of Lille, 2003)

Williams, Thomas Wyn, 'The Conservative Party in North-East Wales, 1906–1924' (PhD dissertation, University of Liverpool, 2008)

Windscheffel, Alex, 'Villa Toryism? The making of London Conservatism, 1868–1906' (PhD dissertation, University of London, 2000)

Internet sources

John Bull's Hearth (1903), www.screenonline.org.uk/film/id/1186859/index.html, accessed on 8 October 2012

Topical Film Co. 310–1, 'Pacifists routed in Brotherhood Church' (1917), www.screenonline.org.uk/film/id/583515/index.html, accessed on 14 March 2011

Index

agriculture 27, 37, 79, 110, 178
Amery, Leo 23–4, 38–9, 47, 62, 64, 74, 76, 105, 118–19, 160, 163, 173, 175, 197
anti-socialist politics
  in Edwardian period 53–7
  in First World War 103, 110–12
  in 1920s 2–4, 9–10, 134–40, 147–8, 154–63, 165, 171–5, 179, 183, 193
Anti-Socialist Union 56–7
anti-waste campaign 3, 142, 154–8, 163, 165, 168–9, 171–2, 175, 185
Anti-Waste League 154, 156, 158, 163, 165, 193–4
Asquith, Henry Herbert 9, 75–7, 126, 146, 171, 177
Atholl, Duchess of 28, 41, 46, 110–11, 180–1, 197

Baldwin, Stanley 3, 5, 9–10, 47, 122, 140, 171–5, 177, 179, 180–5, 191, 195–6
Balfour, Arthur 7, 21, 43, 58, 78
Beaverbrook, Lord 185, 195
Boer War 22, 25, 53
Bonar Law, Andrew 23, 30, 61–2, 74, 77, 79, 104–5, 112, 121–2, 160–1, 171, 173
Boraston, John 30, 106
Bottomley, Horatio 87, 90, 197
Bridgeman, Caroline 24, 28, 64, 72, 110, 112, 125, 135, 197
Bridgeman, William 27, 97, 103
British Commonwealth Union 123, 129, 198
British Covenant 6, 70, 74–6, 78–9, 197
British Empire Union 80, 88–90, 94, 98, 104–5, 114, 123–4
British League for the Support of Ulster and the Union 75–6, 78, 80, 83

British Legion 137–8, 164, 180–1, 199
British Workers' League 80, 88–92, 94–101, 103–9, 112, 123, 126, 129, 193, 198
Brooke-Hunt, Violet 18, 24
by-elections 59–60, 66, 77, 79, 87, 89–90, 118, 124, 154, 156, 195
  Abercromby (1917) 94
  Clapham (1918) 114, 124
  East Cambridgeshire (1913) 61
  East Wolverhampton (1908) 38–9
  Flint Boroughs (1913) 78
  Harborough (1916) 90
  Leeds Central (1923) 143, 162
  Leith Burghs (1914) 77, 79
  Mid-Devon (1908) 1, 39–40
  Poplar (1914) 61–2
  Reading (1913) 61, 77
  South Hackney (1922) 138
  South-West Bethnal Green (1914) 61–2
  Worcester (1908) 36–7

Cecil, Robert 75–6, 78, 83, 158
Chamberlain, Anne 143–5, 147, 166, 172, 181–2, 194, 197–8
Chamberlain, Austen 71, 76, 180
Chamberlain, Joseph 2, 5, 21, 24–5, 27–8, 32, 37, 41, 58, 183, 191
Chamberlain, Neville 103, 106–7, 143–4, 164, 169, 175–6, 180
'Chinese labour' 22
Churchill, Winston 23, 57, 128
Clarke, Peter 59
Clubs and Institutes Union 20, 39
Coetzee, Frans 6, 56, 69–70, 84
Collings, Jesse 60–1, 74, 191
Comrades of the Great War 94, 100, 199
Conservative Central Office 2, 4, 19, 22–3, 30, 62, 70, 81, 104, 107, 119, 125, 140, 148, 160, 181, 183–4, 195

Conservative Party
  appeals to men 5–6, 17–18, 20, 36–7,
    39–40, 44–5, 80, 134–41, 147–9
  in local elections 41–2, 57, 135–45, 153,
    156–9, 162–3, 175
  organisational problems 7, 22–3,
    29–30, 55, 62–3, 72, 164–5
    see also Unionist Reorganisation
    Committee (1911)
  relations with Lloyd George coalition
    102, 119–20
  relations with non-party organisations
    8, 103, 109, 112, 118, 143–4, 159,
    164, 180–1
  working-class appeals 21, 60–4, 104,
    125, 154, 162, 164–6, 173–5
consumer politics, 5, 37, 39–41, 48, 80,
  141, 148, 156, 166, 177, 179, 194, 196
  see also anti-socialist politics; free trade,
  tariff reform; 'villa toryism'
Cowling, Maurice 3, 6
Curzon, Viscount 48, 118

Derby, Lord 94, 198
Devon, Unionism in 1, 22, 32, 39–40, 46,
  58, 63, 179

East Anglia, Unionism in 23–4, 63, 72,
  79, 178–80, 194
elections, culture of 7–8, 23–30, 36–42,
  44–6, 48–9, 54–7, 60, 74, 112,
  117–18, 126–7, 133–4, 138–40,
  142–4, 146, 153–5, 175, 183–5, 195
electoral reform 2, 102, 117–18
empire 17, 26, 58, 60, 77, 125, 185, 195
ex-servicemen *see* servicemen and
  politics

film and politics 3, 8, 22, 25–6, 87, 171,
  184–5
Fisher, Victor 91, 104, 106–8, 120
free trade 22, 24–30, 35, 37–40, 45, 48,
  55–6, 58–9, 66, 69, 72–4, 122–3, 174,
  177–9, 191–2
  see also Free Trade Union
Free Trade Union 7, 27, 37, 45, 63, 118

general elections 10, 173–4, 178
  1895 22

1900 22, 25
1906 19–20, 22, 27, 32, 36, 40, 55, 58,
  63, 71–2
1910 elections 23, 25–6, 29, 38–40,
  42–6, 49, 55, 58–9, 62–3, 66–7, 73–4,
  124
1918 2, 97, 102–3, 107–8, 118–19, 121,
  124, 126–7
1922 133, 160–1, 167, 173
1923 144, 146, 171, 173–4, 177–9, 191
1924 134, 140–2, 147–9, 158, 165,
  171–2, 174–80, 185
1929 153, 179, 184–5
Germany 27, 37–9, 47, 87, 90, 92, 96,
  104–7, 118–20, 123–4
Goulding, Edward 36–7, 118, 198
Green, Ewen 7, 10, 12, 17–18, 60–1, 69,
  74, 123

Hannon, Patrick 123, 198
Henderson, Arthur 96–7
Home and Politics 135, 142, 145–6, 171
home rule, Unionist campaign against 2,
  4, 42–3, 64, 69–80, 119–20, 124–5,
  192
House of Lords 58, 74–5, 78
Houston, Henry 142, 144, 165, 184

Imperial Tariff Committee 24, 28, 30
industry 26, 37–9, 55, 57–60, 73, 94–5,
  103–6, 123, 134–5, 143–4, 155–6,
  160, 162, 164–5, 173–4, 191, 194
Ireland 2, 17, 79, 119–20
  see also home rule

Jackson, Daniel 69, 75–6
Jarvis, David 3, 55, 60, 134, 140
Jenkins, William 28, 30
Junior Imperial League 70, 81, 88, 140,
  196

Labour Party
  after 1918 133–8, 140–2, 145–7, 153–8,
    160–3, 175–7, 180
  appeals to women 133, 141–2, 148
  in Edwardian politics 58, 62, 117
  in First World War 96–8, 102–4, 106–7,
    110–12, 126
  in local elections 57, 153, 156–63

responses to anti-socialism 4, 154, 160–3, 194
see also anti-socialist politics
Lancashire, Unionism in 19, 21, 59, 64, 73–4, 77, 82, 121, 137, 159–60, 174, 192
Lansbury, George 135–6, 157
Lawrence, Jon 37, 49, 98
League of Nations Union 182
Liberal Party
consumer appeals 20, 37–40, 58, 174, 178
decline of 3, 9, 126, 145–7, 158, 171–2, 177–83
Edwardian strength 6, 20–3, 60, 72, 78–9
in local elections 53, 56–7, 158, 162, 182–3
Nonconformist support 9, 21–2, 72, 74, 78, 179–80
organisational problems 63, 146–7, 177, 188
relations with extra-parliamentary organisations 117, 180–2
strength in 'celtic fringe' 9
strength in rural areas 20, 60–1, 178–9
see also National Liberal Federation; Women's Liberal Federation
Liberal Unionist Party 4–5, 17–22, 24, 27, 30, 32, 35, 55, 71, 74
Licensing Bill (1908) 39
Lloyd George, David 9, 26, 38, 40, 57, 60–1, 79, 94–5, 100, 105–9, 119–24, 126, 128, 146, 151, 155–6, 160, 177, 179
London, Unionism in 22, 29, 42, 53–4, 56–7, 71, 156–7

McCrillis, Neal 4
MacDonald, Ramsay 89, 95, 126, 139–40, 171, 174–5
McKibbin, Ross 3, 8, 11, 53, 55, 109, 154, 181
Masterman, Charles 53, 55–6, 61
Maxse, Mary 23–4, 29, 47, 64, 104–5, 110–1, 121, 125, 126, 128, 180, 198
Middle Classes Union 155–9, 163, 193
Millman, Brock, 88, 95, 100
Milner, Viscount 74–6, 78, 95, 100, 105, 120

Morrison-Bell, Ernest 1

National Federation of Discharged Sailors and Soldiers 88, 94, 96–7
national insurance 55, 60–2, 78–9, 166, 191
National Liberal Federation 7, 24
National Party 120–4, 128–9, 193
National Service League 6–7, 47–9, 103–4
National Union of Conservative Associations 23, 63, 72
National War Aims Committee 88, 94–7, 100–1, 105–6, 112, 116, 123
Navy League 6–7, 47–8
newspapers and politics 23, 90–3, 95, 109, 118, 134, 136, 148, 154–6, 175, 182, 184, 188, 195
non-party organisations
during the First World War 103, 112, 126–7, 180, 193
and political culture after 1918 8–9, 109, 143–4, 147, 164, 180–3
Northcliffe, Lord 90, 135, 154, 198

Page Croft, Henry 24, 44–6, 121–2, 183–4, 193, 198
Pankhurst, Emmeline 1, 123
'patriotic labour' 65, 103, 106–7, 109, 112
Pemberton-Billing, Noel 87, 90, 92, 114, 123, 199
plays and politics 8, 26–7, 29, 34, 39, 111, 184
'Poplarism' 135–8, 157–8, 163, 175, 177, 193
Primrose League 6, 18–22, 27–8, 31–2, 38, 40–1, 43, 46, 48, 51, 70–3, 75–7, 81–3, 99, 118, 125, 143, 181, 191–2

'radical right' 6–7, 65, 80, 87–97, 104–5, 123–4, 127, 193, 195
radio and politics 3, 8, 171, 184–5
Ramsden, John 2–3, 11, 30, 63, 69, 124–5, 189
Representation of the People Act (1918) 2, 96, 102, 117, 122, 124–5, 133, 193
religion and politics 3, 8–9, 21–2, 55–6, 72–4, 78, 164, 178–80, 182, 185
see also Welsh disestablishment

Rothermere, Lord 135, 154–5, 199
Ruger, Jan 25

Scotland, Unionism in 4, 9, 21, 28, 32, 43, 77, 89, 93, 96
servicemen and politics 89–91, 93–8, 101, 134–41, 146–9, 158, 164, 180–1, 194, 199
Smedley-Crooke, John 163–4, 166, 170, 199
Smith, Jeremy 75
social reform 9, 18, 32, 56–8, 79, 160–2, 166, 171, 175–6, 183, 190, 194
Steel-Maitland, Arthur 79, 164–5
Stephen, Jessie 133
'stratified electioneering' 5, 55–6, 60, 65, 80, 112, 127, 141, 145–6, 153, 155, 185
Sussex, Unionism in 19, 28–30, 45, 57, 63–4, 75, 82, 111, 156, 158–9

tariff reform
　Edwardian campaign 1–2, 6–7, 18–20, 22–30, 36–48, 51, 55, 58–60, 63–4, 69–73, 80, 153, 173–4, 183–4, 195
　post–1914 3, 120–2, 126, 173–4, 177–9, 191
Tariff Reform League 6–7, 23–4, 26, 29–30, 36–8, 45, 48, 51, 59, 63–4, 72–3, 80, 118, 120–2, 153, 183, 192, 197–8
Trentmann, Frank 24, 37, 196

Unionist Reorganisation Committee (1911) 2, 23, 30, 58, 81, 183, 195

'villa toryism' 5, 53, 55–6, 64, 109, 124–5, 143, 154–62, 165, 193
violence in British politics 38, 44–6, 48–9, 87–98, 101, 103, 106, 110, 126, 134–41, 147, 175

Wales, Unionism in 9–10, 71–2, 74, 89
Welsh disestablishment 74, 78, 180
West Midlands, Unionism in 20–2, 24, 36–8, 63, 69–72, 74, 122, 144–5, 159, 165, 169, 197
Willoughby de Broke, Lord 75–6, 80, 199
Windscheffel, Alex 42, 60
Williamson, Philip 3, 11, 125
Women's Institutes 103, 111, 125–6, 130, 143–4, 180, 188, 194, 198
Women's Land Army 110–1, 125, 130, 197
Women's Liberal Federation 19, 28, 110, 146–7, 181, 194
Women's Liberal Unionist Association 21, 24
Women's Tariff Reform League 24, 43
Women's Unionist and Tariff Reform Association (WUTRA) 1, 5–6, 18, 23–4, 28–30, 34, 38, 40–3, 46–8, 50, 59, 63–4, 70–1, 76, 80–1, 99, 104–6, 109–112, 114, 121, 125, 144–5, 147, 192
Women's Unionist Organisation (WUO) 4, 125, 135, 140, 142, 144–5, 147–8, 159, 162

Yorkshire, Unionism in 59, 74, 77, 82, 95–6, 108–9, 133, 140, 143, 154, 160–3, 166, 169, 178, 192, 194